RHINELAND—WINELAND

Rhineland Wineland

A Journey through the Wine Districts of Western Germany by

S. F. HALLGARTEN

with an Introduction by

T. A. LAYTON

Paul Elek : LONDON

Dedicated to my father
ARTHUR HALLGARTEN
on his 80th birthday
with deep gratitude

CONTENTS

CONTENTS

————— • —————

Foreword

I have consulted the works of many authorities on science and kindred subjects, and from some of them I have quoted freely. A list will be found on page 186.

Special thanks are due to the burgomasters of many wine growing communities for their assistance in my researches.

My heartfelt thanks are further due to Mr. Villforth of the Weinbauschule in Weinsberg and to Director Goedecke in Niederhausen (Nahe) and Mr. Blüme in Wurzburg for having had the great kindness to look through those parts of my manuscript that refer to the wines of Wuerttemberg, the Nahe and Franconia respectively; and to Professor Hennig for acting as my guide at the Viticultural College in Geisenheim and teaching me the latest methods of dealing with wines, in particular the use of physio-chemistry in their examination.

I should like also to take this opportunity of expressing my best thanks to those of my friends who have been kind enough to read the MS and encourage me to publish it—first and foremost to my old friend, G. U. Salvi, the chairman of the Wine Trade Club Education Committee and last but not least to T. A. Layton who also was good enough to write the introduction.

6th June, 1951

Roman Wall House,   S. F. HALLGARTEN
1 Crutched Friars,
London, E.C.3.

Introduction

WANTED, A HOLIDAY. Outside, a little bird is feverishly pulling
off strand after strand from a piece of rope it has found lying on
the path and is disappearing into a tiny hole in the eaves of the
house; on the lawn the blades of grass, emerald green, seem to be
shooting up visibly, while in the hedgerows the buds are just enough
in bloom to advertise, like a film trailer, the glorious technicolour
display they will shortly be showing.

In the woods, in the fields around, the cries of the animals have
that urgency which denotes an impending mating or a new birth;
the monotonous call of the cuckoo, the strident screech of the phea-
sant, and the plaintive bleat of the lamb.

Inside the house, one sits desperate to get out among the new
year which is proclaiming itself, yet anxious to finish the summer
wine list or to work out how much must be added to a single bottle
because bottling charges have gone up three guineas a hogshead;
nothing useful comes from your pen, because no inspiration comes
into your mind; however, you daren't take a walk round the garden,
because you know you won't get back to work for the whole day;
but you know too, that, however hard you concentrate, you won't
do any useful work if you stay indoors.

There is only one time that this can happen and that is early May,
and if you have ever felt like this and also felt that perhaps you
don't quite yet deserve a holiday, that is just when you need it most.

On such a morning did Fritz Hallgarten ask me to tour the
Rhineland with him. Our only previous encounter had been when
he made me a present of a bottle of Red-White Hock, after I had
written certain defamatory remarks about this curiosity. I wavered,
but fell. Anyway, I thought, here is a man who will drive me
leisurely through the vineyards, so that I can learn everything. As
for the leisurely driving—oh! how was I mistaken!—but as for
the knowledge I gained, never was there so fine a tutor.

We started off from London so well that we got to Dover in
such good time that we took morning coffee—and missed the boat.
Still, we got to Brussels that night, and even then I didn't realise
how untiring were the energies of my host.

The next day, things warmed up. We tore through Luxembourg
(lunching en route at an excellent little place outside Marche in
Belgium), dashed through Trier and rested our heads at the Burg

Landshut Hotel in the twin village of Berncastel-Cues, which lies on either side of the—lovelier than the Rhine—River Moselle. We were in the Berncastel part, and as we arrived the sun was setting behind the hills and the lights of Cues were to be seen twinkling merrily across the river. Berncastel was lovely enough, but Cues looked a veritable fairyland. A pity, I thought to myself, as I walked across from Berncastel to look at the other side, that Fritz didn't have the sense to station us in Cues. But when I got over the bridge, there were the lights of Berncastel dancing merrily on the Moselle, even more enchantingly.

Next day, serious tasting began and between each cellar visit I began to understand why Fritz Hallgarten's knowledge and enthusiasm of the wines of Germany was so profound, and why his love for them was more than that of just a wine merchant in pursuit of his living.

The Hallgartens were originally Spanish wine merchants, only leaving the country in 1492 because of the Inquisition, from whence they fled to Holland, and moving by stages up the Rhine, finally settled in Winkel in the Rheingau. Here to remind themselves of their Spanish origin they built themselves a Spanish house, which stands still. From then for the next three centuries they engaged themselves in trades allied to that of wine, and especially acting as Wine Brokers to the big Wine Shippers until just over 50 years ago Fritz's father established himself as a wine shipper.

Fritz, in such a millieu, naturally grew up in vineyards and around wine. As a small child he used to play in the vineyards. Later, when he went to school at Geisenheim, he passed some of the most famous vineyards in the world on his way home on his bicycle and at that date it was probably safe to say that he often sampled the grapes before their owners did! Year by year he watched the wine making and followed the processes with eager interest. When he reached the top form all his classmates were intimately connected with the wine trade, and were sons of wine growers, the father of one of them being in addition a wine merchant, another a manufacturer of sparkling wine and the third a brandy distiller. Under these circumstances it is hardly surprising that wine became his hobby at an early age. He tells of one memorable occasion when wine was consumed even during school hours. It was in 1922, while he was in the top form. The last break of the day lasting twenty minutes, there was time enough to rush round to a grower's cellar a few doors away from the school, where Arthur Hallgarten, Fritz's father, had stored some Geisenheimer Rothenberg 1921, as fine a Rheingau hock of as fine a year as was ever made. The youths happily tasted and approved the delectable beverage, and then returned to school for a mathematics lesson. Called upon to prove the Cosine formula, Fritz collected his wits, began, as he thought, as well as could be imagined. Disillusionment came swiftly and the Professor interrupted his discourse, saying "You have made so many mistakes one might have thought you were drunk." Bursts of laughter followed this remark, and as the son of a Geisenheim wine grower himself, he dealt leniently with the topers when they told him the story.

All through his undergraduate years and later as auxiliary judge at Ruedesheim (Rhein) and then barrister in Wiesbaden, young Hall- garten kept up his interest in wines, attending every auction possible, and then joining the distinguished Circle of Wine Friends composed entirely of University men who had distinguished themselves in various walks of life.

But the Nazi creed was beginning to make itself felt: and a treatise on the German Wine Law written by the young barrister was suspended and then on the morning of his 31st birthday, there arrived the enforcement of the recent law, forbidding him to practice in the legal profession—Fritz was now jobless. There was only one thing to do, and that was to take up as a profession that which had been his hobby all his life.

So much I learned from Fritz as we dashed round hairpin bends, darted into cool cellars, or sipped a glass of Wehlener Sonnenuhr on a terrace overlooking the Moselle. By the time we had got to Wiesbaden I had found out more. In 1937 he wrote for Harpers Wine and Spirit Gazette an article on German Wine Law which had failed to see daylight under the Third Reich. I remember it well, and so must many more, for he was inundated with requests for copies. It was these requests which contributed to his decision to write this present book. But the fire can well be laid; the tinder may be there; still a spark was needed and this was supplied by his children who had listened with interest so often to their father's anecdotes of his Rhineland youth as he took them along with him on his wine buying tours, that one day they politely suggested he put them down and turn them into a book.

Was it because they felt such a book would succeed? Or was it, Fritz confided in me, because they didn't want to hear the stories repeated again?

No matter; all that does matter is that here is a book written by a man who really knows his subject, who knows how to present it in a readable manner, and—here comes the highest praise of all— who has produced a work which anyone seriously in the Wine Trade is bound to need as a reference book, yet which the enthusiastic amateur will read with instruction and delight; this may be because he has so admirably avoided any semblance of self-advertisement in the whole work. As for the glossary of good and bad wine terms in Appendix VI, I find this pure gold. Had it been my companion, perhaps it would have saved me from making a curious 'gaffe'— Fritz was tasting a row of twenty hocks one morning, and with less than a smattering of German I was having the cheek to act as interpreter to a friend who knew even less German than I. Suddenly Fritz tasted a wine and said 'Amerikanisch'. Eyebrows were raised, and then, again, he said 'Amerikanisch'.

There was silence.

'What does he say?' said the non-speaking English friend. This took place at the home town of a courtier outside Wiesbaden, a town stiff with Americans, as it was the Air H.Q.

To conclusions I jumped. 'Hallgarten is saying that that wine is one which would appeal to American palates', I replied, and added, 'I can't quite make out whether it is a compliment or not'.

As we drove away I asked for corroboration of my translation.

'No, Tommy, the wine I tasted was not suitable for Americans. What I said was that the fact that it was made from American stock was rather more noticeable than usual'.

Thereafter I held my tongue, and the tasting tour continued. We visited the Hotel Schwan in Oestrich, we tasted asparagus at Ingelheim and tried Rhine salmon at the famous 'Krone' at Assmannshausen. I was unable to enthuse over Rhine fish in the same way that Hallgarten has done in this book, but see now by the great number of varieties obtainable that I condemned before I had all my facts; but anyway, the meat is superb. And all the time, while we drank Hock, Fritz talked wine; he talked it unaffectedly, enthusiastically and knowingly, and I learnt more in that fortnight than I had learned in all the years before.

Thank you for a splendid holiday and may your readers learn from your book as much as I did from you.

T . A . L A Y T O N

Rhineland — Wineland

The Rhine is one of the most beautiful highways created by any of Europe's rivers. At its source near the Alpine glaciers it appears as a young and turbulent mountain stream; then, after flowing through the gentle Lake of Constance with its vine- and rose-covered shores, the river moderates its pace as it passes through Southern and Western Germany on its way to the North Sea. Joining its bold sweep from the east are its eager tributaries, the Main and the Neckar, while from the west the Ahr, the Nahe and the Moselle hurry to meet and do homage to their nobler brother. All these streams are lined with vine-covered slopes. Blue skies enhance the charm of the orchards, birds sing in the beechwoods, blue cornflowers and red poppies show amidst the golden corn, while the violet hills of the Kaiserstuhl, the Taunus, the Black Forest, the Westerwald, the Siebengebirge and the Eifel in the background make a perfect foil for the colourful scene. It is a unique region which in the course of German history has collected a number of stately cathedrals, proud castles and picturesque wells built under lime-trees—not forgetting the figures of romance. For it was here too, that the legendary Nibelungen resided, here that the fairies held their revels. Rain-washed and fertile, the soil emits a scent to match the visual joys awaiting the traveller.

Before starting our journey through the wine country, let us first clear up a few points, study the arts of wine making, of wine tasting and drinking in order to enhance the enjoyment of our journey.

What is wine? The German Wine Law gives this precise definition: 'Wine is the product of fermented grape juice, made from freshly gathered grapes.' This places very definite restrictions on the meaning of the word 'wine' and excludes its use to designate concoctions made from raisins, currants, or other fruits worked up into alcoholic liquids. Wine, then, is the beverage produced by alcoholic fermentation from the juice of fresh grapes.

History of German Viticulture

Prototypes of the vine existed in primeval times. In particular, remnants of vines have been found among the strata of the tertiary formation.

There is no doubt that the knowledge required for the manufacture of wine reached Germany through the Graeco-Roman sources from Gaul. Gallic viticulture had been founded by Phocaean Greeks in pre-Roman times (approx. 600 B.C. in the region of what is now Marseilles), who extended it to cover the Garonne district and up the river Rhone. Apparently very soon after, viticulture spread towards the north and west, after Gallia Narbonnensis had become a Roman province (121 B.C.), and particularly under the influence of Caesar's conquest of the whole of Gaul (58-51 B.C.). The Roman wine-merchant preceded the conquering soldier. These were followed by the colonist and the settler who never failed to plant vines, even if only for their own use. In this way, viticulture made its way to the North—probably near the Rhine-Rhone Canal—and into the valleys of the Rhine and the Moselle. All kinds of vines were introduced in this way, but it is quite possible that the cultivation of the native wild vines was also started about that time. Certain laws restricted the extension of viticulture in the Roman province, but apparently they were never properly enforced (e.g. the lex Domitiana, 91 A.D.) —and under the Emperor Probus (276-282) they were abrogated. And not only that. Probus rendered further service to the cause of viticulture by employing his legions to lay out extensive new vineyards.

In any case, from the first centuries A.D. the Romans produced wines in many German districts : Beside the great military roads along the Rhine via Speyer and Worms as far as Mainz; along the foot of the hills via Neustadt, Deidesheim, Gruenstadt, and Alzey, to Bingen. In proof of this, numerous Roman utensils for wine cultivation have been found, as well as inscriptions, sculptures, etc. Many technical expressions, too, are of Latin origin, for example: the word 'wine' itself (German 'Wein'), from vinum; the German Most (must) from mustum; Keller (cellar) from cellare; Kufe (coop) from cupa; Kelter (wine press) from calcatorium; Schemel (stool) from scamellum; and many others.

The documentary proofs of viticulture in Germany become more numerous after this early period. In the Palatinate 70 villages are known to have planted vines from Carolingian times, and during the subsequent decades German viticulture was widely extended— even to Northern Germany and the Baltic provinces—mainly through the monasteries which were obliged to produce their own wines for celebrating Mass. Later the volume of their production went beyond their own needs, and others besides monks began to perceive the value of possessing and enlarging vineyard properties. Such people included not only abbots and ecclesiastical princes, but also hard-drinking knights and secular authorities. And thus, in the early Middle Ages, the area devoted to the culture of vines increased considerably, reaching in the early 15th century a maximum which has never since been equalled. Giant casks and drinking-vessels bear testimony to the immense consumption of wine at the drinking-bouts and various festivals customary at the time.

A second peak of prosperity of viticulture occurred in the 18th century. Better transport created better sales for the products of good wine districts, but the competition proved too formidable for the less favourably situated villages. Simultaneously the increase in the population led to a rise in the importance of agriculture, which in many districts in the plains began to displace viticulture. Gradually the restriction in the extent of the cultivation areas led to an improvement in the quality of the products, enforced by the planting of superior vine species.

In the Wine Museum at Speyer, which is well worth a visit, we find illustrated the whole history of German wine-lands and their age-old culture. Until the city was destroyed in 1689, Speyer was the main centre of the wine trade and it was in recognition of this fact that the Museum was established there. It contains striking proofs of Roman viticulture in the Palatinate—in particular Roman shapes that originated in Greece and were favoured by the vintners' utensils found on Palatinate soil, knives of the Gallo-Roman Phocaeans of Marseilles. Incidentally the same shapes are used in

Greece today. Tools, documents, coats of arms of the Palatinate communities are exhibited in the Museum; so are old wine-presses and casks, hose-pipes, wine-vessels. The last named include an amphora—two-handed vessel—made in the 3rd century which was found in a Speyer sarcophagus still filled with wine, dating from the Roman era.

The Wine Museum in Trier (created in 1925) used to contain exhibits from the whole of Germany and from all wine regions. Its viticultural and statistical material was unique, and it also made a speciality of cultural history. It would have taken anyone a good two hours even to glance at the wealth of exhibits illustrating anything and everything connected with wine. But the contents of this Museum were wantonly destroyed, and with them invaluable material for research workers and writers. The historical wine-presses were burnt and the rest of the collection was stolen. Nothing remains but the building itself which is intact, and the library, most of which was unharmed. There are plans afoot for re-stocking the Museum.

Two new Museums have been established since the war, viz., the Main-Franconian Museum in the fortress of Marienberg above Wuerzburg (which has an imposing hall in which wine-presses are housed); and the Wine Museum in the Bromserburg at Ruedesheim on the Rhine. Here students can hear impressive lectures with physical exhibits on the 2,000-year old history of viticulture on the Rhine.

In these 2,000 years the extent of the German wine area has varied considerably. From the 11th to the 13th century it extended to the northern and north-eastern provinces, wherewith it reached its maximum. According to the latest statistics the viticultural area of Western Germany now covers approximately 58,000 hectares. France—including Algeria—has thirty-five times as much, Italy thirty-four times as much, Spain twenty-seven times as much, Portugal seven and Greece three times as much. The viticultural area of the whole of Europe amounts to more than 6 million hectares of which Western Germany has only 0.8 per cent.

Since 1900 the wine area in Germany has been reduced by about 40 per cent., but the wine production in Western Germany is nevertheless a most important branch of German economy. In 1950 Western Germany had 151,649 Wine-growers, owning together 58,237 ha. vineyards (in 1939—159,500 with 66,600 ha. vineyards). The area is distributed as follows: Palatinate 14,000 hectares, Rhinehessia 13,200 hectares), Nahe (1,929 hectares), Moselle (7,528 hectares),

Rheingau (2,316 hectares), Wuerttemberg-Baden (14,522 hectares), Franconia (3,081 hectares) and Ahr (370 hectares).

There is a certain amount of viticulture in Eastern Germany, viz., in Thuringia, Saxony and Silesia, but these districts will not be included in the following survey.

The Grape-Harvest

The most picturesque process in the manufacture of wine is the gathering of the grapes. Many a traveller has been attracted to a particular locality in the hope of watching activities during the harvest season in the vineyards. Few, however, suspect how much the quantity and the quality of any vintage depend on the proper selection of the date on which the fruit may be gathered. And yet it is vitally important, a fact that has been recognized by wine-growers from time immemorial. In feudal times it was the seigneurs who set the date and kept a strict eye on the peasant to see that none entered the vineyard without special permission, particularly when the grapes were nearly ripe. This was not only to guard against pilfering, but in order to ensure delivery of a flawless harvest of fruit and grape-juice (must), for no berry was allowed to come off the vine before it was fully ripe. Incidentally, even when the grape-harvest was in full swing, the vineyard might only be entered at specified times, the object being to hinder any grower from trespassing on his neighbour's ground and taking his fruit.

The same ancient rules are still in force, though for different reasons. Harvesting dates are set by the Commissions which exist in every grape-growing community and are composed of the leading growers. Their main object is to secure the best possible vintage in every respect by choosing the most favourable date. The riper the grapes, the more juicy they are and the richer the wine, not only in sugar and acid content, but also in the etheric substances on which its bouquet and flavour depend. Even when the grape-gathering has officially started, the growers are not allowed to harvest their fruit when they please. Wine must never be watery, so the Commission, concerned to prevent the gathering of grapes which may be wet with dew or raindrops, takes careful meteorological observations and in accordance with these and other conditions orders the daily ringing of local church bells to denote the beginning and ending of picking-time. At the sound of the early bell, whole families—men, women, and children—stream forth to the vineyards, their vine-cutters in their hands. There is work for all and to spare.

In order still further to enhance the quality of the wine, other special procedure is habitually taken during the harvesting. There is, for instance, the Spaetlese (late gathering); one speaks of a Spaetlese when the gathering of the grapes takes place a good time after the normal period of harvesting, so that all grapes of the vineyard are fully ripe. 'Auslese' of grapes is made that only the choicest fruit is used for the wine-making, to the exclusion of any specimens that may be diseased, damaged, or less than fully ripe. Beerenauslesen are Auslesen of berries, over-ripe and 'sleepy' from good 'Lagen' for separate pressing.

Trockenbeerenauslesen are Beerenauslesen as described above, but the collection of these 'sleepy' berries takes place only after these have been semi-dried by the sun while still on the vines and have attained an almost raisin-like consistency. 'Sleepiness' in grapes is caused by the fungus known as *Botrytis cinerea*, which is apt to attack the fruit in a mild and sunny autumn. Its action is beneficial and greatly improves the quality of the grape. Needing for its existence large quantities of acid, it destroys the grapeskin by means of its mycelial filaments, causing the water in the berry to evaporate in the dry, sunny autumn air; the fruit-pulp thus becomes more concentrated with a relatively higher sugar-content until the berry is finally sun-dried into a natural raisin. The dehydration process may result in the evaporation of as much as three-quarters of the water content, bringing the harvest down to one-quarter of its normal amount.

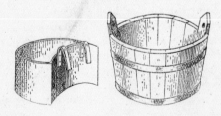

When gathering the grapes, the harvesters collect these rarer dried-up raisin-berries in special sickle shaped containers hung in the punnets into which they throw the rest of the fruit. A foreman in charge of every 8 to 10 (female) workers keeps careful watch to see that no ordinary grapes are mistaken for the genuine sleepy berries and wrongly placed in the special containers. In this process, it takes anything up to 100 workers (varying with the size of the vineyard a full two weeks to gather enough fruit from a vineyard of 3 hectares (nearly 7½ acres) to make 300 litres of must.

The highly concentrated must from the over-ripe berries dried on the vine is so rich in sugar that it may fairly be described as syrupy, and this makes its fermentation and after-fermentation a difficult task which can only be entrusted to an expert with long experience and specialized knowledge. Once it has been accomplished, however, the result is a dream of perfection. The fineness, the delicate aroma, the rare bouquet, and the noble quality are indescribable. Honey sweet richness tempered by the clean, pure, finely-acidulated flavour of the grape make this wine the connoisseur's joy. Not easily obtainable, it is of course correspondingly high-priced.

The partial dehydration of over-ripe grapes which turns them into raisins is an ancient process. It is mentioned in the Old Testament, and Homer has a description of it. He speaks both of allowing the grapes to hang on the vines till they are over-ripe and partially dried, and of the process by which they are dried (after picking) by being exposed to the sun on hurdles or beds of straw.

The ancient Romans were familiar with the respective processes of sorting out over-ripe and partially sun-dried fruit as already described but in the course of time the knowledge was lost and was not recovered till the beginning of last century. The revival, so the story runs, was due to chance. The Bishop of Fulda, owner of vineyards in the Rheingau, is said to have delayed sending his permission to begin grape-harvesting until 'too late,' in other words, until the fruit had become over-ripe. To everybody's amazement, the resulting vintage was superb.

To the 1920 Steinberger belongs the distinction of having attained the record weight of must of any selected dry-berry vine—its specific gravity was found to be 268 degrees Oechsle standard (see below).

When the grapes have been gathered, they are tipped into large barrels and driven to the wine-presses. Here they are first crushed in grape-mills, after which the juice has to be separated from the mash. In Germany, mechanical presses—worked hydraulically or by electricity—are generally used for this purpose. The amount of must obtained by pressing 100 kilogrammes of grapes varies — according to the kind of grapes, the year and the degree of ripeness of the fruit—from 65 to 80 litres.

The must is then pumped from the presses into its appointed vats in the fermentation cellar. Vats in Germany are usually made in two sizes, holding respectively 1,200 and 600 litres (as in Rheingau and Rhinehessia, where the full size is designated as 'Stück' and the half-size as 'Halbstück'), or else (as in the Moselle district and the Palatinate) holding respectively 1,000 (220 gallons) and 500 (110 gallons) litres and known as 'Fuder' and 'Halbfuder."

From Vine to Cellar

Having deposited the must in its vats, there to await fermentation and the rest of its gradual transformation into bottled wine, it is time to consider more closely some particular aspects of wine-making.

What, for example, is must (grape-juice) ? Clear must is an aqueous solution of various substances, the most important quantitatively being sugar and acids. The average sugar content is from 14 to 22 per cent. A seasonal crop of unripe berries can bring this down to 6 or 7 per cent., while a crop of sleepy grapes will yield a sugar content of 35 per cent. or more. Selected 1921 vintages showed as much as 52 per cent., and those of 1949, 43 per cent.

The sugar content is not uniform, but is composed on the one hand of grape-sugar (dextrose, glucose) and on the other of fruit-sugar (levulose, fructose). Fully matured grapes contain about equal quantities of the two kinds of sugar; unripe grapes have a preponderance of grape-sugar, while over-ripe and sleepy fruit has more fructose.

The more noteworthy acids found in must—some free, others combined with mineral substances such as potassium and calcium—are tartaric acid, malic acid, and tannic acid. Tartaric acid, absent in almost all other fruits, is characteristic of the grape. Its quantity increases till the fruit begins to ripen and then remains practically static till full maturity is reached. At first, much of this acid is free, but it has an increasing tendency—during the ripening process—to combine with potassium to form potassium bitartrate (cream of tartar) and also lesser quantities of other bases.

Malic acid, a very frequent phenomenon in nature, plays the main part among wine acids. It is almost always present in free state, and increases rapidly in quantity up to the moment when the fruit begins to ripen. At that point there is far more malic acid than tartaric acid to be found in the grape. During the ripening process, however, the malic acid content decreases through exhalation, until in a good year it may drop below that of tartaric acid; even in the ripe grape it does not disappear entirely.

The amount of tannic acid in must depends on the way the mash is treated. In any case, only traces of it are found in the fruit-pulp, while the skin, pips, and stalks contain respectively 1.5 per cent., 4 per cent., and 2.5 per cent. The longer the mash is allowed to stand, therefore, the more tannic acid is present in the must and the wine itself. Where the mash has been put through the wine-presses immediately, the resulting wine is poor in tannic acid; where the mash is allowed to stand and ferment (red wines), there is a high tannic acid content.

Besides sugars and acids, grape-juice contains traces of numerous other substances all of which have their part to play in determining the development and the quality of the wine. Among these are the nitrogenous compounds: albumen, peptones, amides, ammonium salts, nitrates—which provide the ferment with its nitrogen; and the mineral components from which the ferment derives the bases needed for its development, namely potassium, phosphoric acid, calcium.

Of inestimable value to the wine are the substances which give it its bouquet, or peculiar aromatic odour. In the must the only recognizable aroma is that of the primitive grape-bouquets, the chemical origin of which is still unknown. Their nature is decisive for the value of the wine, and in certain kinds of grapes, such as Muscats, Gewuerztraminer ('spicy traminer'), 'Riesling', the primitive bouquet is particularly strong and characteristic.

The original grape aroma increases with the maturing of the fruit.

Finally, the must contains colouring matter. White and red must invariably absorb decomposition particles from the chlorophyll in the grapeskin and stalks, and these latter give hock its yellow colour. White wines derived from mash which has been put through the wine-presses immediately, are always lighter in colour than those from mash which has been allowed to stand, because in the latter case more of the decomposition matter from the chlorophyll has been absorbed.

When grape-juice is transformed into wine by fermentation, the most noteworthy chemical change is the resolution of the sugar content into roughly equal quantities of alcohol and carbon dioxide. The alcohol content of any wine is somewhat less than half the sugar content of the must.

Sweetening

Unfavourable climatic conditions in many German Wine-growing districts often prevent a (varying) proportion of the grapes from reaching full maturity. In most years therefore many German wine-growers are unfortunately compelled to take steps to improve a large part of the crop. This consists of adding sugar or sugar solution to the defective juice up to one-third of its quantity. Unripe grapes produce a wine which not only keeps badly, falling an easy prey to acidification and other diseases, but which is unpalatable, because alcohol and acid are blended in the wrong proportions and there is a lack of 'body'.

But the effect of the climate in these districts is not all bad. It is also largely responsible for the variety in the types of these wines, their robust flavour and other individual characteristics.

The addition of sugar to German wines is regulated by the Wine Law of 25th July, 1930. Article 3 states:—

> Sugar (or sugar dissolved in pure water) may be added to grape-must or wines (in the case of red wine also to grape-mash) derived from home-grown grapes, provided that this is done for the purpose of supplementing a natural lack of sugar or alcohol, or counteracting a natural excess of acid, to an extent sufficient to produce in the said wines a composition equal to that of wines derived in a good year from grapes of the same kind and origin without extraneous additions.
>
> Such addition may however in no case make up more than one-fourth of the whole quantity of the liquid.

The legality of the proceeding by which a lack of sugar or alcohol or an excess of acids is cured, through the addition of dry sugar or an aqueous sugar solution is dependent on the fact that these defects are due to natural causes. Intentional unnecessary premature grape-gathering bars any such possibility of improvement. This shows that it would be unfair to suspect all German wines of being doctored simply because in certain specified cases it is permissible to add extraneous sugar. It should also be noted in this connection that Germany is not the only country in which it is permissible to improve wines. Other countries too, even those with more favourable climatic conditions than Germany, make similar concessions to their growers, French growers, for example, are permitted to add sugar or sugar-water to their wines, with the proviso that in the latter case they lose the right to market their products with the original 'appellation controlée'. Tarragona wines are usually sweetened with grape juice, while the sweet taste of port-wine is only preserved by interrupting fermentation through the addition of brandy.

In Germany, as has been seen, the law limits the amount of extraneous sugar (or sugar solution) to a quantity which makes the composition of the improved product equal in alcohol and acid content to that of wines derived in a good year from grapes of same kind from same site without extraneous addition. This does not mean that a particularly good year like 1921 or 1949 may be taken as the standard, but it does mean that the best years may be included in computing the average according to which any wine may be improved by the addition of sugar or aqueous sugar solution. Where dry sugar is added, this is the only limitation, but in the case of sugar solution a further limit is imposed, viz., that in no case— however high the acid content of the original produce—may more than one quarter of the total liquid be made up of added sugar solution; in other words, not more than one-third of the quantity of the defective must or wine may be added. The highest permissible ration of sugar-solution to wine (or must) is thus 250 litres of the former to 750 litres of the original liquid.

In order to simplify the calculations attendant on the sweetening practice, the various grape-growing districts in the Rhineland have been divided into three categories, each with its own sweetening maximum. This maximum is fixed according to the so-called Oechsle standard, which is a convenient designation for the specific gravity of any given must. It indicates the number of grammes by which one litre of must is heavier than one litre of water, the sugar content representing about 25 per cent. of this calibration. Thus, with a reading of 100° Oeschle, 100 litres will contain about 25 kilogrammes of sugar. Districts in Category One are those with the most favourable sites. These are allowed to add sugar solution up to a maximum alcohol content of 98° Oeschle standard. For Category Two the limit is 92°, and for Category Three 85°. Poorer vineyards in these districts are restricted to a limit still lower than that of their category, while particularly good sites in categories two and three may exceed by a small margin the limits of their respective categories.

The final alcohol content of any wine can be calculated with fair accuracy by dividing the specific gravity of the must by ten. The figure thus obtained denotes the number of grammes of alcohol that will be generated in 100 cubic centimetres of the wine.

Owing to the great number of variations from year to year in the quality of the musts produced by each of the many kinds of grape, it would be impossible—even if for no other reason—to use the same recipe that did duty for any one season for the following year's vintage. The quality of the product depends not only on the district and the site, which may be favourable or otherwise, but also on the specific gravity of the must (the variations of which are considerable), the degree of acidity produced by the stage of maturity at which the grapes are gathered, the kinds of manures used, the methods adopted to destroy pests, etc. It is therefore essential for the assessment of the permitted amount of additional sugaring, that the specific gravity of the must and the proportion of acidity are measured in each individual case.

While it is illegal to 're-sugar' a must or wine which has already been treated, pure wines of previous vintages may be 'improved' in the period between 1st October and 31st January. After 31st January sugaring is forbidden. Other regulations laid down in the Wine Law are aimed at simplifying control. Thus sweetening may only be carried out within the German wine regions, and the authorities must be notified of the proposed sugaring of all grape mash, must or wine. In the case of natural wines, such notification must be given at least eight days in advance, while a single 'block' notification is sufficient to cover the whole produce of a new crop. The sugar used must be pure and free from colouring matter; subject to this condition it may be the product of cane, beet, starch, or a mixture of fruit-sugar and grape-sugar ('invert' sugar) such as is often used for this purpose. As already stated, no wines may be put on the market as wines if there has been any contravention of the law in their treatment. Such wines are also liable to confiscation.

Wine control is efficiently organized. Trading in wine is supervised from the moment it reaches the wine-presses till it is sold for consumption. Wine Controllers with expert knowledge are appointed for all German regions. They have wide powers and can, at their own discretion, visit growers and wine-merchants, check their books, correspondence, price-lists, etc. (there are detailed provisions for the obligatory book-keeping), taste the wine in storage, and so on. If the Controller finds anything amiss or has suspicions of any of the products, he can take away samples for chemical examination. If these show grounds for objection, the wines may be confiscated and the owner prosecuted.

The Fermentation

To return to the must. Soon after it has been deposited in the vats, the vital process of fermentation starts. This acts on the fermentable sugars and generates not only alcohol and carbon dioxide, but also glycerine, succinic acid, volatile acids, ethylic alcohols, and various esters.

Fermentation is a gradual process. By the time it ceases, the sugar has been broken down, and the expiring yeast precipitated to the bottom of the vessel. About January the young wine can be separated from this sediment and can be racked-off, i.e., drained off into another cask. This racking-off is repeated two or three times (second racking approximately 6 weeks, third racking approximately four months after the first racking), and is usually supplemented by a mechanical clearing of the young wine by 'fining' or filtering in an asbestos filter which retains all the sediments and impurities. Success or failure may depend on the proper and well-timed application of these measures and on the selection of the right moment for bottling the finished wine.

Another important factor in determining the quality of the wine is the manner in which it is stored. For many centuries theory and practice followed the principle of allowing wines to ferment in wooden vats and of storing them in the same way, the idea being that wine must 'breathe' and that the porous wood allowed it to do so. Recent years have, however, brought great changes in this matter. Immense progress has been made, and experiments are still continuing. Here are some examples.

A 1948 Kreuznach Riesling which had been allowed to ferment in an enamelled high-pressure tank (under the auspices of the local Academy for Viticulture) fetched 60 per cent. more at an auction held in June 1949 than wine which had been freely fermented. The explanation was that the cellarer had watched over the development of the wine from beginning to end and had, by using the high-pressure tank, preserved the natural carbon dioxide which was generated by the wine in the course of fermentation. This process also increased the volume of those substances which give the wine its full maturity and reduced the escape of those which enhance the bouquet, and also of alcohol.

The carbon dioxide that develops in the hermetically sealed tank is the best medium for regulating the fermentation. If it can then be preserved in the wine itself, the result is a mild pleasant drink which is just perceptibly sweet. Wines which are bottled with a relatively high natural carbon dioxide content are less likely to suffer from a slight sediment of sugar particles than others which are poor in carbon dioxide content. Their flavour is also more aromatic.

I myself had occasion to note these differences while in the Niederhausen Domain. I tasted and compared wines which had been fermented as just described and others produced on the same day by the same vineyard but fermented in the old-fashioned way. The difference in quality was indescribable. The Lehranstalt in

Geisenheim used the same procedure for the fermentation of their
1949 Geisenheimer Mauerchen Spaetlese (Cask No. 4932) and the
Geisenheimer Altbaum Auslese (Cask No. 4948); the result was
elegance, finesse, fullness and fruitiness, so that leading growers
decided to change over to their modern art of wine making as soon
as their financial situation allows. Actually, the Domain at Eltville
stored part of the 1950 Vintage in tanks (9 tanks of 8,500 litres each
and one of 21,000 litres), and so did Schloss Johannisberg with approximately 10 tanks of 6,500 litres each.   It will take years until all
wines are treated this way, but the beginning has been made, and
great and pleasant surprises are in store for all wine-lovers!

When fermentation is over and the wine has been drawn off from
the lees—first racking—growers and wine-merchants start its treatment for bottling. In old days this process was left to nature, i.e.,
wine was left in cask till it became impervious to air and had lost
every vestige of cloudiness.   This usually entailed a succession of
rackings and often operated to the detriment of the consumer, the
wine having lost its freshness by the time it was finally bottled.

The Cellaring

Nowadays wine is bottled much earlier. This is a great progress,
made possible by advances in science and long experience of cellaring. New methods of treating must and wine, involving in some
cases the employment of new materials, have replaced the old practices. It must be borne in mind in this connection that it is no
simple matter to produce a good wine. Wine in its early stages may
easily be attacked by disease and may exhibit defects that can only
be cured by what amounts to an operation. But not all 'curative'
methods are legal; wine legislation limits the processes that may be
applied to wine in cellars to a selected range. It lays down what
substances may be added and in what quantities, with the further
limitation that such additions may never exceed genuine cellaring

requirements. Here are some examples of the restrictive provisions :

Defects of colour and flavour may be rectified by the addition of liquid wine lees, but these must be the product of the same cellars. The amount added may not exceed 15 per cent. of the volume of wine treated.

For starting or accelerating fermentation, lees may be used, but they must be pure liquid lees with a maximum volume of 2 per cent. of the liquid treated.

It. has often been found necessary to neutralize excess acidity in wines with a high acid content by adding calcium carbonate. While no legal limits are set to quantity to be applied in such cases, practice has shown that no more than 2 grammes acid per litre may be thus neutralized, as otherwise the alkaline addition produces an unpleasant chalky taste. The chemical used in such cases must be 'pure precipitated calcium carbonate'. This combines with the tartaric acid in the wine to form calcium tartrate, a salt which is only slightly soluble in wine and which is therefore speedily precipitated in the form of hard crystals. The carbon dioxide in the calcium carbonate, freed by this chemical reaction, escapes into the air in the effervescence generated in the process.

Sulphurization. Other permissible treatments of, and additions to, Wines.

Sulphurizing of wines is also regulated by law, a very necessary precaution in the interest of viticulture, to keep the wine sound. The wine law does not say how much sulphur may be used. As will be recalled, even those substances with which it is permissible to treat the wine may only be applied if their use is necessitated by the requirement of good cellarage. Sulphurization fulfils this condition, as it is needed to keep the wines sound and prevent the formation of organisms which might cause decomposition. The quantity which is absolutely necessary depends upon the type of wine. Rich wines need more to mature than ordinary wine. Food chemists have agreed that it is essential for the quality of the wine, that a maximum should be set for the use of sulphur. The limit should stand at 200 milligrammes per litre, of ordinary wine, to include no more than 50 milligrammes of the free (sulphuric) acid.

There are, however, exceptions to this rule, particularly when a wine is affected by a disease. In these cases sulphur must be used more liberally in order to preserve the wine or counteract the disease. Similarly the sulphurization of musts can exceed the limit when necessary to maintain a predetermined grade of sweetness, particularly in musts produced from selected 'sleepy' or 'dry-berry' fruit.

It may be interesting to show the limits of sulphurization in various countries:—Germany 200 mg/1, France 450 mg/1, Spain 450 mg/1, Portugal 350 mg/1, Italy 200 mg/1, South Africa 200 mg/1 for dry wine, 357 mg/1 for sweet wine, England 450 mg/1.

Sulphurization may be carried out by means of the following processes : Burning sulphur or sulphur wafers, with the exception of sulphur containing spices; employment of pure sulphuric acid in gaseous form or of solution containing a minimum of 5 per cent. sulphur dioxide (made of liquid sulphurous acid in distilled water); employment of commercially pure potassium pyrosulphite (in tablet or other form).

Carbon dioxide is sometimes added to wine that has grown rather stale and flat, in order to 'freshen' it. There are no quantitative restrictions on the addition of this gas.

A maximum of 10 grammes of *tannin* per 100 litres may be added to wine. This combines with the albuminous matters in the wine and tends to make it more durable. It also promotes the precipitation of substances inclined to cause turbidity.

White clay (kaolin) may be added in some circumstances, chiefly in the case of viscous wines.

Another permissible addition is purified *charcoal* prepared from wood or bones. It is used to remove certain defects, counteract some diseases, and also to improve the wine's appearance.

Wine-drinkers are becoming increasingly inclined to prefer young, fresh wines and to demand their complete limpidity—they expect them to be 'bright as the stars'. Wines can be clarified either by 'fining' or by filtering.

The ancient method of *clarifying* wine by the use of isinglass (obtained from sturgeon or shad) is still very much to the fore. Other materials used for clarification are gelatine, agar-agar (also known as Bengal or Japan isinglass), white of egg, and white clay.

Addition of Alcohol. When wine is to be sent in barrels to tropical countries, it is permissible to fortify it by the addition of spirits of wine or of high-grade spirit (90 per cent. alcohol content or more), up to a maximum of 1 per cent. of the volume of the wine.

Filtering. Filters used for clearing wine of impurities may not contain any soluble substance that might be absorbed by the wine.

Sugar standard. It is a long-standing practice to cater for the taste of some consumers by maintaining certain wines as far as possible at a consistent level of sweetness. The technics of cellaring have now reached such a high state of development that it is possible to do this in two ways. One: lees and bacteria may be eliminated from wine by filtering it before the fermentation process has been concluded. In that way part of the sugar content is preserved unfermented. But for this to succeed the conversion of malic acid must also be interrupted. Where therefore wine has to be treated so extensively for technical reasons that it loses all its sugar in the process, the second method is used, viz.: the addition to completely fermented wine of small percentages of sterilized sweetened must, sufficient to attain the desired standard of sweetness.

Blue-Fining

Some wines are apt to prove recalcitrant when treated for turbidity with the fining substances just mentioned or when subjected to filtration. One cause of this may be the presence of copper particles— not, be it said, a normal or frequent phenomenon. When this does occur, it may be due to the use of unsuitable vessels; or it may be the result of employing a wash of calcined copper, copper oxychloride, or copper acetate to combat vine-mildew (a disease caused by one of the fungi). Most of the copper is precipitated during fermentation, probably as cupric sulphate or phosphate, or possibly through combination with yeast-gum. The copper traces that remain can be eliminated by what is known as 'blue-fining.' So, incidentally, can any zinc particle (only found in wine when zinc-coated apparatus has been used), as well as the traces of iron always present in natural wines. In combination, as iron phosphates, the last frequently produce a whitish-grey turbidity in the wine which shows an obstinate tendency to recur when (temporarily) removed by filtration.

What is 'blue-fining'? The layman may be surprised to learn that it denotes treatment with potassium ferrocyanide which in certain combinations produces the deadly poison, prussic acid.

The use of potassium ferrocyanide was legalized as far back as 1923, and for the following reason :

Other clarifying media merely remove substances in solid form which are making the wine cloudy. But to deal with the heavy metal salts *dissolved* in the wine, it is necessary first to turn them into solids. And the action of potassium ferrocyanide on the metal salts does just that. The precipitated solids are then easily removable. But if more of the reagent is added than is necessary for the purpose, the remainder combines with acids present in the wines to form the deadly prussic acid. It is obvious that expert dosage is needed, graduated in relation to the volume of the wine. To guard against the deleterious effect of possible inexpert handling, the law, which does not recognize any effective method of removing prussic acid from the wine, has laid down that on completion of the treatment the wine may not contain in solution any cyanide compounds whatever; it must be analysed by a 'wine chemist'.

Experiments had been undertaken by which the iron content of wines was to be precipitated in the form of ferrous tannin by the addition of oxygen. It turned out, however, that wines thus treated with oxygen took on a very dark colour and were apt to age very quickly. This method was therefore abandoned in favour of bluefining.

Sterilization Filters

It has been mentioned above that bacteria may be eliminated by filtering. Obviously the filter used for this purpose cannot be one of the ordinary asbestos filters used for clearing the wine of impurities, but must be specially constructed. Sterilizing filters are made on the model of the cellar-presses which were formerly in common use in wine-cellars. Sealed off between two covers there is a fixed number of so-called 'clear' and 'turbid' chambers, arranged alternately. Separating the chambers are so-called 'sterilizing sheets' held in place by a simple device. It is these sheets that give the filter its peculiar character. They have minute pores that not even the smallest microscopic particles can penetrate, which means that they are capable of excluding from wines or other filterable liquids even bacteria and fermenting fungi. In other words, this method makes it possible to sterilize liquids without heating them—i.e., by a 'cold' process. The replacement of the pasteurizing apparatus (till lately employed for sterilizing wines) by these 'filters' represents an immense improvement. The 'pasteurization' of wine meant heating it to 167°F., the temperature at which all undesirable bacteria and fermenting fungi might be considered to have been rendered harmless; the filter achieves the same object at normal cellar temperature, thus removing the risk of change in the character of the wine inseparable from the application of heat.

Sterilization filters may also be used to prepare for bottling wines which—though perfectly healthy and fully matured—still contain a quantity of unfermented sugar. The use of the filter eliminates the risk that such wines will later become clouded with lees or turn acid.

Blending

In the Rheingau, the principal wine-growing centres of Rhinehessia, the Palatinate, and the central Moselle region, most growers keep the wines produced by each vineyard separated from each other. Some of them even go so far as to keep in different casks the wine made from grapes gathered on different days. Thus the individuality of the wines is meticulously preserved.

It is however a well-known fact that the quality of the grape harvest varies from year to year, even in one locality. On the other hand, once the wine-drinking public has become accustomed to a wine with particular qualities, it is apt to expect the wine merchant to continue delivering the same wine. Sometimes the blending of various wines may achieve the desired result and this has been found

1. Idyllic wine corner in the Wine Museum in Speyer.

2. & 3. Roman wine-jugs
(Museum Speyer).

4. Amphora (3rd century
A.D.) still filled with wine
dating from the Roman
era.

5. Roman wine-ship (3rd century) found in the Moselle near Neumagen.

6. Roman wine containers (200 B.C.).

7. Wood carving (Museum Speyer).

10. (*Opposite*) Old winepresses in Eberbach (Rheingau).

8. Cellar in Eberbach.

9. Old wine press (Museum Speyer).

10.

11. & 12.
Harvest preparations.

13, 14 & 15.
Grape picking near Ruedesheim
(Rheingau).

16. Grapes arriving at the pressing house.

17. Grapes being unloaded and put through the grinding mill.

18. View of the pressing house.

19. Grape mash.

20. The hydraulic press can be handled by a child.

21 & 23 (*Opposite*). From the press into the cask which has been sulphured beforehand.

22. Fermentation in cask and tank, side by side. (Viticultural College, Kreuznach, Nahe.)

24. (*Opposite*) Casks with glass heads to show how the young wine becomes clear (Viticultural College, Geisenheim).

25. Cellar.

28. (*Opposite*) The young wine (Federweisser) is tasted.

26. & 27. The young wine is racked.

29. Wine Tasting.

30.
The wine
(after more
rackings and
finings)
is bottled.

31.
The wine
finally goes
to the cellar
to mature.

32. Wine
Tasting.

33 & 34.
Work in the vineyards.

35. New vines, one
and two years
old, in a greenhouse
(Geisenheim).

36. New vines,
(crossings) planted
in the open
(Geisenheim).

37. Wine chemical
laboratory
(Viticultural College,
Geisenheim).

the best way of meeting the wishes of the consumers. For this reason the law permits the blending of wines of different origins.

Blending is a very difficult and intricate part of cellar work, an art that requires many years' experience and a first-class sense of smell and taste. It is undertaken as has just been observed, in order to make possible the delivery of wines of consistent quality; it is also a method by which prices can be regulated and inequalities adjusted.

It is, for example, permissible to blend wines of low acid content with others rich in acids. For this purpose any wines of German origin of any vintage year may be blended with each other. To give extreme examples: a Rhine wine may even be blended with a Moselle or a Stein, or a 1936 vintage with a 1921 crop. Certain limits have however been laid down and these rules must be strictly observed. Red wines, for instance, may only be blended with each other—the admixture of white wine to red is illegal. Nor may any foreign wine be blended with one of German origin.

Curiously enough, many laymen are prejudiced against any blending of wines. Perhaps the above explanation may serve to show that such prejudice is unjustified. Not only is blending perfectly legal, but it is in the interest of the consumer that it should be undertaken by any wine merchant who is not committed to selling exclusively 'original' wines. No one can reasonably expect every cask of wine to be perfect, to possess all the qualities desired by the eyes, nose and palate of the purchaser. But if the wine-expert is able to perfect the quality of the wine by blending two or more kinds and thus place on the market an irreproachable and completely natural product at a comparatively low price, surely that is all to the good and quite unobjectionable from the consumer's (or indeed from any) point of view.

Nomenclature

Very strict regulations control the naming and marking of wines intended for sale. In fact, owing to the wide possibilities and the large number of rules that have been gradually evolved to prevent unfair practices, the subject has become very intricate. As an aid to understanding, it is well to remember certain basic principles on which the rules are founded and to regard all other regulations in the light of modifications of these principles, tending to greater or less severity as the case may be.

The first principle is embodied in an enactment forbidding misleading nomenclature and all deceptive marketing devices. A second enactment is founded on the basic rule that topographical designations of wines may be used solely for indicating their origins. Blends are dealt with separately.

Thus, if extraneous sugar has been added to a wine, it would be illegal to call it by a name that might induce a purchaser to assume its purity or to believe that special care had been used in its production. Again : To put up a Rhine wine in a 'Bocksbeutel' (a flask of distinctive and peculiar shape) which by long custom is used only for Stein wines, constitutes a clear case of fraudulent marketing. Similarly, when wines are designated by invented names, it is illegal to print a landscape on the label, as this might create the impression that the fancy appellation was a designation of origin.

A natural wine may have attached to it any description referring to its purity, vintage, etc., which is customarily used in marketing, provided it is in no way misleading.

The main examples of such descriptions (implying the purity of a wine or that especial care has been used in procuring the grapes) —and which, as has been mentioned, may not be used in connection with sweetened wines—are the following :—
Naturwein (natural wine); ungezuckerter Wein (nonsweetened wine); rein (pure); naturrein (purely natural); echt (genuine); Wachstum, Kreszenz [my] own vineyard; Gewaechs, Eigengewaechs (growth); Originalwein (original wine); Originalabfuellung, -abzug (original bottling) or any other combinations with the word 'original'; Kellerabfuellung, -abzug (bottled in cellar of the proprietor); Schlossabzug ('castle-bottled'); Fass Nr. (Cask No.); Fuder Nr.-Spaetlese; Auslese; Beerenauslese; Trockenbeerenauslese; Hochgewaechs, Spitzengewaechs, Edelgewaechs (superb, supreme, noble growth); Edelwein, Edelauslese (noble wine, noble select); Cabinetwein or Kabinettwein (cabinet wine).

APPLICATION OF TERMS. The terms 'Original-abfuellung' und 'Originalabzug' may be applied only to unsweetened wine developed and bottled in the grower's cellars. The term 'Spaetlese' is reserved exclusively for unsweetened wine from fully ripened grapes gathered later than the normal harvesting period. The designation 'Auslese' is strictly limited to unsweetened wines produced entirely from carefully selected berries, to the exclusion of any that are not fully ripe or are in any way damaged or diseased. 'Beerenauslese' denotes a wine made from specially selected single berries which have been allowed to become over-ripe in good vineyards, while 'Trockenbeerenauslese' refers to wines made exclusively from the shrivelled raisin-like berries obtained by allowing over-ripe grapes to become partially dried on the vine. Only 'Beeren-' and 'Trockenbeerenauslesen' may be designated as 'Spitzen-' or 'Hochgewaechs'.

No wine may be marketed as 'natural' if the unsweetened, i.e., natural, product has been adulterated by the addition of an 'improved' wine, however small a quantity of the latter may have been added.

Place Names and Site Names

German wines are named after the villages, or other locality at or near which they are grown. Often the suffix '-er' is added to the name of the locality to designate the wine. Thus a wine may be called 'Ruedesheim'—the actual place-name—or more 'usually, Ruedesheimer, meaning 'the wine of Ruedesheim'. (It has sometimes been mistakenly thought that the '-er' denotes the comparative form, indicating a better quality. This is not the case.)

The vineyards of a village are divided into several 'Lagen' (sites) with special names distinguishing them from each other—e.g., Ruedesheim Schlossberg, Roseneck, Berg Burgweg, Hauserweg, etc.; Berncastel-Lay, Altenwald, Doctor, etc. Any wine grown in the borough of Ruedesheim may be called 'Ruedesheimer', but it may only be called 'Ruedesheimer Roseneck' if it has been grown in that district of the borough of Ruedesheim which is known as Roseneck.

I have frequently been asked what significance should be attached to the site-names. What, I have been asked to explain, does 'Lage' really mean ? The term denotes a piece of land. Where one 'site' or piece of land ends the next begins, and the sites keep their distinctive names even where they overlap the local community boundaries. In other words, the names of 'Lagen' within the wine district are like the names of municipal districts within a town or city. Like all names, they are used to distinguish their owners and make them easier to find.

Despite the similarity of the geological structure and of the vine-yard sites, the quality varies greatly. The slightest differences in soil, in the Lage, or its situation in respect to the sun, produce differentiations in the wine. Even Goethe bore witness to this when he wrote in 1814: 'The quality of a wine depends on its Lage'. An investigation into the meanings and origins (with appropriate classi-fication) yields an astonishing fund of discoveries and unsuspected connections. In addition, there are names embodying historical memories; names with ecclesiastical flavour that carry allusions to churches, church dignitaries, ecclesiastical institutions, monasteries; or names that recall theological conceptions, picturing for example various aspects or phenomena of heaven and hell. At times a name has been inspired by the particular colour of some vine-bearing rock or mountain side, and—naturally enough—vineyards, specially favoured by the sun's rays are frequently the bearers of names indi-cating either the sun itself or the effects of its light and warmth. Other sites have been given the names of birds or other animals.

Then again we find vineyards with poetical, humorous, or grotesque appellations. (To give a full list of 10,000 sites would fill a book. I therefore give in appendix a short list, under the various headings, of the sites known in this country.) The famous vintage 'Forster Ungeheuer' is derived from the name of former owners of the vine-yard, 'a patrician family called Ungeheuer. Although the word 'ungeheuer' (literally 'monstrous') is commonly used to denote some-thing 'overwhelming', it has in this case nothing to do with the fact that the wines from the Ungeheuer Estate are in truth 'over-whelmingly' full and rich. So may many other sites have been named after their proprietor.

Names of Lagen were often taken from such obvious points of contact as the shape of a hill, the rock formation, or other natural features *on* or *near* which they were situated. Hence the numerous combinations with:— berg (hill, slope); Weinberg or Wingert (vineyard); -feld (field); -Acker (field, etym. acre); -bach (stream, rivulet); -lay (form of 'Lage', site. Etym. 'lair'); -stein (stone); -kopf (head, summit); -mauer (wall); -strasse (road, high-way); -weg (way); -pfad (path), etc.

Examples of such original site-names are the following (to be found in Nierstein):—

Am Hinkelstein, auf dem Domtal, am Geisenberg, Hinter der Warte, Ober dem Fockenberg, in der Rehbachersteig, im unterer Hipping, bei dem Kiliansberg, im unteren oder oberen Auflangen etc. In time these names were shortened to *Hinkelstein, Domtal,*

Many mementoes of cultural history are preserved in the names of vineyard sites. Both the names themselves and the language from which they are taken, point to the history of the Rhineland which in the course of centuries was in the hands successively of, the Romans, the French and various Germanic races.

Latin names still survive as remnants either of the Roman viticultural period or of the 'Monks' Latin of the Middle Ages. Here are some examples:

Calmont, from calido monte, meaning 'hot mountain' (Eller, Bremm);

Camp, from campus, meaning 'field' (Waldrach, Poelich);

Kranklay, from the grande lay, meaning 'great site' (Urzig, Bremm);

Kunk, from conca, literally 'shell', in this case 'valley' (Wittlich);

Laudamusberg, from the first word ('laudamus', let us praise) of a hymn (Neumagen);

Monteneubel, from in monte nobile, meaning 'noble mountain' (Enkirch);

Pichter, from petitura, meaning 'common land allotted to a vineyard' (Longuich M, Forst P);

Pomerell, from pomerellum, meaning 'little applegarden' (Zell);

Zeppwingert, probably from cippus, meaning 'summit' (Fr. ceps, meaning 'grapevine'—Enkirch M);

Old Germanic or mediaeval German names.

There are still a number of these to be found, either alone, or in combination with other terms. Examples:—

Im Wuesten (Uerzig); Neuberg (Forst P); Olk, Celtic: Originally meant 'fruit garden', later 'vineyard' (Trittenheim, Bernkastel); Boehl, meaning 'hill' (Gm. 'Berg'); Bruehl, meaning 'meadow' (Trier M, Erbach R); Held, from halde, meaning 'pasturage' (Poelich, Bernkastel, and others); Bungert, meaning 'orchard' (Baumgarten) (Poelich); Pichter, orig. meaning 'uncultivated land' (Forst); Steig (Steeg), meaning 'footbridge'; Wingert, same word as Weingarten, meaning 'vineyard'.

In almost all Moselle districts we find the name 'Lay' or 'Ley' sometimes alone, sometimes in combination—as in Urlay, Busslay, Rotlay, Muenzlay, Baerlay, Stablay, Kirchlay, Huettlay, Geierslay, Guenterslay, etc. The word ('Lay') denotes the slate rock of the Devonian formation. It occurs particularly frequently on the Middle Moselle, on the Saar and the Ruwer, and on the Middle Rhine. The

Devonian slate has its origin in the deposits of the Devonian Sea and can therefore be described as fossilized sea-foam. The slaty structure of the Moselle hills arose through the pressure of folds in the earth-crust, and through the remnants of other (higher) strata which have since for the most part been removed. Indications of this origin are still to be found in the slate in the form of fossilized flora and fauna : sea-lilies, sea-roses, sea-weeds, bracken, crabs, sea-spiders, etc. Their age is estimated as about 20 million years.

In the Lagen rejoicing in the name of 'Lay' the vines stand on slate. Slate is both warm and moist, contains potassium, and promotes growth and maturity. To this, and to the species of grape from which it is grown, the Moselle wine owes the distinctive flavour that marks it off unmistakably from the other wines of any other district. 'Lay' then means that the soil of the Lage thus designated has a pronounced slaty character. Wines from these sites are characterized especially by a strong bouquet and the typical delicate flavour of 'slatiness'. The name 'Lay' is usually applied to small sites situated round rocks, in places that are well protected and have a favourable aspect.

These site-names, some of which have great originality and charm, may be so strung together as to constitute an invitation to what might be termed the Rhineland equivalent of a merry pub-crawl. In Franconia, for instance, where the very names induce dreams of luscious wines, you can start by seating yourself on a *Kitzinger Sonnenstuhl* (sun-chair), magically placed in an *Iphofen Kammer* (Parlour); here you converse gaily with draughts of Franconian nectar, and if the conversation has been a little too much for you, you take the Thuengesheim cure known as *Thuengesheimer Scharlach* (scarlet). Then soothed by the pleasant strains of a *Wuerzburger Harfe* (harp), you tread lightly across the *Randeracker Spielberg* (Play hill), passing the *Eschendorfer 'Hengstberg'*, and, having descended into the valley, dawdle your way through the vinelands on the Main. Do not fail to look in on the *Roedelseer Kuechenmeister* (Kitchenmaster), who will provide you with sustenance for your Wuerzburger *Innere Leiste* (Inner Man). Possibly while you are thus taking your ease, someone will pluck a dunce's cap from the hill of the *Schalksberg* (Imp of Mischief) and cram it down over your ears; but most certainly that will not make such a fool of you that you will omit your visit to the *Wuerzburg Stein* (Stone), where with the help of the philosopher's stone you will regain any wisdom you may have lost. And what fun you will have watching a *Sommer-acher Katzenkopf* (Cat's Head) seeking its prey in the *Sulzfelder Maustal* (Mouse Valley). You are no snob and will therefore not object to sharing your table with the *Eschendorfer Lump* (Raga-muffin), nor are you a coward to be frightened away by the flames ascending from the *Randersacker Teufelskeller* (Devil's Cellar). But should your participation in the sinful pleasures of the cellar at any time lead you too far astray, do not forget to seek forgiveness on the *Hoerstein Abtsberg* (Abbot's Hill), after which you may pass blissfully into the *Randersacker Ewiges Leben* (Eternal Life).

It has already been mentioned that topographical descriptions of wines may only be used to designate their origin, i.e., the country, the place or district, and also the name of the 'Lage' (site). To avoid confusion which might arise owing to the duplication of names (or pronunciation of names) in different wine-growing districts, it has been laid down that where this possibility exists, descriptions must include supplementary qualifications to show the actual geographical origin of the wine. Thus : Ruedesheimer is an insufficient appellation in itself—it is either Ruedesheimer-Nahe or Ruedesheimer-Rheingau; Zeller is either Zeller-Pfalz (Palatinate), Zeller-Mosel (Moselle), Zeller-Baden, or Zeller-Franken (Franco-nia). Wachenheim is either Wachenheim-Pfalz (Palatinate), or Wachenheim-Rhinehessia.

Wine Growing Centres

The very large number of wine-growing localities and sites makes it impossible for all their names to be familiar to the public. In view of this, the law permits certain deviations from the basic regulations in order to assist the wine trade and facilitate marketing. It has therefore been enacted that certain wine-growing localities whose products are distinguished by their volume and equality should be looked upon as so-called 'centres'. This means that the names of these places designate particular brands of wines and have in fact become the generic names for the wines produced in whole districts. Such centres are :

(a) *All* wine-growing localities in the *Rheingau*, e.g. Ruedesheim, Johannisberg, Winkel, Geisenheim, Oestrich, Hallgarten;

(b) in *Rhinehessia* : Alsheim, Bechtheim, Laubenheim, Bingen, Dienheim, Nierstein, Oppenheim, and others;

(c) on the *Moselle;* Zeltingen, Graach, Piesport, Traben, Wehlen, Berncastel, and others;

(d) in the *Palatinate* : Duerkheim, Forst, Deidesheim, and others.

(For full list, see Appendix 1.)

A wine grown in a locality 'adjacent or near' to one of these centres may be labelled with the name of such centre, provided that the character and quality of the wine may fairly be described as identical with the products of the centre itself. A site is as a rule considered to be 'adjacent' when it is actually contiguous to the locality in question. The term 'near to' has not been strictly defined in this context—no fixed distance (as the crow flies) has been laid down as a maximum. Given, however, a reasonable similarity in growing conditions, it may be assumed that a minor locality on the outskirts of a centre would be entitled to use its name.

Vineyard 'Class' Names

The regulations pertaining to nomenclature according to centres did not satisfy the wine trade, because they did not allow for distinctions (in the description) 'between the products of the various sites ('Lagen'). The trade's wishes were therefore met by further legislation to the effect that wines could be classed and named, not only according to topographical centres, but also according to the vineyard sites. Names thus given are not necessarily strictly individual designations of origin, but may be used for all wines coming from a group of adjacent or neighbouring localities in which vineyard products are similar in character and quality.

As has been noted, vineyard sites may belong to more than one village, and in such cases the 'vineyard class name' may be derived from either side of the local boundary. The Kroetenbrunnen vineyard, for example, overlaps the boundary between Oppenheim and Dienheim, and the wines produced therefrom may be called either 'Oppenheimer Kroetenbrunnen' or 'Dienheimer Kroetenbrunnen' (For further Vineyard Class-Names see Appendix 2; Page 150).

Are class-names derived from the names of districts affected in any way if one district, formerly independent, is incorporated into another? In 1939, for instance, the village of Eibingen was incorporated into Ruedesheim on the Rhine. The vineyard sites known as Kiesel and Haeuserweg overlapped the boundaries of Ruedesheim and Eibingen, and their names had therefore legitimately become class-names for the wines grown thereon. It can hardly be assumed that the political fact of the incorporation made any difference to this classification.

Restrictions on Nomenclature

The enactments outlined above allow a certain latitude in the giving of class-names to wines. But once a name has been given, the right to change it is lost. The classification of a wine under a particular designation is determined by origin, quality and characteristics, and it would constitute an abuse of the law if, for example, a whole string of names were to be applied to products from one and the same vat. In exceptional circumstances—and *only* in exceptional circumstances—a second name may be chosen for a wine. Such an exceptional circumstance would be a change in the quality of the wine during treatment. The wine merchant who has occasion to lower the price of a wine may by law rename it according to its changed quality.

Where a wine is labelled 'Originalabfuellung' (Estate bottled), the regulations are extremely strict. No latitude is allowed in the use of the names of districts or sites; 'Class-names' are excluded, and the appellation must be an accurate indication of the wine's true origin. A *Geisenheimer Steinacker Originalabfuellung*, therefore, must have been grown at Geisenheim in the Steinacker vineyard, and bottled in the Proprietor's cellars.

When a class-name is used for a wine grown elsewhere than in the named district it would be misleading within the meaning of the law to print on the label a landscape of that district.

Invented Names

Invented names must not be used in conjunction with a geographical designation, as this might be taken to indicate a district of origin. Such arbitrarily chosen names may not be so formed as to mislead the purchaser, i.e. the quality of the wine must not be inferior to that which he is entitled to expect from the label.

LIEBFRAUMILCH. In this connection, a word about *Liebfraumilch*, which is always in great demand. Contrary to popular belief, Liebfraumilch is not a district at all, but an invented name which may be applied to any pleasant Rhine wine of good quality. The name is derived from the Liebfrauenkirche (Church of Our Lady) at Worms, which is surrounded by vineyards. These vineyards produce an average of 20,000 bottles a year, a quantity which is obviously insufficient to cover the demand for *Liebfraumilch*. And incidentally, the wines produced in Worms in an average year are not even of specially good quality. A wine sold as *Liebfraumilch* may be a Rhine wine from any Rhine district whatever. It may come from the Rheingau, from Rhinehessia, from the Rheinpfalz (Palatinate), from the Nahe and the Middle Rhine (as far as Coblenz).

As *Liebfraumilch* is an invented name, nothing may be added to it that might be interpreted as an indication of origin—neither the name of a district, nor the picture of a village or church (in particular, of the Liebfrauenkirche at Worms), with or without vineyards around it. On the other hand, additions like 'Spaetlese' and 'Auslese' are of course permissible where the implications coincide with the facts.

Naming of Blended and 'Improved' Wines

By way of preface to this category of nomenclature it is necessary to mention two kinds of 'improvements' to wines, apart from those dealt with in an earlier chapter. Due to a change in the preference of consumers (who in recent decades have been increasingly inclined to demand mild wines), scientists have evolved two methods of creating milder products. By the first method the wine is sterilized before fermentation is completed, so that part of the unfermented sugar remains in the wine; by the second, grape juice is added to the fully fermented wine. The first method has been fairly extensively used of late years in some districts, while the second has been abandoned. Both methods are unnatural and neither is to be recommended. Any wine merchant importing casks of wine which have been treated in this way, is taking the risk that the wine, despite its sterilization will come into renewed contact with fermentation bacilli; if this happens and a second fermentation takes place, the wine is ruined. It is however true that these wines have an exquisite flavour and legislation has taken this into account.

Wines which have been sterilized before fermentation is complete, and wines to which grape-juice' (must) has been added, may only be marketed if the words 'sterilized by filtering', or 'sterilized by filtering (containing supplementary grape-must)' are added to their description. This is to forestall any competition which might be detrimental to the producers of sweet, high-grade wines. The additional description is however only required in the case of natural wines, not where the wine has been 'improved'. Wines to which must has been added are 'blended' products. But the addition of pure must does not detract from the *natural* character of the wine—it still is and counts as a natural product.

In principle, a mixture of several ' products may only be named after the component which forms at least two-thirds of its volume and determines its character. The name of a vineyard may only be used if the component, after which the mixture is called, is unsweetened. Descriptions such as *Wachstum, Gewaechs,* (growth) are prohibited in naming blends.

These restrictions in naming blends would operate very severely if the volume of harvests in individual vineyards were insufficient in lean years to allow storage, at least in some of the vats, of wines which can legitimately be sold under their respective vineyard names and vintages. For this reason there is an express supplementary provision, that when grapes, grape-mash, or grape-must of the same kind and originating from the same or near-by district, or when a grower blends wines of his own production and of similar character, originating from the same near-by districts, the above mentioned restriction shall not apply.

In such cases the origin may be stated according to the component forming two-thirds of the volume, and the vineyard name may be used even if the two-thirds component has been improved; and reference to Wachstum or Gewaechs may be made.

In regulating the nomenclature of blended wines, the law confined itself to the case of blends 'between products of different origin' (meaning different geographical origin), and makes no mention of the blending of different *vintages.* Writers on the subject are however, agreed that such blends should be subjected by analogy to the same rules. This means that a blend of several vintages may only be named after one of them if that vintage forms at least two-thirds of the blend's total volume and determines its character. If no single vintage forms two-thirds of any given blend, the latter may only be marketed as non-vintage wine.

All wines may be marketed with corks bearing the brand of the producer or distributor.

But the words 'branded corks' may only appear on price-lists, labels, etc., referring to a particular wine if that wine is a natural product, developed and bottled by the producer. The words may not be included in the description of 'improved' wines or of wines which have not been bottled by the grower.

General Conclusions

Perhaps surprisingly, the main significance of all the above informations of the law—nomenclature only deflects the literal truth in the case of estate bottlings. Quality is the only criterion to be considered. To judge the quality of a wine the prospective buyer tastes it carefully and then takes into consideration the development of the product in the past and any well-founded expectations he may have of its prospects for the future. For the rest, the wine-merchant's advice to a private buyer is: buy and store the wine you like whatever its name or vintage.

Kinds of Vine

Even the most poetical titles are not worth very much. . . . A vine-yard name, though it may truly reflect and symbolize an ideal, carries no guarantee that the quality of the wine from that site will always remain the same—vintages in Germany vary far too much from year to year for any such expectation.

A good pointer to the quality of a wine is to be found on its label in the designation of the *species of grape* from which it is produced, in conjunction with that of the place of origin.

German wine-growers are aware that they can only justify the immense costs of their vocation and indeed their own right to exist if they produce high-grade wines. The authorities supervise the establishment of any new vineyard and have enacted general rules limiting the kinds of grapes that may be planted. Some species of grapes may be planted anywhere, others only in certain districts, while others again may only be planted under a special licence from the authorities. The various species of grapes are detailed in an official list called the *Reichsrebsortiment* (Government List of Vines).

White Wines

Burgundy White (White Klevner)
Burgundy Grey (Grey Klevner, Rulaender)
Elbling White (Kleinberger)
Elbling Red
Gutedel Red
Gutedel White (Schienedel)
Malinger Early (Malinka)
Malvasier Early Red (Early Red Velteliner)
Mueller Thurgau (Riesling X Sylvaner)
Muscatel Yellow
Muscatel Red
Muscat Ottonel
Nueburger
Ortliever Yellow (Knipperle, Kleinraeuschling)
Raeuschling White
Riesling White
Sylvaner Green
Traminer Red (in Baden Klevner)
Velteliner Green
Velteliner Red-White

Red Wines

Affenthaler Blue
Blue Franconian (Limberger)
Burgundy Late Blue (Blue Klevner)
Burgundy Early Blue (Early Burgundy)
Faerber Grape
Hangling Blue (Sweet Red, Tauber Bleck)
Mueller Vine (Schwarzriesling)
Portuguese Blue
St. Laurent (Lorenzi Grape, St. Lorenz Grape)
Trollinger Blue
Urban Red.

The permission to plant these species of grapes for vineyards is restricted to pure strains. It is an offence to mix them with other kinds.

The Sylvaner

The Sylvaner is said to originate in Austria, and in the Rheingau it is known as 'Oesterreicher', meaning Austrian, but actually its origin cannot be reliably ascertained. It is the main strain used in many German viticultural districts, such Rhinehessia, the Palatinate and Franconia. It is also cultivated in Baden, Wuerttemberg, the Rheingau, and on the Middle-Rhine. It may safely be assumed that in Germany it is more widely planted than any other species of vine.

It is also one of the most valuable kinds, as it is very fertile and ripens comparatively easily. It is known to mature on sites and in regions in which the Riesling never attains full maturity; in such places it yields fuller and mellower wines.

Its wine is mild and agreeable, often full-bodied. Its light table-wines are fine-flavoured, while in good years and on good sites wines of rich sweetness with exquisite bouquet are produced from it, including the great *Ausleseweine* of the Palatinate and Franconia.

The Riesling

The best-known of German white wine grapes is the white Riesling —the grape that has made the Rhine and Moselle wines world-famous. It produces distinguished wines with a rich bouquet and its Trockenbeerenauslesen are the greatest of all German wines.

The Riesling vine is the noblest that anyone in Germany has hitherto succeeded in cultivating for the production of white wines. It is distributed over all German wine regions; and on the Moselle, with the exception of the Upper Moselle, the Saar and the Ruwer it is the only kind of vine that is cultivated at all.

It produces the small healthy berries that ripen to a brilliant brown-yellow colour; it grows more slowly and ripens later than other kinds of grapes.

Once the grape has attained its full, sweet maturity, it develops to highest perfection the delicate elements of its exquisite bouquet— the incomparable aroma, the entrancing taste which are somehow reminiscent of all the best in other kinds of fruit. Peach, walnut, pineapple, blackberries, black currants—the Riesling fragrance seems compounded of them all. Pleasantly sweet, not too strong in alcohol content, stimulating and refreshing through their acidity, the Riesling wines at their best have earned a world-wide reputation.

The Mueller-Thurgau Vine
(Riesling X Sylvaner)

This is a seedling vine raised by crossing the Riesling with the Sylvaner and called after its inventor, Mueller-Thurgau. It has become popular in many parts of Germany, particularly in Rhinehessia, Franconia, Baden and Wuerttemberg. Attempts to cultivate it are being made in all German wine growing districts.

The wine produced from the Mueller-Thurgau grape can be described as mild, aromatic and pleasant; grown on suitable sites its quality, particularly in a generally poor season, exceeds that of Sylvaner and even of Riesling wines. At auctions in Rhinehessia and on the open market it attains good prices and can be recommended if intended for consumption not more than two years after pressing. It is certainly not a wine that improves in the bottle. But that is not to say that even in this particular some Mueller-Thurgau wines cannot compete with Riesling and Sylvaner products. Possibly their quality will one day surprise the connoisseurs when the vine-sites are older and can infuse a greater strength into the ripening grapes.

The Traminer

Nowadays the main cultivation areas for the *Traminer vine proper* is in Baden where, particularly in the neighbourhood of Durbach, it is extensively grown, producing good rich wines. It is seldom found in any other German wine regions.

The *Gewuerztraminer* (spiced or aromatic Traminer), said to have been developed from the Traminer proper, and superficially very like it, used to be widely cultivated in Rhinehessia and the Palatinate, contributing greatly to the fame of many districts and many sites. Excellent Gewuerztraminer wines were for example formerly produced in Deidesheim, Wachenheim, Ruppertsberg, and in Rhinehessia in Gau-Algesheim (near Nierstein and Worms). The famous *Zeller Schwarzer Herrgott* owes its great reputation to the Gewuerztraminer vine. Except for fragmentary remains, all these cultivation centres have disappeared, but attempts are now being made to cultivate it in other districts. I have come across it in Guntersblum, in Bingen-Buedesheim (Hessian Domain, Binger Scharlachberg) and even in Hallgarten in the Rheingau. In these districts however the wine is not marketed as a pure Traminer, but blended with Riesling.

The ordinary Traminer is rich in alcohol, soft and velvety with a fine aroma. The Gewuerztraminer has a truly magnificent bouquet, which may even become rather too overwhelming but which makes it eminently suitable for mixing with other wines with less natural bouquet. The result, even with small quantities of the stronger wine, is a delicate aroma; such blends are very popular in Germany. The Gewuerztraminer is all the more sought after because it is so sparsely cultivated and therefore comparatively rare.

The Rulaender

This strain comes from France and was formerly more widely culti-vated in Germany than is the case to-day. The Rulaender is a genuine Burgundy, sometimes called Grey Burgundy, and is to be found mainly in Baden and Franconia.

The grape has a recognizable Burgundy taste—delicate, noble, aromatic.

The wine is mellow, with a delicate bouquet; its appeal it to a refined palate and its acid content is usually low.

The Muscatel

This is nowadays seldom found in Germany.

The Gutedel

This grape, like its counterparts in France and Switzerland, produces agreeable table wines with low acidity and a delicate aroma.

The Elbling

This vine, which can be grown on the Upper Moselle, in Wuerttem-berg, and in Baden, produces lower-grade wines which in most cases have to be 'improved' before being sold for consumption.

Diseases of the Vine

Wine-growers work all the year round, as anyone may observe who tours the wine-regions. Vines need constant attention, and from one harvest to the next there is vital work to be done almost every day. In the Spring there is digging and setting up props, and immediately afterwards the old wood must be hewn away. Soil must always be kept loose, so that, like the pores in a human skin, it may be penetrated by light, warmth and moisture. This means that it must be dug over again in the summer, to avoid the formation of clumps of grass-roots and weeds. And in summer too, superfluous wood must be hewn away, fresh wood this time, so that the vines do not dissipate their strength in developing a number of rank, unfruitful branches.

In recent years great progress has been made in finding ways and means to facilitate such work.

Those engaged in viticulture, like others in every form of industrial activity, have been at great pains to find more economic ways of working, to simplify and rationalize its methods, and not to be outdone by neighbouring or other trade rivals. Vine pests are combated by the most modern media known to science; only such fertilizers are employed as have been thoroughly tested; cellars are equipped as far as possible with latest improvements; and so on.

In many communities a network of paths has been built through the vineyards; in others, plans have been drafted for a system of paths, also for regulating the water supply, and particularly for collecting water from springs, draining pools, etc.

The community of Piesport is a shining example in this respect. The new vineyard paths in Piesport have been constructed in such a way as to facilitate the distribution of slate. A path leading up from the slope to a slate quarry enables the vineyard sites to be provided from above with nearly all the slate they need. And it is good slate. Where there is a lack of communicating paths, these have been planned.

This arrangement has not been without its good effect on the quality of the wine, particularly in enabling greater loads of fertilizer to be brought up than formerly when sites were less approachable.

The vine is a child of the South, and as such is very susceptible to damage through severe winter cold. In some wine districts spring

4

frosts often destroy all the young shoots. Hailstorms—fortunately —are usually confined to certain regions, but they cause more harm among vines than among other cultures, because they not only destroy whatever grapes may have been on the vines, but also weaken the growth for years to come. In two nights—9th and 11th May, 1947—a whole year's work was destroyed in many places. The loss due to the frost was computed at 400,000 hectolitres. The reports of the damage done by hailstorms in 1950 will be fresh in everyone's memory. All such dangers mean extra work.

Apart however from vagaries of the weather, the wine-grower has to be on his guard against pests and against vine diseases. Often he has a hard fight on his hands. Viticulture is no easy matter at best, and the continuous struggle against difficulties and disasters can bring the grower almost to the point of despair.

Every year the authorities publish a list of officially sanctioned remedies against the pests and diseases that attack vines. The 1950 list contains 142 names of such remedies.

It is clear that the danger from pests and diseases means constant inspection of the vines—all the year round—over and above the normal hard work connected with cultivation. Enemies of the vine, such as various species of caterpillar, weevils, beetles, maggots, mites, larvae of various kinds, and fungoids such as oidium, are apt to appear at any time and must then be attacked immediately by chemicals such as blue vitriol or sulphur.

The greatest enemy of the vine is the insect phylloxera (grape louse). In Germany it was discovered for the first time in 1874— on the Annaberg near Bonn. The pest spread quickly and was soon found in all German wine regions. No individual wine-grower can tackle the phylloxera single-handed, and the State had very soon to intervene. A service of inspectors has been set up, whose duty it is to keep German vineyards under constant observation and to take the necessary steps against the phylloxera where it appears. This service is maintained the whole year round and the vineyards of the various wine regions are systematically examined at stated intervals. Nevertheless it has hitherto not been found possible to prevent the spread of these insects altogether.

During the war years it was not possible to carry on the war against phylloxera with the desirable intensity. In the Palatinate alone, a comparison of the year 1948 with the years 1895-1940 showed an increase of infected vines of not less than 150 per cent. Many of those affected had to be completely destroyed. In Baden the phylloxera pest has brought viticulture down to 60 per cent. of its productivity as compared with the year 1937. And in the whole of Western Germany, no less than 35,000 hectares of its 51,000 hectares of vineyards are infected by phylloxera. In the Palatinate only 3,000 ha. remain free of phylloxera, in Rhinehessia 13 only of the 107 villages have not been infected.

For a long time the Moselle regions were spared this plague. It is true that before the First World War the Upper Moselle region near the Luxembourg border had suffered considerably from phylloxera, but for some time the trouble was confined to this district. Curiously enough, the Middle Moselle region, the part that produces the best quality wines, was at first not affected. It was in 1947 that phylloxera was discovered for the first time in vineyards between Trier and Coblenz.

What are the facts about these dangerous insects? In the Summer, the winger females of the species, carried by the wind over wide stretches of territory, lay their ova on the stems of the vines. The ova develop into wingless 'grape-lice' which penetrate through the soil to the vine-roots and there suck out the vitality of the plant for their own subsistence and that of the countless generations which they produce with incredible rapidity. In one year a phylloxera may have anything up to 24 million 'offspring'. Where the vine-roots have been attacked, they become knotted and deformed, the surest sign that they are victims of the phylloxera. Again with unimaginable fertility the phylloxera spreads underground from root to root, from vine to vine, and in a very few years the sick vines, from which the best juices have been sucked away, wither and die.

To combat this scourge, the earth is saturated with petroleum, bisulphide of carbon, and other poisons, so that it seems inconceivable that grape-lice or any other vermin could survive. For six years no vines may be planted on soil that has been so treated.

Usually the phylloxera has been carrying on its subterranean devastation for years before it is found. Long before remedies are applied, the warmth of summer days will have attracted it to the surface, a puff of wind has carried the tiny thing possibly miles away. And if where it is finally dropped, it happens to land on any part of a vineyard, then the procreative process begins anew, a fresh phylloxera focus is established and the deadly work goes on in the new locality. Again it may be years before the first signs of withering—caused by the constant deprivation of vital juices—appear on the vines and are discovered by the 'Phylloxera Commission' on its regular visit of inspection.

It has been observed that certain American species of vine are either never attacked by the phylloxera or are not noticeably affected by its depredations. On the other hand, these vines do not yield drinkable wines. It was therefore found necessary to graft some of the best German vines—Riesling, Sylvaner, etc.—on American vine-stock or apple-shoots of comparatively worthless but robust and easily-grown wild strains. The grafting of the vines is carried out by the English method (tongue-grafting). The experiments were long and tedious, and many failures had to be recorded. But today —in the affected areas—many a vineyard contains the vine with American roots proof against phylloxera. Since 1926 vine-grafting stations have been at work in all wine regions; growers in infested districts establish 'Vine Rehabilitation Associations', and the State gives the maximum aid.

Germany has now started a systematic rebuilding of her vineyards on phylloxera-proof foundations. The rapidity with which the pest spreads, thus affecting vast areas, has made this project a vital necessity. It has been estimated that strongly infected areas must be completely reconstructed within 15 years, less badly infected within 30. Consequently there is a tremendous demand for root-vines. In 1940 the demand reached the figure of 35 million, but has now risen to 40 million, so that about 32 million must be imported annually. Main producer-countries are Italy and France.

The quality of the wines produced from grafted vines has been the subject of much controversy, and expert opinions vary. In respect of *French wines,* it must be remembered that the famous Champagne and Bordeaux wines have long been products of grafted vines. For the rest, my own experience of these wines is too small for me to give a personal opinion, particularly as I had no acquaintance with them before they were attacked by the phylloxera and cannot therefore judge whether their quality has been affected by the grafting process.

On the other hand, I have 30 years' experience of tasting *German wines* and have followed their development closely. As regards these therefore I feel qualified to form an opinion on the basis of my own unbiased observation. In particular, I have tasted several thousands of wines of the years 1943, 1945, 1946, 1947, 1948, 1949, 1950, among them a large number produced from old European vines, as well as many others obtained from grafted stock. I have also carried out the specific tests of comparing the two kinds with each other, in particular when both have been products of the same vineyard.

One quarter of the Schloss Bockelheimer Kupfergrube from the State Domain, for example, is still derived from pure European vines.

It has thus been possible to come to certain conclusions:
The wines derived from grafted vines are milder than the others

and therefore—having regard to present trends of taste—on the whole more popular both inside and outside Germany.   On the other hand, *some* of these wines have entirely lost the characteristics —at least as far as their bouquet goes—of German products, showing that in these cases the American stock was stronger than the German and decisive for the nature of the 'wine. Such wines age more rapidly and have a shorter life than those from European vines, which often have an outstanding durability. In the years 1947 to 1949, for instance, I bought 1921 Rhine wines—including 1921 *Niersteiner Pettenthal Riesling Allerfeinste Goldbeerenauslese*—and 1934 and 1937 Rheingau wines—including *Rauenthaler Langenstuck Riesling Auslese,* and *Erbacher Siegelsberg feinste Auslese*—all of which were outstandingly fresh and fruity, while much younger American-based wines were undrinkable. I feel quite certain that the American vines are incapable of producing wines with any such expectation of life as the pure European just named. Wines from Americanized sources must be treated quickly and should, I am convinced, be bottled before they are a year old if they are to have an even average life. Over and over again I have found when visiting vintners and growers' co-operatives, that their wines which have been stored in casks for less than two years and have certainly received the best of care and attention, show signs of ageing while still in the cask. They already have that special flavour peculiar to old well-seasoned wines that even the lesser European wines do not attain before they have been stored for 5 or 6 years.

Great hopes for preventing early ageing in casks are put in the new method of storing the wine in hermetically sealed vessels, where the wine is prevented from breathing and actually kept as if bottled.

It must of course be remembered that the vineyards producing these wines are still young, and it may well be that in a few years their products will be richer. Another reason for the inferior quality of these wines as compared with those of European stock is likely to be the quantity in which they are produced. In some cases—in the year 1949—Americanized vines produced almost three times as must as the former yield from European vines, and even more in 1950. The 'Steinberg' vineyard of the State Domain produced 5 times the average quantity compared with the average quantity before 1925 ! It is therefore not surprising that the quality cannot compare with wines from the same vineyards of 20 and 30 years ago. Altogether I am of the opinion that the Rheingau in particular has not yet found the ideal vine for its viticulture. Its wines from the hybrid plants are far more reminiscent of Nahe wines than of the old Rheingau wines as they used to be.

As a rule young vineyards yield quantitatively large crops in the first ten years of their existence; but, qualitatively speaking, these are inferior to the products of older vineyards on the same sites. This is in conformity with the general rule that greater quantity means lesser quality and vice versa. The American vines have brought forth far greater quantities than the growers ever dared to hope.

These remarks refer, as said above, to those vines where the American root proved to be stronger than the European graft. Where the European vine proved to be the stronger partner, I am of the opinion that wines from grafted vines are of similar quality and do not differ much in character from those obtained from genuine European vines, though their staying power is smaller.

Incidentally, the grafted vines themselves do not live nearly as long as the pure European plants; while the expectation of life of the former is estimated at—at most—25-30 years, the others are known to flourish at least twice as long.

A vine may live 100 years or more. Vines over a century old are to be found in the Rheingau today, and the mayor of Rhodt in the Palatinate assured me in November 1949 that his district can still show Traminer vines which are 200 years old. The nature of the soil plays a major part in determining the duration of the vine's life. The average age is said to be fifty years. When the decayed vines have been removed, the land is given over to agriculture for a few years, and then—after about five years—re-planted with young vines. For this purpose the soil is completely turned over to a depth of about one metre (3.37 feet); the top vegetable soil is thus brought to a low level, in order that it may strengthen the development of the delicate roots of the vine cuttings (previously cultivated for two years in a 'vine plantation').

In Rauenthal and on other sites in the Rheingau, vines a century old still bear grapes of exceptionally high quality.

Possibly the Rheingau will have to abandon its cultivation of the Riesling grape and adopt other kinds. A report from wine regions outside Germany encourages this opinion. In the Banat for example, new varieties of grapes, specially cultivated for a high sugar content, have been grafted on American vines, and the old kinds—Sylvaner, Kleinberger, Mueller-Thurgau—completely abandoned. The change-over was accomplished comparatively quickly and without great expense. In the mountainous regions, where the Ruelaender grape was favoured, and on the Banat plains, where the so-called 'Zackel-weiss' was used, it was found that the resulting wines had an increased alcohol content of from 13-15 per cent., a finer bouquet, and a better colour than the old kinds. Encouraged by the Growers' Associations, the Viticultural Institute in Alzey and Geisenheim have for the last 20 years undertaken grafting experiments with a view to producing new hybrids which would yield richer musts with a higher sugar content. The new products are examined at regular intervals by a Commission composed of representatives of Hessian Viticulture, who select the varieties that show any improvement on the normal local vines.

Experiments are being continued, and it is hoped that success will crown the efforts to find 'thoroughbreds' suitable for cultivation and wine-production in Germany.

The importance of this for West Germany may incidentally be deduced from the establishment in August 1950 of a Federal Committee for Viticultural Research. Its purposes emerge from the following quotation from the *Deutsche Weinzeitung* (German Wine Journal) of 31st August, 1950:

> The Federal Ministry for Food, Agriculture and Forests has re-established the Viticultural Research Committee which had existed for over 40 years till the Capitulation as Reich Committee for Viticultural Research, under the auspices of the former Reich Health Ministry. The Committee's terms of reference establish it as research centre for the development and treatment of wines and the promotion of German viticulture. In addition, the Committee is entrusted with the investigation of methods for testing wines and musts; with issuing authoritative expert opinions for Government offices and courts of law; with the submission of material for the enactment of new legal provisions; and, finally, with the compilation of annual reports on the scientific investigations and other scientific work carried out by its members. The Committee is composed of representatives from all German wine regions.

The above observations may serve to show what complicated processes are necessary for producing wines, treating them correctly, and preparing them for bottling. It is a work requiring scientific training which must include a certain amount of geology and of course of chemistry. German viticulture and German wine industry could not have attained their present eminence without scientifically trained wine-growers. All German wine-regions have their training colleges for viticulture. There is one in Geisenheim (Rheingau), others in Trier and Berncastel (Moselle), in Neustadt (Palatinate), Weinsberg (Wuerttemberg), Veitchochheim (Franconia), Oppenheim (Rhinehessia), and one in Freiburg (Baden).

The purpose of these colleges is to train young people who wish to become wine-growers, in all subjects relating to viticulture and the treatment of wines. In addition, there are special courses for older people—practitioners with some knowledge and experience—in which new methods and discoveries in various fields are explained and discussed.

Then there is the experimental and research branch of viticultural science, which is of inestimable value. New apparatus, new machines must be tested; fertilizers and pest-destroyers investigated; there are samples of soil, of wines, of sweet musts to be checked—and so forth. The usefulness of this kind of work was strikingly demonstrated in the case of the difficulties encountered by wine-growers with the 1947 vintage.

In the teeth of long experience and despite the application of all the known fining methods, the 1947 vintage remained cloudy, or—if it cleared at all—became cloudy again after a short period. When the scientists took over, they found that the cloudiness was due to an excess of albumen. The albumen had become so thoroughly disintegrated in the wine that it was barely discernible even under the ultra microscope. Extremely unstable, the particles of albumen were precipitated as soon as they were disturbed from within or from without. The scientific workers soon discovered the right remedy for such persistent cloudiness. It was betonite, a substance found in a small corner of the State of Wyoming, U.S.A.

The training colleges also act in an advisory capacity to any wine-grower with a problem. They tell him what fining media to use and later test his products to make sure that the fining has been correctly undertaken.

Anyone interested in wines could not do better than pay a visit to the training college in Geisenheim, Rheingau, which is a model for all the other institutes. I myself take every possible opportunity of consulting Professor Hennig and am indebted to him for much valuable advice. I shall always remember my amazement when he first demonstrated to me how it is possible to find an exact chemical determination of acids with the help of physical apparatus.

Coopers play a very important and responsible part in the treatment and care of wines. This is especially so in the case of the small wine-grower who may be too much occupied with the rest of his agricultural work to give proper attention to his cellars. In such cases it is the cooper who steps in with advice and help.

It follows that the cooper is not just a man who makes casks—he has to be thoroughly well acquainted with the nature and treatment of the liquid with which they are destined to be filled. He is an indispensable link in the chain of those who keep watch over the nurseries and schoolrooms of infant and developing wines.

How to Judge Wines

The quality and the value of any wine depend first of all on its chemically ascertainable components. Much might be written on this question, but here it will perhaps be sufficient to give a typical analysis of a German Rhine wine, and, as a matter of interest, I give two analyses of the same wine, one produced by the old-fashioned method of fermentation, the other by fermentation in an hermetically sealed tank (as reported by Dr. Geiss in *Wein und Rebe*, of 15th September, 1950)—

	Tank Wine.	Vat Wine.
Specific gravity	1.0027	0.9954
Alcohol, g/1	82.5	81.8
Alcohol, volume %	10.45(a)	10.36(b)
Extract indirect, g/1	43.1	24.0
Sugar, g/1	16.0 under	1.0
Sugar-free extract, g/1	28.1	24.0
Volatile acid, g/1	0.19	0.28
Total acid as tartaric, g/1	7.6	8.1
Free sulphurous acid, mg/1	16.6	6.4
Total Sulphurous acid, mg/1	79.3	56.3
Original gravity (Oechsle°)	85.0	85.0
Original gravity calculated	90.4	82.0

(a) 18.2° or % Sikes.
(b) 18.2° ,,

g/1 = Grammes per litre.
mg/1 = miligrammes per litre.

Further components are tartaric and lactic acid, glycerine, ash and nitrogen.

In many countries it is customary for ordinary table wines to be marketed exclusively according to their alcohol content. But here it must be stated that the tasting test is preferable to the chemical method and is decisive. A chemical analysis can never succeed in conveying a wine's essential overall quality. Professor Hennig has even succeeded in finding by chemical analysis what substances—including cinnamon, vanilla, aldehyde, glucose, pectines, and vitamins—make up the bouquet aroma of a wine. In Germany it is the expert taster with his tried and experienced palate who asseses the value of a wine, judging it by its intrinsic qualities—especially its bouquet and flavour—to which of course its alcohol content and the rest of its chemical make-up contribute.

Tasting

Wine-tasting is an art, and the prime requisite for a good wine-taster is a sensitive palate. The condition is ineluctable, the quality usually inborn. Palate, nose, and tongue must form a triumvirate of sensitive—preferably supersensitive—organs with which to perceive the most minute differences in the substance and the bouquet of the wines on trial and to detect unerringly and at any time the slightest fault or deficiency.

So much for the personal qualities required of a taster. Apart from this, conditions are simple. The test-glass must be clear, colourless and fine-spun. The wine must not be ice-cooled; white wines should have a temperature of from 52-54° Fahrenheit.

The method of tasting a wine is well-known. Having alerted the senses of sight, smell and taste, the taster fills one-third of the glass, using his eyes to test the colour and clarity of the wine; he gently rotates the fluid and then sniffs, allowing his nose to breathe in the full aroma.

JUDGING WINES BY SENSE OF SMELL. The olfactory cells, situated in the mucous membrane of the nose, are stimulated by aromatic emanations from the bouquet of the wine and pass on this aroma by nerve-oscillations to the brain. The resulting sensation is called smell, scent, or aroma. No one suffering from a common cold with consequent catarrh and sneezing can judge a wine with any accuracy.

The judging of a wine by sense of smell must be carried out systematically. First the health of the wine must be gauged, then its age; next come the general wine-aroma and the particular bouquet-aroma, and finally the aroma of any other substances the wine may contain.

1. *Healthy Wines.*

The smell of a wine is a fairly safe guide to its age. Young wine smells fresher and lustier than old wine, old wine has a pronounced 'alcohol smell'. An expert wine-taster can even tell the individual vintages apart by the smell alone. Certain vintages have a characteristic aroma which immediately reveal themselves to the expert.

A strong smell of wine is a sign of a good well-flavoured product, a faint smell indicates a thin, 'empty' wine. The general 'wine-smell' may sometimes be overlaid by the bouquet-aroma, if the latter is very rich and the wine contains a large proportion of alcohol.

The bouquet substances vary greatly in different wines. The value of a wine is largely dependent on its bouquet.

Healthy wines always have a bouquet, which may be noticeably strong. Those of certain wines are immediately recognizable, for example, Riesling, Spiced Traminer, Muscatel, Gutedel, and *Bukett-riesling*.

Alcohol content, proportion of sugar, natural purity of wines can also be ascertained by the sense of smell.

2. *Sick Wines.*

The expert's nose can reach a high degree of certainty in detecting and diagnosing wine diseases. Vinegar flavour, mousiness, tawniness, a smell of sulphuretted hydrogen, a yeasty or a mouldy or a woody smell—none of these present any difficulty to the expert. Often his sense of smell will even tell him whether a Boeckser comes from the soil, from the lavish fertilization with hot stable manure, from the sulphurization of the vineyards, or from over-sulphurization of the wine.

The sweetness, astringency, or acidity of wines, or the presence of other foreign substances, can easily be detected by the sense of smell.

JUDGING BY TASTE. Finally, the taster sips, employing tongue and palate to judge the flavour.

But even sipping is a more complicated process than it sounds. Tongue and palate must be moistened with the wine, then a few drops are sucked in and *chewed* thoroughly, the mouth being left open in order that the wine's bouquet may be fully developed with the help of the accompanying air. Moreover—as it is quite common for the anterior part of the palate to react differently from the posterior (8- or 9,000 little taste-buds lie in the mouth, mostly towards the tip of the tongue), and some taste-buds are alkali-, others acid-producing (sweetness in general is detected at the tip of the tongue, bitterness at the sides and the back); it is therefore necessary for the sample to come into contact with both parts of the palate and both kinds of buds.

The effect of smoking on the palate is a controversial question.

There must of course be no smoking in the tasting-room, but otherwise smoking does no harm to a taster's personal equipment for his job. On the contrary. My father, for instance, likes to smoke part of a strong cigar in the open and then go to the tasting-room. His theory is that a short, good smoke heightens the sensitivity of the palate. I agree with him and follow his example. If I have a wide range of samples to taste, I leave the tasting-room now and again and have a short smoke. With me this takes the place of the piece of bread that other tasters commonly eat between samples. Incidenally, any bread eaten during a tasting session must be white; black bread contains acids and is too highly flavoured altogether. No spicy foods of any kind may be taken from beginning to end, as that would interfere with the functions of nose and mouth. It is a good thing to rinse one's mouth from time to time with water, thus removing any wine particles.

The following anecdote, told of the Eberbach monks, will illustrate the height of sensitivity which a connoisseur's palate can attain. The cellarmaster Father, making a cask test of a new vintage, remarked that the wine was excellent, but that it had a peculiar taste, reminding him of iron. He made repeated tests, and then, finding himself unable to make up his mind, consulted the Father responsible for the cooking who was renowned for his fine sense of taste. The latter in his turn made careful tests and came to the conclusion that that faint alien taste was not ferrous, but leathery—he too considered that the wine was otherwise excellent. In order to settle the dispute, the two of them finally consulted the Prior who, after yet another investigation. gave it as his opinion that the wine, undoubtedly good in other respects, tasted unmistakably of wood. The dispute continued and so did the tests, until finally there was no wine left in the cask. And at the bottom of the empty vessel they found a small key attached to a little leather strap fastened to a stump of wood. A cooper had accidentally dropped it into the cask.

A well-known story in the Rhineland is that of a wine-taster who expressed his conviction that the wine to which objections had been raised (in a trial for wine-faking) had been sugared, while the chemist who had analysed the wine denied that this had happened. After the wine-faker had been found guilty, he confessed that he had added sugar to the wine.

Professional wine-tasters are capable of detecting a particular brand of wine among a number of different kinds.

POINTS TO BE OBSERVED WHEN TASTING WINES. The general character of a wine is judged by its colour, its aroma, and its taste.

Colour. White wines should be a shade ranging from greenish-yellow of the Moselle to light gold of the Rheingau and amber of the Palatinate. A dark yellow or—even worse—a brownish colour shows that the wine has been wrongly treated and will probably have an acrid, raw taste. The golden shades, formerly so dear to the hearts of the poets, are a good sign only in the case of old wines which have been bottled for many years.

Aroma. The 'bouquet' of a wine is the collective designation for all aromatic emanations perceptible by the sense of smell; it varies greatly according to the brand and the vintage of the wine. Essentially it must be delicate, pure, and characteristic. In the case of grapes like Riesling, Traminer, Muscatel, and Burgundy, they must be clearly recognizable by the bouquet alone. The fine aroma of a wine is destroyed by excessive sulphurization (causing a taste and smell of rotten eggs), or the formation of aldehyde (caused by the oxidation of alcohol). Unsuitable blending too may change the bouquet considerably.

The actual taste of the wine is the coping-stone of the series of impressions made by all its components on the sense of taste. Tasting is not a mechanical function—on the contrary, the brain must be working at full strength in order to co-ordinate the messages received through eyes, nose and mouth, and weld them into a considered judgment. That is why some wine-tasters will not reject the whole mouthful of the wine they are tasting, but will swallow a little of it, in order that their judgment should not be in any way impaired by some after-effect of the rejection. Final judgment on a wine is not passed until several samples have been tasted and a period has been allowed for consideration.

The following points must be noted in the order shown:
State of the wine's health; full flavour of the wine; harmony of its components; bouquet substances; general verdict.

Taste. It is practically impossible to distinguish between the taste and the smell of a wine. Nose and tongue appreciate equally and simultaneously the peculiarities of a Riesling, a Traminer, or a Burgundy. Our sense of taste reacts equally to all components of the wine, such as alcohol, acids, tannic substances, glycerine, and all the bouquet elements; but even more does it realize the pleasant and soothing effect of the harmonious blend of all these ingredients.

Clarity. Nowadays wine-consumers are greatly attached to very clear ('star-bright') wines and anyone judging a bottled product must take this attribute into full consideration. Any cloudiness in the wine denotes that it was not properly handled before being bottled. In most cases re-bottling will cure the defect.

When turbidity in bottled wines is caused by tartar or albuminous tannic particles, the defect is apt to be merely transitory. In these cases the bottled wine should be watched for a few weeks, not re-bottled in a hurry.

Tartar, in small crystals, is formed in the bottle in the course of the further development on the wine. As they are heavier than wine, they fall easily to the bottom of the bottle; in any case they do no harm to the wine, and the connoisseur likes to see them.

To obtain a general evaluation from the various tests, eyes, nose and tongue must co-operate harmoniously, following the magic formula evolved by Horace and known as COS—*colore, odore, sapore.*

The fine distinctions drawn up by experts may be arranged in the following groups:

According to colour: Green, coloured, highly coloured, cloudy, turbid.

According to age: Young, fresh, fruity, yeasty, mature, over-ripe.

According to weight: Light, thin, shallow, heavy, thick, bulky, oily, fat.

According to smell: Flowery, aromatic, inclined to be sour.

This also indicates the approximate age of the wine.

According to taste: In combination with the above-named categories, the nature of the wine may be described as: Effervescent, volatile, delicate, mild, soft, full, fully-rounded, hard, strong, finely fermented, pithy, steely, pungent, bitter, earthy, sour, sweet, fiery, dry, blunt, smoky, fusty, racy, amiable, elegant, harmonious.

It is a well-known fact that there is a sympathy between the wine in the cellar and the vine. When the vine puts forth its buds, the wine is observed to show signs of fermentation. That, therefore, is not the proper time to taste wines in cask.

Professor Hennig of Geisenheim has evolved a points system for the evaluation of wines which is extremely interesting, especially for a beginner in this field. He has drawn up a table on which a fixed number of marks is assigned to each of the possible qualities (or points) of a sound wine. (No diseased wines are considered). When judging any given wine, the examiner lists its points and adds up the appropriate marks. The sum total then amounts to assessment of the wine's quality as a whole. Thus:

(1)   For full Glossary see Appendix VI
(2)   For Table see Appendix V.

How Wines Should be Drunk

Many people who would like to be connoisseurs of wine and to enjoy its delights to the full, do not realize that there is an art in wine-drinking. This art must be studied.

To begin with, there is the wine-glass. This must be adapted to its content. German wines, like all wines with a rich or a delicate bouquet, require a glass which, full-bellied at the base, grows slender at the top. It should not be more than two-thirds full, the surface of the liquid just reaching the widest part of the bowl; the wine is thus able to 'breathe the air'. To facilitate the breathing process, the liquid should be gently swirled in the glass before being drunk. The aroma thus released—the 'bouquet'—is not lost in a glass of this shape, but is on the contrary collected in the narrow top part of the vessel and thus provides the maximum enjoyment and benefit. It goes without saying that the part of the glass that holds the wine must be clear, transparent and colourless, so that the eye may rejoice in the golden splendour and clarity of its delectable content.

Wine must be drunk at exactly the right temperature—not too warm, not too cold. In the case of new wines, the bottle should be left open for a short 'breathing-space' before the beverage is poured. These preparations made, a sip of the wine may be taken and allowed to roll over the tongue. When dealing with a high-class wine, the connoisseur only sucks in a few drops with which he moistens the upper part of the tongue, the palate and the sides of the tongue—in that order. Not until he has enjoyed the process of slowly 'chewing' these drops, does he allow them to slip down his throat, thereby testing the 'flow' of the wine. No good wine should be swallowed straight from the glass. Students of wine-drinking should watch the habitues in any of the many pleasant little wine-taverns in Germany. Those are the people who know how to get the last ounce of enjoyment out of their wine. They act on the principle:

Don't drink in haste, it's not a game.
No wise man over-shoots his aim.
Drink slow, but deeply all the same!

When to Drink German White Wine

Wine should always be taken with food or after a meal; on an empty stomach it is apt to act as an irritant. In the evening, after a day's work, wine is refreshing and invigorating and that is therefore the best time to enjoy it.

There is a prevailing idea that Rhine or Moselle wines should be drunk with the fish course, or at best with poultry. A fallacious doctrine that may lead to great disappointment! One wine merchant is known to have been profoundly shocked at the results of his hospitality when, wanting to give his guests a special treat, he arranged a dinner for them at which he served a *Trockenbeeren-auslese* with the fish. The guests drank the wine, but failed to eat their fish, and when the meat-course came round, they were incapable of appreciating the noble red Burgundy which accompanied it.

Oysters and fish require pungent, semi-pungent or mild white wines, never Trockenbeerenauslesen. These should be served with dessert or the sweet, or, better still, after dinner, instead of a liqueur. Strictly speaking, Trockenbeerenauslesen are a kind of natural liqueur.

Sweet white wines, Spaetlesen and Auslesen, are very suitable for serving with *pate de foie gras,* pullets, or lamb, or with boiled fish. Incidentally, no good wine should be served with salads or vinegar sauces, as these acid dishes do not mix well with wines. Cheese, on the other hand, because of its basic alkaline content, is very well suited to enhancing the excellent qualities of good wines.

Rhine and Moselle wines can be drunk throughout any meal with any course, including red meat, provided that the right kind of wine is selected. Suitable for this purpose is a dry wine of the Palatinate.

Nothing is more enjoyable than a refreshing bottle of Hock or Moselle when one is listening to the wireless or viewing a television show or playing bridge. It is a deplorable custom to serve spirits on such occasions. I offer my friends a fine Hock or Moselle. When I start regaling them with spirits or liqueurs, they know the day has come to an end and it's time to go home.

Wine-merchants are often asked whether an opened bottle of wine must be finished at one sitting. That is not absolutely necessary—a good wine will keep for several days after un-corking, provided that it is well-stoppered and stored in a cool place. Indeed I have repeatedly found that a young wine, properly cared for, tastes better on the second day than on the first. As a rule, bottled wines should be stored lying down; this keeps the corks moist.

It is not advisable to try out a wine for the first few weeks after bottling. The new development process in the bottle affects the wine strongly, making it temporarily 'bottle-sick'. Again, after a case of wine has been consigned to the purchaser by rail or sea, the recipient should allow it to settle for a week or two before tasting and judging it.

TEMPERATURE. Icing a wine kills its bouquet; moreover, the poorer qualities of any vintage are likely to be disguised if it has been too strongly iced. In no case should a wine be cooled beyond the strictly necessary point. Where a wine-cooler seems indispensable this should at least be of approximately the same shape and length as the bottle, in order that the effect on the wine may be evenly distributed. If a shorter vessel is used, so that the upper half of the bottle protrudes from the cooler, the first glasses poured will still be too warm, while those from the lower half of the bottle will be too cold. I am afraid I must often have made a nuisance of myself in restaurants, trying to modify the effects of such mistake by playing about with unopened bottles in the cooler, or taking them out and putting them back head first. My remonstrances with the wine-waiters were, however, bound to be ineffectual, as none of the restaurants in question possessed the right coolers for Rhine wines.

Wine Journey

Now we can start our journey through the various wine districts of Germany in order to learn more about the manifold characteristics of their wines. Let us remember once more that wine is a product of climate, soil, grapes, and the technique used in its making, and hence the great differences in quality.

We shall start in the well-known districts first and then visit the lesser known wine districts of South Germany.

Our Wine journey begins in the

Palatinate (Pfalz)

Coming from the Rhine into the Palatinate, the traveller sees a fertile plain spread out before him. This is so to speak the advance guard of the Palatinate—known as the 'forward' (Vorder-) Palatinate. Towards the west this plain is separated from the Western Palatinate by a long chain of hills which (at its southern end) is a continuation of the Vosges mountains, while to the north it is known as the 'Haardt' range, or simply the 'Haardt'.

The English designation 'Palatinate' for the German 'Pfalz' is linguistically and historically well-founded, for 'Pfalz' is derived from the Latin 'Palatinus', the name of the first of the seven Roman hills to be inhabited and the one on which the Imperial Palace was built under Augustus. This, the site of the first Imperial Palace, then gave its specific name to the whole genus of royal residences. Wherever a Roman Emperor rested his head in the course of his Imperial travels, the building that housed him became a palatium. And hence of course the English word 'palace', the German word 'palast', and also the derivative 'Pfalz' The person responsible for the administration of the 'Pfalzen', or royal residences, was known as the Pfalzgraf. The title *Pfalzgraf bei Rhein* (Pfalzgraf by the Rhine) first appears in documents of the year 1136. Like other offices, that of the Pfalzgraf became hereditary and assumed an increasingly territorial character in the course of years, so that finally it came to include local sovereign rights. From 1354 till 1803 (with the exception of the years 1635-1648) the land was known as *Kurpfalz,* and in that period the territory was more extensive than the Palatinate today. To the right of the Rhine it stretched beyond Mannheim and Heidelberg, to the left of the river as far as and including Bacharach. The peace treaties of Campo Formio (1797) between Austria and France, gave all German territory on the left bank of the Rhine to France, and it remained French property under the Republic and the French Empire. In 1814/15, when Napoleon's fate was sealed, a mixed Austrian-Bavarian Administration was appointed for the disputed territory to the left of the Rhine, until in 1816, it was handed over to Bavaria. In 1817 it was called *Bayrischer Rheinkreis* (Bavarian Rhine District). Since 1838 it has been known (geographically speaking) as the *Pfalz.*

The eastern strip of the Palatinate—about 86 km. in length and 30 km. wide—lies on the left bank of the Rhine. It comprises about 160,000 square kilometres of vineyards with about 160,000,000 vines, tended by about 35,000 growers who are distributed among about 200 communities. The Palatinate alone has more vineyards than the whole of the Rhine-Moselle-Saar-Ruwer- and Nahe territories taken together. It also has more vine plantations than Hessia, Baden, and Wuerttemberg.

The wine region of the Palatinate lies about 210 metres above the chilly mist-wrapped Rhine Valley. The eastern slopes of the Haardt afford a natural protection against the cold winds from west and north.

The vineyards of the Palatinate are nowadays almost entirely confined to sites which are particularly suitable for grape cultivation and as a rule guarantee a good mature crop.

A good many of the vine plantations are to be found in the plain. In consequence, the inhabitants of the Palatinate seldom speak of their *Weinberge* (lit. Vine hills—the usual German word for 'vineyards'), but mostly of *Wingerten*—i.e. *Weingaerten,* meaning wine gardens. The geological and climatic conditions in the Palatinate account for this difference. The Rhine Valley from Muehlhausen to Bingen is like an immense sunk trench. The Vosges and the Haardt on the one side, the Black Forest and the Odenwald on the other, form the sides of this mighty 'ditch' through which the River Rhine flows. In the whole region of the Rhine plains the climate is outstandingly warm and dry, but particularly so in the Palatinate. In the summer there is almost tropical heat, and the winters are

mostly mild and free from snow, so that the traveller may well think
he has struck a patch of the 'warm South'. Fine chestnut trees
decorate the hills and bear good fruit. Almond trees are scattered
about the vineyards, or line long stretches of the roads; mulberries
and fig-trees flourish in the gardens; peach- and apricot-trees are
weighed down by the weight of the fruit they bear, while other fine
fruits are to be found everywhere in great profusion; even lemons
are sometimes grown here.

Such a favourable climate obviously promotes the growth of vines,
which here put out their shoots and blossom earlier, and bring their
grapes to an earlier maturity than in any other German district.

Particularly in years when the sun has been sparing of its rays do
the wines of the Palatinate usually outshine their rivals in other
German wine regions. As a rule they are milder, have less acidity,
are somewhat mellower but also richer than comparable products
of different regions. Anyone therefore whose digestion is inclined
to be intolerant of acids will find that these wines suit him better
than others. The present tendency to prefer sweeter richer wines has
enlarged the market for Palatinate products.

The nature of the soil in the whole of this Palatinate wine region
varies considerably, sometimes changing more than once within a
very short space. The vineyards in the southern part of the *Vorder-
pfalz* are mostly constructed on loess soil, i.e., a diluvial deposit
of fine loam. This, sometimes light, sometimes heavy, frequently
collects in such immense deposits that cave-like cellars can be dug in
it. Along the Haardt, which has a coloured sandstone soil, vineyards
are to be found on its detritus, i.e., a rather poor, dry sand. But
sandy soils of older origin also occur, as well as shingle and gravel
soil. The sites built thereon often take their names from the soil—
that is why we find Kieselberg (meaning shingle-hill, shingle).
Excellent wines are produced on such grounds.

Then again within the same region we find limestone soils, sometimes only as small reefs of tertiary lime, interrupting the loess or
sand stretches. In these cases it may happen that we find a vine
plantation of only a few acres. There is however a more extensive
stretch of limestone soil bearing north from Bad Duerkheim via
Ungstein, Kallstadt, and Leistadt to Herxheim a Bg. Other lime sites
of considerable extent are to be found in Zellerthal (Harxheim,
Zell, Niefernheim). In some places almost every site lies on different
soil—sand, clay, slate, and porphyry. And finally there is the soil
composed of a younger eruptive rock, viz. basalt. This is found
near Forst.

It has long been the custom of wine-growers to take away for

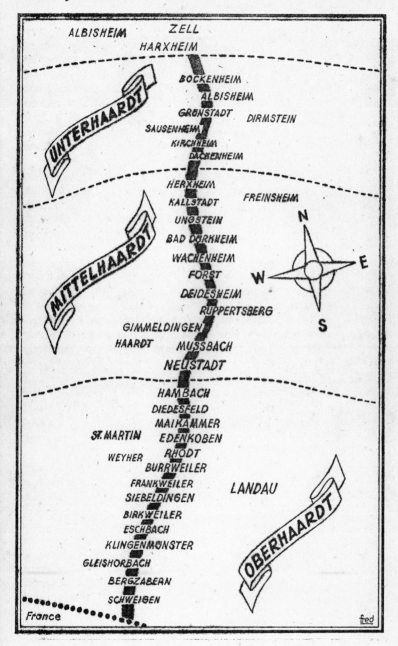

their own use the so-called 'pitchstone deposit', i.e. the rubble found
in basalt quarries.. This substance, on account of its potassium content and it dark colour, has been found very useful for improving
vineyard soil. Large tracts of the Forster and Deidesheimer vineyards have been so treated, and the high quality of their wines may
well be partly due to this.

The main species of grapes to be found here are the Sylvaner (in
this district known as *Oesterreicher* or *Franken*—'Austrian' or 'Franconian'); then the Riesling, which is grown in large quantities,
mainly in the finest production region of the Middle Haardt; the
Traminer and the Gewuerztraminer, which used to be the main
product of the Palatinate, but is now only sparsely grown as a pure
strain; and the blue Portuguese, from which a light red wine is
made.

Close to the French frontier we pass through the *Weintor*—Wine-
Gate—near Schweigen. At this point the road begins which takes
its name from the millions of vines lining its borders: *die Weinstrasse.*

In the Rheingau and in the Moselle district the whole landscape
of the grape country is dominated by the river; here it is the road—
the Wine Highway—that, taking the place of the flowing stream,
guides the traveller through the fertile wine-lands.

Upper Haardt

The Upper Haardt is the wine-cellar of the Palatinate, or rather
of the whole of Germany, for nowhere are such record harvests
garnered as here. Medium wines are produced which are marketed
as 'small' to 'medium', mostly in casks, but sometimes in bottles. A
goodly proportion is devoted to the preparation of sparkling wine.
A few sites in the upper country may be said to produce medium—
more raredy good—table and bottle-wines (Hambach, St. Martin, a
few sites on Weyher and Burrweiler, on Edenkoben and Maikammer
have a good reputation); but for the German exporter and the foreign
importer the wines are uninteresting and classed as 'mass-produced'.

Middle Haardt

North of the Upper Haardt and adjoining it, we find the Middle
Haardt. This is the district north of Neustadt and Haardt. It is the
region where the quality wines of the Palatinate are produced.

Less rain falls in the country between Neustadt and Duerkheim than anywhere else in Germany, and it has more sunshine than any other part. Moreover, the soil is unsuitable for anything but the growing of vines, so that the whole region has been turned into what seems to be one vast vineyard. The main species grown is the Riesling, cultivated as a pure strain and selectively gathered, and producing *Hochedel Auslese* wines, *Trocken-* and *Edelbeeren-Auslesen* of superb quality. Gewuerztraminer and white muscatels are also cultivated here. In the lower, moister sites there are Sylvaner and in some few cases White Gutedel plantations. Neustadt is the hub of the Palatinate Wine Trade, and a tourist centre.

The communities between Neustadt and Bad Durkheim and their sites are all worth knowing; to visit only the most important in quality, we have to go to the Neustadter Vogelsang, Grain Kies, the Haardter Herzog and Mandelring, the Gimmeldinger Meerspinne, Schild and Kieselberg, Hofstuck, Schloessel and Neuberg, Konigsbacher Idig and Satz, Bender and Weissmauer, the Mussbacher Pabst and Spiegel, the Ruppertsberger Reiterpfad, Hoheburg, Spiess, Goldschmidt, Linsenbusch and Hofstuck. Our next stop is Deidesheim. This is the site of the Bassermann-Jordan wine estate, to whose owner (Dr. Friedrich von Bassermann-Jordan) we are indebted for a historical survey of German viticulture. The soil in Deidesheim is suitable for fine quality wines, consisting as it does of volcanic primary rock, shingle, sand, and lime. Deidesheim is the centre of the highest grade wine production in the Rhine Palatinate. The best 'peak' wines in the world prosper here on the sites: Grain, Hohenmorgen, Kalkofen, Leinhoehle, Kieselberg, Kraenzler, Langenmorgen.

In the Middle Haardt, near *Forst,* there is an impressive natural formation which is of inestimable importance for the local wine production. This is the so-called 'Pitchstine Head' (*Pechsteinkopf*), a basalt cone created by eruptive rock. The dark-coloured basalt rubble from basalt quarries is frequently used (as mentioned earlier) for treating the soil of vineyards. It has the effect of generating warmth in the shingle soil, and this is extremely favourable to wine production; the vintages from soil thus treated are particularly good, sweet, full and fiery.

To range the Middle Haardt wines in order of quality is a very tricky matter. Certainly none but the Forster wines can compete with the Deidesheimer. World-famous are the sites: Kirchenstueck, Freundstueck, Jesuitengarten, Ungeheuer, Fleckinger, Granich, Elster, Ziegler, Langenmorgen, Pechstein, Musenhang, and others. The Reichs Valuation Law of 10th August, 1925, which fixed values per hectare of wine-producing lands, assessed the site Forster Kirchen-stueck at 16.000 Marks per hectare—a higher value than that given for any other site. It is here that the grapes reach their highest degree of maturity.

One-seventh of the whole Forst vine-area pertains to the vine-estate Reichsrat v. Buhl, the model estate of the whole Palatinate. It was here that the colossal feat was accomplished of moving vine-plantations from northern to southern slopes by transferring the soil. The Forster Auslesen and Trockenbeerenauslesen are world-famous. The *Trockenbeerenauslese* 1921 had 256° Oeschle (must) specific gravity; the 1949 208°; the 1921 *Forster Ziegler Riesling Beeren-auslese* cost 70 RM (£3-10s.) per bottle, the *Forster Ungeheuer Riesling Beerenauslese* 90 RM (£4-10s.) per bottle at the grower's cellar when sold in cask and the 1949 *Trockenbeerenauslese* 50 DM (£4-5s.).

If you visit the cellars—1 kilometre long—the cellar-master will point with pride to a blackish substance covering the wall and will explain that the excellence of his wines is in part due to this. The substance is cellar-mould. This fungus is only to be found in good cellars. It cannot develop if the cellar is either too dry or too moist. It cleanses the air of the cellar, lives literally on air, mainly on alcohol in gaseous form. Thus the fungus absorbs the volatile components of wine which are given off in the process of fermentation, tapping, etc.

Other villages in this region are: Wachenheim (*Goldbaechel, Baechel, Geruempel, Altenburg, Boehlig, and Wolfsdarm*); Bad Duerkheim (*Spielberg, Michelsberg, Fronhof, Feuerberg, Hochbenn, Hochmess, Geiersboehl, Schenkenboehl, and Proppelstein*). The ex-cellent sites of the neighbouring and very ancient wine village of Ungstein are of a similar character (*Spielberg, Herrenberg, Nuss-riegel, Kreuz, den Kobnert*); the vineyards on the last-named site extend to the neighbouring Kallstadt, with its sites *Leistadt*, Horn, Nill, Saumagen, Steinacker, Trift, and Kronenberg. Then comes Herxheim with sites: *Sommerseite, Himmelreich, Steinberg, Gold-berg;* and finally Freinsheim, with sites: *Oschelskopf, Hahnen, Hochgewann, and Rosenbuckel.*

Unterhaardt (Lower Haardt)

Merging into the fertile Rhinehessian plain, the German Wine Highway comes to an end with the following well-known viticultural communities in the Unterhaardt region: Dackenheim, Weisenheim, Kirchheim, Sausenheim, Dirmstein; and finally, Bockenheim.

The soil on which the Unterhaardt (Lower Haardt) vines grow is heavy and rich in lime (clay, loess and sand). This tends to produce milder wines, less elegant and patrician and with less body than those from the Middle Haardt, but nevertheless fruity and racy, extremely pleasing to some palates.

Gruenstadt is distinguished by a 'Wine-Market Association'. The wines produced by the members of this organization are judged annually during the Gruenstadt Wine Festival by a special panel of experts, and are drunk in enormous quantities by the tens of thousands of visitors to the Festival.

We shall be referring to this again in connection with our survey of German Wine Festivals.

Gruenstadt is the end-point of the Wine Highway, but not of the viticultural area of the Palatinate. Adjacent to it lie the winelands of the Northern Palatinate. There—in the Zell valley, on lime-soil mixed with clay and cement—grows a wine very different from all other Palatinate wines, a wine both robust and steely. The Zell product known as *Schwarzer Herrgott* has an excellent reputation in Germany itself, but is so far unknown in other countries. (Place of production : Harxheim-Zell).

In conclusion it may be said that of all Palatinate wines, those from Forst, Deidesheim, Koenigsbach, Ruppertsberg, and Wachenheim are in the top class; the second class is composed of those from Duerkheim, Ungstein, Gimmeldingen, Haardt, Kallstadt, Mussbach, Neustadt, Winzingen, and Niederkirchen, while all others are third class.

Rhinehessia

Emerging from the Palatinate we immediately find ourselves—near Worms—in the wine district of Rhinehessia.

The designation Rhinehessia is used to denote the origin of all wines grown in the Province of Rhinehessia with the exception of a small area along the river Nahe. (*See page* 68.)

Round the east and north of Rhinehessia flows the River Rhine in a wide semi-circle (Worms-Mainz-Bingen), while the Nahe flows to the west of the province. The region comprises 13,000 hectares of cultivated wine-lands, and here we find the greatest possible variety of wines—ranging from 'small' table-wines to the most exquisite 'peak' wines (Spitzenweine) produced not only in Germany, but all over the world.

Rhinehessia has been called 'God's Garden'. The fertility and wealth of this strip of land has been famous from time immemorial. The Carolingians made sure of owning large tracts of land here.

whereon they built their royal castles; their successors took over the estates as imperial property. They were well aware of the treasures they secured thereby. A 'Vogt'—governor—administered these estates and collected tithes and other dues for the imperial household from tenants and neighbouring landowners.

As we have seen while discussing other German wine-regions, the quality of a wine depends not only on the climate, the species of grape, the degree of attention devoted to caring for the vines, and the treatment of the wine itself when it has reached the cellars—but also on the kind of *soil* on which the vines are planted. The soil exercises a decisive influence on the quality of the wine and is responsible for manifold differences in taste which the wine connoisseur knows how to appreciate. The same species of grape planted on various soils produces entirely different wines; in particular, it is the bouquet—that indefinable quality—that is dependent, not only on the kind of grape but also on the kind of soil on which it is grown. Different soils contain different kinds of nutriment—the varieties in even neighbouring patches of land are sometimes astonishing—and that is what ties the taste of the wine so closely to the nature of the soil.

In considering the wines of Rhinehessia with its 162 wine-growing communities, from the point of view of soil, it is necessary to distinguish between the wines of the 'Rhine Front' from Worms to Oppenheim and Nierstein-Nackenheim, the wines that originate near Bingen on the Rhine, and those from the high plateau lying farther back, and of Alzey and Gau-Bickelheim.

On arriving at Worms, we find—near the Rhine bridge—the Church of Our Lady (*Liebfrauenkirche*) which is surrounded by a few vineyards. It has already been mentioned that the wine marketed under the designation Liebfrauenmilch does not come from these vineyards. Incidentally, the entire annual output amounts only to about 110,000 litres. The wine is of medium quality and has a decidedly earthy taste to which most wine-drinkers object.

In the extensive vine-covered hill-country to be found on the left bank of the Rhine from Osthofen to Oppenheim, vines are planted almost exclusively on loess. This applies to *Bechtheim* (site Woelm); *Alsheim* (site Goldberg); *Guntersblum* (site Steinberg); *Dienheim* (sites Kroetenbrunnen, Goldberg, Saar), and *Oppenheim*. Here the tertiary marl and lime assist the growth of first-quality vines, particularly in dry years, as this kind of soil is capable of storing considerable amounts of finely distributed moisture.

Red sandstone striated with sandy clays is also found. It is easily warmed by the sun's rays, and in wet seasons is capable of storing superfluous moisture in such a way that the vines are not harmed.

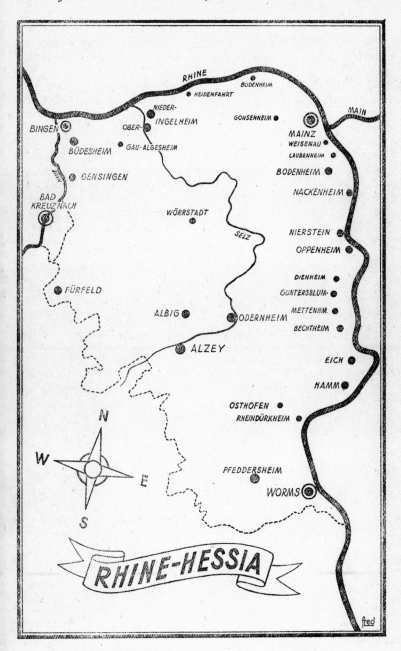

In Schwabsburg, Nierstein, and Nackenheim we find clayey sandy soils of a violet-red colour.

VITICULTURE IN NIERSTEIN. Nierstein boasts a population whose ancestors have been settled there for many generations and all its families are dependent either directly or indirectly on the cultivation of vines. There are about 500 individual owners of vineyards—both large estates and small plantations. Almost every Nierstein family owns at least part of a vineyard, but only about twenty of the wine estates play a significant part as producers of world-famous and 'peak' wines. It is almost entirely owing to them that the name *Nierstein* has such a good reputation as designating the place of origin of superb vintages. Foremost are the estates Franz Karl Schmitt (whose owner is the president of the Rhinehessian wine-growers), Anton Balbach Erben and the State Domain.

Vineyard sites of Nierstein on the Rhine are: *Rehbach, Mersch, Spiegelberg, Fockenberg, Hipping, Flaschenhahl, Kehr, Pettenthal, St. Kiliansberg, Auflangen, Oelberg, Heiligenbaum, Bildstock, Patersberg.*

Generic site names: Domthal, Monzenberg. Site names of the nearby community *Dexheim* are Koenigsberg, Doktor, and Hoelle.

Literary allusions to the quality of Niersteiner wines are not infrequent. In Goethe's *Ur-Faust* for instance, where the scene is laid in Auerbach's Cellar, one of the 'jolly topers' calls for a glass of 'genuine Niersteiner'. Then there was K. J. Weber (1767-1832), who wrote in his slim volume *Demokritos* under the heading 'The Delights of Drinking': 'In my opinion *Niersteiner* heads the list. If, now that I am old, I could drink a bottle of it a day, I am certain I should live 10 years longer.'

Where, leaving Nierstein behind them, the Rhinehessian hills draw quite close to the Rhine, we come upon *Nackenheim,* clustered around its vineyards in the form of a horseshoe—at one point the well-known Rothenberg—at another the Engelsberg with an old mountain chapel, and, pushing right down into the village, the Kirchberg with its baroque Church. The houses are built down to the very bank of the river, crowded close together, among them imposing homesteads with tall stone-arched gateways.

It was not till the end of the 18th century when the growers were freed from serfdom, that the whole of the land to the last patch became dedicated to the cultivation of the vine.

Today here is no room for the cultivation of any but the highest quality products. Climate, situation, nature of the soil, those three determinants for the character and quality of a wine, are all so favourable in Nackenheim that nothing but the best need be or is produced. Sun-kissed slopes and hills of red sandstone and clay slate (so-called 'Red-lier') are here the homes of the Riesling and Sylvaner grape which are also favoured by the vaporization, light reflexes, and warmth-conveying influence of the broad stream of the Rhine. Small wonder that they bring forth a wine which combines depth, fire, spiciness and delicacy in delicious and noble harmony. Hard work is needed to attain these results. In an average year the quantitative yield in this region is less than in any other part of Rhinehessia.

For a long time—far too long—Nackenheim wines were used for blending with others. In giving of their maturity and sweetness to wines from other regions which were deficient in these qualities, they descended into anonymity—the name of Nackenheimer was lost. It is only in recent years that people have begun to recognize the peculiarity, the special qualities and the exquisite taste of the wines fathered on the Nackenheim slopes. (The estates of Gunder-loch-Lange, Dr. Gunderloch-Usinger produce wines, which showing all the finesse of the best Rhinehessian wines, have some of the characteristics of good Rheingau wines.) Next we come to

BODENHEIM which produces mild wines with a fine bouquet. They are good wholesome wines, though they never attain the excellence of a top-quality Niersteiner. *Sites*: *Westrum, Burgweg, Hasenmaul, Leistenberg, Neuberg, Hoch, Kahlenberg, Ebersberg, Bock.* The same applies to the wines of Laubenheim, with its sites: *Hitz, Dammsberg, Kirchenstuck, Steig, Burg, Edelmann, Secker-grund, Kalkofen, Johannisberg, Hausschen.*

Journeying along the Rhine we come first to Mainz, a centre of the Rhinehessian wine trade. Not very much can be said about the wines of Rhinehessia between Mainz and Bingen and the plateau lying to the South of this strip, with not less than ninety-eight wine-growing communities. Names connected with this region are: Ingelheim, Gau-Algesheim, Ockenheim, Gaubickelheim, Wallert-heim, Worrstadt, Alzey.

The vineyards of *Alzey* are to be found widely scattered over the sites of the Selz Valley and the plains of the Alzey Plateau. The wines there produced are: Sylvaner and Mueller-Thurgau (White), and St. Laurent (Red). Their quality varies. The district is cold and windy and therefore unfavourable for the production of quality wines. It is the 'little' wines that are cultivated here, those sold in open containers; they are seldom bottled (except when blended with other wines). It is here too that grapes for the table are produced and sold to health resorts for 'grape cures'. The wines from this region are not suitable for export.

The municipality of Bingen-Rhine lies actually on Rhine and Nahe and comprises the vineyard sites :
Bingen-Stadt : *Schlossberg, Eisel, with Eisel and Schwaetzerchen, and Morsfeld, Rochusberg with Rochusweg, Hungerborn and Rosengarten. Mainezerweg with Rheinberg, Ohligberg, Mittelpfad and Kalbskopf.* Bingen-Kempten; *Kempter Berg, with Gaensberg, Schnack, Wolfskraut, Pfarrgarten, Kapellenberg; Grosse Lies, with Hofwingert, Mauer, Treffelsheim and Moerdershoelle.*
(*Red wine*) *Hagelkreuz.*

Although the Bingen vineyards are separated from the Rheingau only by the width of the river, they produce quite different wines. The vines along the railway line and on the slopes around Bingen are distinguished by a certain 'smokiness', derived from the smoke of the engines. I myself do not care for the taste, but the wine has found many lovers; it is well-suited to the preparation of a good, racy, sparkling wine.

Bingen is a city with a long wine-tradition going back to the 14th century. One of the many anecdotes originating from this city is the following :

One day the Bishop of Mainz called a meeting of the clergy in Bingen. During the meeting the Bishop wanted to make a note and asked someone to lend him a pencil. Hastily all present scrabbled in their pockets and each one of them brought out—a corkscrew. Since then corkscrews have been dubbed 'Bingen pencils'. A popular saying is, 'I've done no "bing-ing" today', meaning, 'I haven't been intoxicated today'. Curiously enough, both forms of this remark could be expressed in English by 'I haven't been on the *binge* today', although Partridge's Dictionary of Slang gives no indication that the English and the German expression could be etymologically connected.

On the Rochusberg near Bingen we find clay-slate, lightly mixed with devonian quartz. The slate disintegrates easily, producing a clayey soil which though poor in lime is rich in vegetable mould and has a medium potassium and high nitrogen content. The large dark slabs of slate and the quartz keep the soil loose, which is a good quality because it permits the passage of air, the easy circulation of water and the rapid assimilation of warmth—all of which have an excellent and characteristic effect on the surface soil of these vineyards.

The Rochusberg is crowned with a chapel which was rebuilt in the year 1814. Its consecration was celebrated by a popular festival (which incidentally is now repeated annually). Goethe, who was present at the consecration, has given us a description of the festival, including a sermon preached on that occasion by a suffragan Bishop. An extract from it seems both appropriate and amusing enough to be included here.

The Bishop had been preaching on the vice of drunkenness. After he had described it in drastic terms, he ended the sermon as follows :

> You, my devout hearers, who have already been pardoned and directed to show repentance and do penance, will realize from all that I have said that he who abuses God's glorious gifts in such a manner commits the greatest sin. But abuse is by no means the same thing as use. Has it not been written that wine delighteth the heart of man! That shows that we can and should enjoy wine, in order to give pleasure to ourselves and others. Now, among you here today there is possibly no one who could not take unto himself two measures of wine without thereby causing his senses to become confused. But if anyone who has taken but three or four measures (Mass) should so far forget himself as not to recognize his own wife and children, as to wound them by abusive words, by blows or kicks, in fact if he should treat his dearest and nearest as if they were his greatest enemies, then let him immediately take counsel with himself and in future refrain from such excess, for it causes him to become unpleasing and contemptible in the sight of God and his own fellow-men.

> But should anyone after taking four measures, yea, five or six still remain unaffected—should he still be able to give kindly assistance to his fellow-christians, to regulate his own household, should he even still be capable of carrying out the orders of his clerical and lay superiors—then let him enjoy his modest portion and thankfully accept it. But let him beware of going forward without further tests, for here as a rule weak humans reach their limit. It is very rare that our Gracious Heavenly Father grants anyone the special gift of being able to consume eight measures, as He has granted it to me, his faithful servant. Since, however, no one can say of me that I have attacked anyone in an unjust fit of wrath, or that I have failed to recognize the members of my own household or my relations, or still less that I have failed to perform any of my spiritual duties or offices— since indeed you will all testify that I am at all times prepared to act in praise of and to the honour of God Almighty and to the benefit and advantage of my neighbours—therefore I may

with a good conscience and in sincere gratitude continue in future to enjoy this gift which has been vouchsafed to me.

And you, my devout hearers—each and every one of you—take your modest portion, in order that you may be refreshed in body and rejoiced in spirit, according to the Will of the All-Highest Giver. And in order that you may do this and on the other hand banish all excesses, I beg you all to act according to the command of the Holy Apostle who has said : Examine all and retain the best.

Nahe

Leafing through an old book of student drinking-songs, I found one commending the wines of the Nahe. This is how it begins :

> Here's to Monzinger—smooth and fine,
> Like satin (only wetter),
> First cousin to a Rhenish wine—
> I don't know which tastes better.

It might have added that the Nahe wines are also first cousins to the Moselle products. This would have made the description accurate, as Nahe wines are reminiscent both of Rhine and of Moselle wines, which is not surprising when it is remembered that their geographical origin lies between the two. Nahe wines yield an annual average of 100,000 hectolitres in 82 wine-growing communities.

Looking down from the Ruedesheimer Berg vineyards on to the Rhine, you will see—just opposite and coming from the South—a little stream slipping past the two watchful hills known as the *Scharlachkopf* and the *Elisenhoehe* and winding its peaceful way towards the Rhine. That is the Nahe. Its source is near Birkenfeld on the Hunsrueckhoehe and its path to the Rhine takes it through one of the most beautiful valleys in the region.

The products of this valley however are not the only ones sold under the name of 'Nahe wines'. The name includes those from the districts of Kreuznach, Baumholder, and the Alzenzthal.

Far back along the valley when the little stream cascades into the Rhine, almost all its banks (at least those with southern aspect) are planted with vines. The Nahe wines are comparatively little

For names of all Nahe communities and their vineyard sites, see Appendix III.

known, though in olden days they appear to have been popular. There are many stories of imposing drinking tournaments held in the vinelands of the Nahe, as a result of which whole estates were often wagered and lost. The lords of the castles, the heads of the monasteries, and the city mayors—all interested in cherishing and protecting the Nahe vineyards—are said to have been concerned in these gambles.

Nowadays quality is more important than quantity, and in this more peaceable form of rivalry, the Nahe can certainly hold its own in competition with other German wine regions. Both the Domains and the carefully cultivated ancient private estates produce wines which have a distinctive character, which are racy, fiery, and patrician. But more on this subject later.

What does the Nahe region look like?

Dominating the landscape is the height known as the Burgklopp rising up from the town of Bingen and standing out behind the vine-covered Scharlachkopf. The Scharlachberg belongs to the community of Buedesheim and the inhabitants claim its robust products as their own. They are probably right.

The ancient Roman Drusus Bridge that once spanned the Nahe was destroyed by the Nazis during their retreat in 1945. At present its only replacement is an emergency bridge thrown up by the Americans. Crossing this from Bingen, we reach the western bank with its numerous picturesque villages : Muenster near Bingerbrueck, Sarmsheim, Laubenheim (not to be confused with the other wine-growing locality mentioned above, viz., Laubenheim near Nierstein), and Langenlonsheim with its rich, sun-drenched slopes.

At Langenlonsheim the Guldenbach valley rises to Stromberg and on to the Hunsrueck. In this valley we find the villages of Heddesheim, Waldhilbersheim and Windesheim. In all these there is extensive vine cultivation.

The next wine-village is *Winzenheim* with its famous sites Rosenheck, Honigberg and Metzler. And then come the great vine plantations of *Kreuznach*—Kreuznach, the 'city of roses and nightingales'.

In the lateral valleys branching out from the Kreuznach district, vines are also widely cultivated. Here, for example, is the territory of the *Amtsbezirk Ruedesheim/Nahe*. It lies in the heart of the Nahe vineyard country, about 10 miles as the crow flies from Ruedesheim/Rhine. Its wines are of good quality.

To this 'Amtsbezirk' (local government centre) belong twelve communities, of which the most important is Niederhausen on Nahe. Its best and most widely known sites are : *Hermannshoehe, Klamm, Kerz, Rosenhecke, and Rosenberg.* As a viticultural Domain (State

6

property) it is world-famous and worth a visit. The administrative buildings of the Domain are picturesquely situated on the western spur of the hill and afford a delightful view of the River Nahe framed in vine-covered banks. Straight ahead lie vineyards rising in a series of terraces to the highest point of the Kupferberg (Copper Mountain) and comprising the sites: *Schloss Bockelheimer Kupfergrube* and *Niederhauser Hermannshoehe*. The terraces are separated from each other and buttressed by strong fortress-like walls; they run from north to south so as to catch every ray of sunlight, thus giving the grapes the best possible chance of ripening. Director Goedecke, born in the Nahe region and an expert in viticulture and the treatment of wines, showed me an old painting of the Kupferberg as it was before 1902. At that date not a single vine grew on the Kupferberg. Its slopes, now so harmoniously covered with beautifully cultivated vineyards were then a mass of oak-scrub and brushwood, cleft by deep gorges. It was the Prussian State which, using convict labour, later planted these model vineyards.

When Director Goedecke had told me the story of the Domain (while I was on a visit there in the year 1949), he invited me to a tasting session. We started in the cellar where the 1948 and 1949 cask-wines came under review and then went on to his office, where we began with wines in bottles dating from the year 1947, and 1943 and ended with the pride of the Domain—the 1945 *Schloss Bockelheimer Kupfergrube Trockenbeerenauslese* which, at the 1948 auction, had sold for 66 DMarks per bottle (£5-10s.).

Its copper content has given the soil of the 'Kupfergrube' a curious earthy colour. (The name 'Kupfergrube' means 'copper mine'— and at one time it was actually mined, but uneconomically). The wine has a taste which is reminiscent of black currants. For this reason when I first tried it I thought it was impure, but later I gladly and wholeheartedly changed my opinion. The earthy element gives the beverage a certain delicate piquancy. To be understood and enjoyed this particular wine must be sucked rather than drunk in the normal way.

The vineyards on these slopes are now at the height of their productive capacity. The Niederhaeuser sites of *Steinberg* and *Hermannsberg*, and neighbouring sites *Kupfergrube, Felsenburg, Muehlberg*, and *Koenigsfels* belonging to Schloss Boeckelheim are among the best to be found along the whole of the Nahe.

Ranged close behind them come *Norheim* (with its sites: *Dellchen, Kirschheck, Goetzenfels,* and *Henterfels*), and *Traisen am Rotenfelsen* where some glorious vines grow from among porphyry rocks.

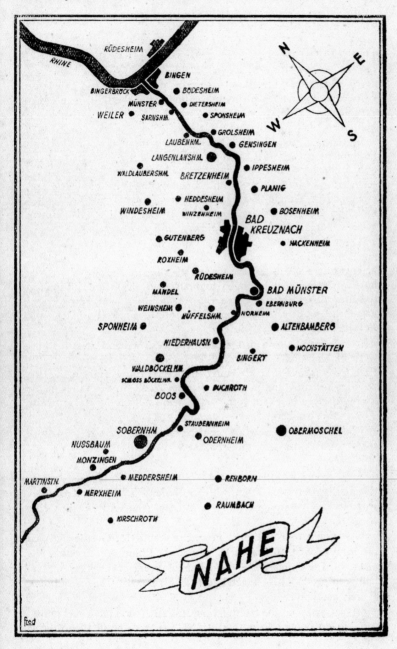

The other vines in the Amtsbezirk produce wines of the same or very similar quality. They are:

HUEFFELSHEIM which once changed hands as the result of a wager when one Ritter Boos von Waldeck drank a whole bootful of must in one draught; *Weinsheim,* the wine village par excellence as its name indicates, with its sites named after the hills, here rather grandiously called 'mountains' (Berge): Kellerberg, Muehlberg, Hinterberg, Nauenberg, and Holzberg.

Ruedesheim, with Rosengarten, Koenigsberg, and the Haardt heading its list of sites; Mandel, likewise with a Rosengarten, and also Schlossberg and Dellchen; then; Hargesheim, Roxheim, Sankt Katharinen, formerly a convent, Braunweiler, which calls its best vineyard site simple Weingarten (wine garden) and Gutenberg, with the sites Schlossberg (on which an old castle stands), Rosengarten, Margarethenberg, Bangenberg, and Bingergrube.

Through the beautiful *Salinen* valley we come to *Bad Muenster* am Stein, with its wine sites: *Rotenfels* and *Felseneck.* On the heights of the opposite bank we see the ruins of the Ebernburg, the mighty fortress that belonged to Franz von Sickingen. There (on the sites: *Weidenberg, Erzengrube, Schlossberg,* and *Pfarrwinger*) grow the vines that produce Sylvaner, Riesling, Traminer, and Portuguese grapes.

On the warm slopes of the porphyry rocks we find sites that bear signs of high-grade cultivation. The wines produced are peculiarly racy, have an individual bouquet, are steely, fruity, and, in the case of Rieslings of a fine piquancy. Farther south, in the valley of the lively Alsenz, there are many more wine-cultivating areas, among which Altenbamberg deserves mention.

Waldboeckelheim, slightly off the route along the river, is known for its good sites, exemplified by *Koenigsberg, Muehlberg* and *Welschberg.*

At *Monzingen* we enter a new viticultural region of good repute; this fairly extensive district, which includes *Weiler* and *Martinstein* with its site 'Burgwingert', is practically the end of the Nahe wine-lands.

While on a tour of the Rhine in the year 1815, Goethe attended the festival of St. Rochus at Bingen-on-the-Rhine. At that time the 1811 vintage enjoyed the reputation of being about the best that had been produced for several years. This is what Goethe said of it at that occasion:

> Gazing on the fruitful vineyards all around me, I feel moved
> to do honour to our great 1811. The name of that wine is

like the name of a great and beneficient ruler. When praise is
due for anything that befalls in his country, it is the name of
the ruler that is on everyone's lips. And so it is with a good
vintage. The people who dwell on the Nahe greatly praise
a wine that grows on their land, and to which they have given
the name of Monzinger. It is said of this wine that it is
pleasant and easy to drink, but that before a man is aware
of it, it goes to his head. We were invited to partake of its
delights and it has been so highly recommended that we are
all eagerness to taste it in such good company and to put
ourselves to the test, even though the experiment may be
attended with some risk.

In the valleys on both sides of the Nahe, there are many more
places with a thriving wine culture—for example, on the Glan near
Offenbach, and Odernheim. Although the vine centres on the
Alsenz and some of those on the Glan, are politically speaking in
the Palatinate, their wines belong in the Nahe category.

The wine-lands on the Nahe cater for all tastes. The high-grade
wines of the vintage-year 1949 from this region are the equals of
the best anywhere. In fact, they attained higher prices from German
wine-merchants than many kinds from other districts.

In conclusion, it may be said of the Nahe wines that their value
for export is certain to rise.

Rheingau

The most beautiful landscape in Germany, wrote Heinrich
von Kleist in the year 1801, which the Great Gardener must
have fashioned with the most loving care, rejoiced our eyes
as we moved along the Rhine and beheld its banks from
Mainz to Coblenz. The whole region resembles a poet's dream
and nothing more beautiful could be conjured up by the most
fertile imagination than this valley with its changing aspects—
now open, now closed, now flowery, now bleak; smiling and
frowning in turn. Swift as an arrow flows the Rhine from
Mainz, hurrying straight ahead as if its goal were already in
view, as if nothing could prevent its arrival there; impatiently
it strives to reach it by the shortest route. But a vine-covered
hillock, the Rheingau, rises up in its path and diverts its
impetuous stream.

The natural conditions for wine-growing are very favourable in
this district. The cluster of vineyards on the right bank of the Rhine
(which at this point flows from east to west) has a southerly aspect
and is protected against the biting east and north winds by the

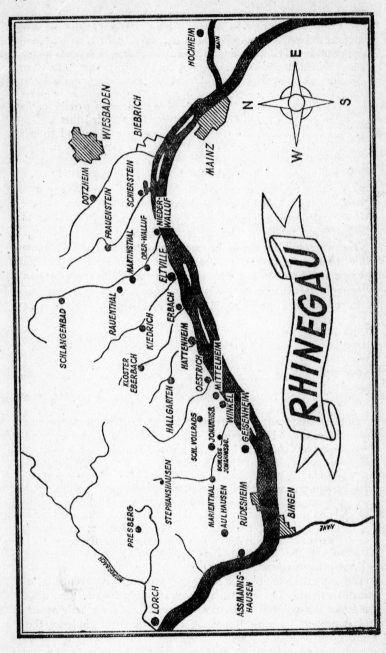

semi-circular wall formed by the thickly-wooded Taunus mountains. The effect of the sun's rays on the more or less steeply inclined vineyard slopes is heightened by their reflection from the surface of the Rhine. Moreover, the high proportion of moisture in the air, caused by the broad surface of the river, has an extremely stimulating influence on the whole development of the plantations, being particularly helpful when the grapes are ripening in the autumn. And finally, the advantages of the site are still further increased by the composition of the soil; this is for the most part very fruitful and particularly well adapted to viticulture.

The designation 'Rheingau' is used for wines originating in the wine-growing communities of the district of Ruedesheim (Rheingau-kreis), and extended to include those from the municipal district of Wiesbaden, the localities Frauenstein and Schierstein, and even the wine-growing centre of Hochheim together with its immediate surroundings; these are situated on the right bank of the river Main and strictly speaking therefore belong to the Main rather than the Rhine.

It was in the Rheingau that I spent my youth, on friendly terms with all the growers, familiar with every vineyard and its products. Of all wines my favourites are those grown on that piece of earth. The princes of viticulture who have brought the art of tending vines to its highest perfection have their home there, and it was there that I myself began to make wines my special study Every year from 1916 onwards I tasted wines from nearly all the Rheingau sites. Memory recalls the names of Erbach, Marcobrunn, Johannisberg, Ruedesheim, Asmannshausen, and many others, and pictures for me the vineyard slopes that I knew so well.

The Rheingau is still the home of descendants of the old patrician families who devoted their lives to furthering viticulture. In Eltville we have Freiherr Langwerth von Simmern and Graf zu Eltz, in Erbach there is Prince Friedrich Heinrich; in Hattenheim: Graf Schoenborn; in Hallgarten: Fuerst Loewenstein; in Johannisberg: Fuerst Metternich; in Winkel we find Freiherr von Brentano and Graf von Matuschka-Greiffenclau; in Ruedesheim: Graf von Franken-Sierstarpff—and many others.

Then there are many small, medium, and large Growers' Associations whose work is entirely devoted to the cultivation of wines. They look upon it as their duty to produce high-grade wines. I have tasted and bought many an excellent cask of wine from some of the small and medium concerns and found such products in no way inferior to those offered by the large undertakings. Superior even to these however are the State Wine-Cellars which developed out of the originally Nassau, later Prussian Domain. In the best vine-yard districts in the Rheingau—and always on the best sites—the State owns vineyards extending over more than 130 hectares in Hoch-heim, Rauenthal, Eltville, Kiedrich, Hattenheim, Erbach, Steinberg, Ruedesheim, and Asmannshausen. Domain Bensheim of the Berg-strasse (see p. 117) is now included with 10 hectares. The vineyard and cellar economy here are beyond praise and the resulting wines have been known to attain—and in fact still attain—fabulous prices.

The most easterly town of the Rheingau is—as has been men-tioned—Hochheim, and it is odd that this place on the river Main should have given the name 'Hock' in English-speaking countries to Rhine wines as a whole. But is is a fact and perhaps not so strange as it seems, for Hochheim wines have all the typical features of the Rheingau products. Several dozen sites in Hochheim produce wines which, together with a slightly earthy taste, are found to be mellow, delicate and well-balanced. Here are the names of some of these sites: *Hoelle, Bein, Reichesthal, Wandkaut, Stein, Kirchen-stueck, Domdechaney, Daubhaus, Koenigin-Viktoria-Berg, Kohlkraut, Falkenberg, Laut Weiler, Hangelstein, Neuenberg, Rothensee, Raber. Gans, Sommerhell, Berggasse, Schlicht, Kolben, Rossgaenger, Eber-land, Wiener, Bremenbusch, Rauchlock, Stiehlweg, Im Heiligen Haeuschen, Huehnerberg, Bettelmann, Hochmeister, Loch Goldberg, Ruesselheimer, Bickei. Orben, Steinern Kreuz, Eberland.*

Since the secularization of the Carmelites in 1803, a large part of the Hochheim Vine estates has belonged to the city of Frankfurt. To this very day *Hochheimer Hoelle* (Hochheim Hell) is drunk in the Frankfurt 'Ratskeller' as the city's own home-grown wine.

Just a word about the estate known as the 'Queen Victoria Vine-yard' (Koenigin Viktoria-Berg). Not that I think particularly highly of this wine; on the contrary, I have always found its earthy taste so prevailing and penetrating that its other qualities are submerged. But this vineyard was christened after Queen Victoria. In 1850 she visited the vineyard which produced her favourite wine. This visit was the cause for asking the permission of the Royal Court to give the 'Lage' the new name. It displays a monument to her within its own precincts. That is its main claim to interest. On the 5th December, 1950, the town of Hochheim celebrated the centenary of the Lage 'Konigin-Viktoria-Berg'.

Nor is there anything of special viticultural interest to note about Wiesbaden. It is of world-wide fame as a spa, but less well-known as a wine-centre. (I advise everybody to let the Wiesbaden local patriots drink their *Neroberger*.) Under the Occupation, Wiesbaden is the home of American Air Force Headquarters.

Passing over Schierstein (which incidentally possesses one of the oldest and formerly important Rhine harbours) and the little village of Nieder-Walluf, which is better known for its horticulture than for its wines, we come to the Rheingau proper. And by way of introduction, here first is a poetical flight of fancy referring to its vinous glories. The poet Emil Ritterhaus, though it cannot be said that he discovered a real connection between the sound of various church bells and the quality of the wine in any given village, composed the following verse which suggests the possibility:

> Along the banks of Father Rhine
> The church bells ring in praise of wine:
> 'It's good', they chant, or 'superfine',
> Each village has its own hum.
> A tinkling note means, 'Something wrong',
> But where the wine is rich and strong
> The chiming bass intones its song:
> 'Come here for vinum bonum,
> this way for vinum bonum' !

Eltville derives its name from the Latin 'alta villa'. Its vineyard area comprises 740 hectares and is the biggest in the whole Rheingau. Sites belonging to it are : *Albus, Kalbspflicht, Setzling, Taubenberg, Messwingert, Alte Bach, Langenstueck, Moenchhanach Neuweg, Klimchen, Freienborn, Sonnenberg, Sterzel, Engerweg, Bunken, Grimmen, Sandgrube, Steinmacher, Auf'm Ehr, Pellet, Grauer Stein, Bornhaeuschen.*

Three well-known wine-centres—*Kiedrich, Martinsthal* and *Rauenthal*—are situated on the heights at the foot of the Taunus Mountains.

The sites belonging to Kiedrich are : *Wasserros, Graefenberg, Norr, Peterschluessel, Sandgrube, Dippenerd, Brueck, Heiligenstock, Osbach, Berg, Dietenberg, Turmberg, Weihersberg, Gangolfsberg, Klosterberg, Huehnerfeld,* and *Kiesling.*

Wines from these sites are compact and have a fine aroma of spicy herbs. When they have been bottled for some time they are found to have gained in refinement and elegance. At the wine auction in Eberbach in 1906 a Graefenberg vintage broke the world price record for any wine sold up to that date.

Wines from *Rauenthal* vineyards always cost 10-15 per cent. more than any other Rheingau products—and rightly so. Here, on the steep mountain slopes are produced wines of supreme elegance— mild and aromatic, rose-scented, with a taste suggesting fruits and spices, and often honey-sweet. In the year 1927 the 1921 *Rauenthal*

Baiken Trockenbeerenauslese attained the price of 101 Marks (more than £5) per bottle. Quantitatively speaking, Rauenthal produces far less than any other Rheingau localities, and—quantity being usually attained at the expense of quality—this may explain Rauenthal's superiority. In 1949, for instance, Rauenthal produced two-thirds less wine—on an area of equal size—than any of her neighbours. This vintage promises to be as great as those of 1934 and 1921. I have my eye particularly on some 1949 Rauenthal wines, which, produced from old European vines, are likely to rejoice the palates even of the next generation. Situated in a valley between Rauenthal and Eltville is the community of Martinsthal—known till 1935 as Neudorf. The inhabitants of Neudorf considered that the name Neudorf (New Village) was too common; it allowed the distinctive quality of their own wines too little chance of becoming known and appreciated. A 1933 Martinsthal which had won a special prize for its superb quality, was a wonderful wine—mature, sweet, fruity, with a delicate bouquet.

Lower down the Rhine comes Erbach. (Sites : *Honigberg, Bruehl, Siegelsberg, Herrnberg, Hohenrain, Michelmark, Seelgass, Katz, Langenwingert, Rheinhoelle, Hetzelweid, Steinmorgen, Bachhell, Weiler, Pellet, Bein, Kablig, Weiler, Kiesling*).

At the western end of the village Schloss Reinhartshausen, property of Prince Heinrich Friedrich von Preussen, owner of an estate which comprises the best sites of Erbach and Hattenheim. Erbach is also well-known for its collection of pictures and sculptures recovered from Italian excavations.

The wines are well-nurtured and the vintages of 1934, 1935, and 1937 are something to remember with pleasure. About 10 minutes' walk farther on—midway between Erbach and Hattenheim, there is a famous old well now neglected and waterless. Semi-circular in shape, it still boasts four grooved Doric pillars and an inscription in large Roman letters with the words : Markobrunnen, *Gemeinde Erbach* (Marco Well, Community of Erbach). The fact that the Markobrunnen belongs to Erbach, not to Hattenheim, inspired a humorist to write :

> To solve the thorny question of 'mine adversus thine' :
> Let Erbach take the water and Hattenheim the wine.

While this book was in course of preparation, I had a letter from the Mayor of Hattenheim about the Markobrunnen. This is what he wrote :

'There have always been disputes between the communities of Erbach and Hattenheim about the Markobrunnen site. The popular version is "Erbach the water and Hattenheim the wine". But actually the site Markobrunnen belongs to Erbach, although it is situated practically on the boundary between the two places'.

In the year 1788 the third President of the United States, Thomas Jefferson, at that time still American Minister in Paris, undertook a journey to the Rhine. His diary, which was most meticulously kept, mentions many kinds of wine, among which the Markobrunn enjoyed his especial favour—in fact, he preferred it to all other Rheingau products.

In my opinion, the Markobrunn wines are neither as elegant nor as mature as the Rauenthaler, but they are particularly robust and spicy. The Markobrunn vineyard is shared by the estates : Schloss Reinhartshausen, Graf Schoenborn, Baron Raitz von Frentz, Baron von Oetinger, State Domain, Langwerth von Simmern.

Situated a little higher up lies the Nussbrunnen, a gracefully sculptured modern well dedicated to the North German Saint Urban.

Then comes *Hattenheim* to which belong the sites : *Aliment, Bergweg, Bitz, Boden, Boss am Steinberg, Boxberg, Deutelsberg, Dillmetz, Engelmannsberg, Gasserweg, Geiersberg, Grabenfeld, Hassel, Heiligenberg, Hinterhaus, Kiedricherweg, Kilb, Klosterberg, Mannberg, Mehrhoelzchen, Nussbrunnen, Pfaffenberg, Pflaenzer, Schloss Reichartshausen, Rheingarten, Rotenberg, Schuetzenhaeuschen, Speich, Stabel, Weid, Weiher, Weisert, Willhorn, Wisselbrunnen.* (Incidentally, Hattenheim is the only community in the Rheingau which owns vineyards.)

Equidistant from Hattenheim and Erbach, but farther from the river, idyllically situated in a wooded valley, lies *Kloster Eberbach*. (Monastery of the wild boar stream). It was founded by Augustinian monks in 1116 and 'modelled' on a wild boar shown with its tusks. It very soon fell into decay and in 1131 was taken over for a time by the Johannisberg Benedictines, and finally, in 1135, by the Cistercians. Then came a prosperous period for the monastery, the first of the Cistercian Order to be established on the right bank of the Rhine. The monks devoted themselves mainly to viticulture. A hundred years later Eberbach's reputation for the organization and extent of its viticulture was second to none. As early as in the 13th century the monastery had its own ships on the Rhine and a branch in Cologne. This had been established to evade the rule that forbade monks to attend markets or to be absent from the monastery for more than three or four days at a time. The monks managed to obtain special privileges from the customs, so that they were enabled to buy foreign wines and send them to Cologne free of duty.

In the year 1200 the monks built a wall encircling their whole premises, including the courtyards and gardens. Most of this wall is still standing. Their most famous vineyard was the *Steinberg* (27 hectares) which is still surrounded by a wall 2-2½ metres high and nearly 2 kilometres long.

The Steinberg vineyard now belongs to the State Domain. It has up-to-date equipment and (operated by Heinrich Jost, an old school-friend of mine) keeps pace with all modern scientific and technical improvements. The cellar alone is worth a visit—it contains nearly 800 Half-Stuck (48,000 litres) of wine.

The favourite Rheingau wine in Germany today is the *Steinberger*. And certainly its Trockenbeerenauslesen represent the noblest and finest of any produced in the whole country. A 1921 Steinberger fetched 15,10 RM; Auslese: 24 RM hochfeine Auslese: 28 RM; Edelbeerenauslese: 89 RM; and the best Trockenbeerenauslese 172 RM per bottle (£1—20 RM). The price differences show how little importance can be attached to a name of a wine, even in combination with a particular vintage year. The content of the bottle is the only thing that matters. However, I have extremely pleasant recollections of the best grades, and the 1943 Trockenbeerenauslese is a worthy successor to the older vintages.

Eberbach lies at the foot of a mountain known as the *Hallgarter Zange* (Pincers). Its summit is crowned with a massive observation tower giving a magnificent view over the Rheingau, Rhinehessia, the Hunsrueck heights, and the Taunus; on a clear day it is possible to see the line of the Odenwald and the Vosges foothills. Sheltering beneath the 'Pincers' lies the village of *Hallgarten*, sunbathed, glorying in the fertility of its vineyards. My family takes its name from that village, but that is not the only reason why I have a particular penchant for its wines. The growers who live there are born and brought up in the wine tradition and produce the racy and distinguished wines that prove an attraction on any wine-list. In the year 1921, that famous year which brought forth fine wines everywhere, the Hallgarten products were superior in body, bouquet and elegance to any others from the Rheingau. The Hallgarten sites are: *Jungfer, Schoenhell, Deutelsberg, Mehrhoelzchen* (adjoining the Steinberg), *Wuerzgarten, Hendelberg, Rosengarten,* and *Kirschenacker.*

In Hallgarten most of the growers belong to one of the three local Associations, called respectively the 'English', the 'Boers', and the 'Germans'. The appellations are now used officially, but have a popular origin, dating from their foundation during the Boer War. The poorer growers, having dubbed the larger owners 'Englishmen', themselves automatically became the 'Boers'.

In the parish church at Hallgarten stands the famous 'Wine

Madonna', a piece of 15th century sculpture and one of the delightful monuments to Rhenish wine culture.

Nestling close together in the valley are the villages Oe Mittelheim and Winkel. Oestrich, which is blessed with very good vineyards, and Mittelheim, share the same railway station, while the Mittelheim-Winkel boundary is practically non-existent. Oestrich's sites are named : *Doosberg, Pfaffenpfad, Hitz, Deez, Raeuscherberg, Kerbesberg, Eiserberg, Hoelle, Lenchen, Gottesthal, Muehlberg, The Mittelheim* sites are called *Edelmann, Gottesthal, Honigberg,* and Winkel has the following long list :

Steinacker, Gutenberg, Rheinpflicht, Jesuitengarten, Steinchen, Berg, Hasensprung, Hellersberg, Erntebringer, Sautt, Plankner, Schlossberg, Marienberg, Lauerberg ,Bohret Ansbach, Dachsberg, Honigberg, Bienenkopf, Neuberg, Greiffenberg, Eckeberg, Oberberg, Ensing, Lett. Scharbel, Weiherhaeuschen.

Schloss *Vollrads,* above Winkel, is tucked away in a little vale half-way up the slope of the wooded Taunus hill. Its wines rank high among the best Rheingau products. Established at the end of the 17th century, Schloss Vollrads is justly proud of its press-house. This contains, in addition to some modern presses, one very old press made from the trunks of old oaks on which a coat of arms has been elaborately carved. The Castle is owned by Graf Matuschka-Greiffenclau, the leading figure of German viticulture. His family formerly inhabited the oldest existing German residence—the 'Grey House' in Winkel.

Schloss Vollrads' 1933, 1934 and 1935 vintages are wines of pleasant memories, and its 1945 products have a great future. They have an exquisite aroma, and the *Schloss Vollrads Trockenbeeren-*auslese has always been one of the highlights at auctions. In this connection an early personal experience may be of some interest. The occasion was the bottling of the 1911 Trockenbeerenauslese; to taste this Graf Matuschka (father of the present Graf) invited my father. I was even allowed to drink a few drops of the delectable beverage myself. My elders however did not content themselves with tasting the 1911. For comparison they had out the finest of the 1904, 1893, and 1868 vintages. My father is now 80, and that was the only time in his life that he was ever drunk. But to get drunk on wines of such superb quality is apparently not a matter for regret, for to this day my father tells the tale whenever a Schloss Vollrads wine is mentioned.

A little farther on we come to *Johannisberg*. Blessed with fruitful vines, it has had a colourful history. A conveniently situated castle at its highest point was used as an observation post during the

Second World War and was duly attacked and set on fire by Allied bombers. It has since been partly rebuilt. The first Benedictine monastery in the Rheingau was erected at Johannisberg on the initiative of Archbishop Ruthard of Mainz (1088-1109) and the hill named the *Bischofsberg*. When the monasteries were secularized in 1801, the hill was made over to Prince William of Orange. Five years later, the French Prefecture in Mainz having claimed it as a Domain, Napoleon bestowed both hill and castle as Imperial fief on his Marshal Kellermann. One summer, the Marshal sold the grapes on the vine—the whole yield—to the Mumm Concern in Cologne for 32,500 gulden. But that happened to be the famous wine year 1811; the crop yielded 65 'Stuck' (one Stuck hold 1200 litres), and the merchants obtained for it 11,000 gulden per Stuck! After the fall of Napoleon, the Emperor of Austria (under a clause in the Vienna Act of Congress) came into possession of the estate and bestowed it as fief on Fuerst Metternich—on condition that one-tenth of the wine yield should be surrendered annually to the Austrian Crown. This tribute is still paid to the Habsburgs—in recent years the wine has been sent to Otto von Habsburg in America. Incidentally, in 1815, when the Emperor took over the estate, there was a celebration which Goethe attended. Drawn by the attractions of Marianne von Willemer, he had been taking the cure in nearby Wiesbaden.

The Metternich family is still in possession of the large wine estates —twenty-five and three-quarter hectares in extent—which is now planted with graft-vines and from which the average crop yield is 100 Stuck.

Beyond the Castle lies the village of Johannisberg with its estates *Nonnenhoell, Erntebringer,* and *Sterzelpfad, Hoelle, Klaus.* Its wines fully deserve their universal popularity.

Johannisberg wine graced the historic occasion when, at the 1878 Berlin Congress, the Russo-Turkish war was brought to its formal conclusion. At the close of the proceedings Bismarck invited the members of the Congress to his house and, raising his glass of 1811 Johannisberger smilingly to Disraeli, gave the toast to 'perpetual world peace and increasing understanding among the European peoples'. He compared the gold of the wine to the honest work accomplished by the Congress.

Close to the river lies the old town of *Geisenheim*, with its two (dissimilar) open-work Gothic towers. It is widely known as the home of the largest German Training Centre for Viticulture, Fruit-growing, and Horticulture (see also p. 43). It was in the castle of Graf Schoenborn at the upper end of the town that in 1648 the

Kurfuerst of Mainz, Johann Philipp von Schoenborn, drafted the peace treaty that ended the Thirty Years' War. Here too, he conferred with Leibniz and others on proposals to unite the Catholic and Evangelical Churches. Sites : *Rotenberg, Kapellengarten, Mauerchen, Kirchgrube, Kosakenberg, Klauserweg, Schröderberg, Spitzenlehn, Rosengarten, Kreuzweg, Hinkelstern, Steinacker.*

Extending a considerable length along the Rhine, lies famous Ruedesheim, with its very numerous and far-famed sites. They are : *Bienengarten, Bischofsberg, Bronnen, Burgweg, Dachsloch, Dickerstein, Drachenstein, Eichenbaeumchen, Eisenenger, Engerweg, Geisberg, Hauptmann, Haeuserweg, Hellpfad, Hinterhaus, Kaisersteinfels, Katerloch, Klosterkiesel, Kiesel, Krachbein, Kreuzgarten, Kroonest, Kripp, Lay, Lindgrube, Muehlstein, Pares, Platz, Rammstein, Rechacker, Ringmauer, Roseneck, Rosengarten, Rottland, Schloss, Stumpfenort, Stoll, Wilgert, Wuest, Zimmglaeser, Zollhaus, Kreuzberg, Sonnenberg.* Sites in the part of Ruedesheim known as *Eibingen* are : *Backhaus, Bein, Boehl, Dechaney. Dummchen, Flecht, Hangeloch, Hasenlaeufer, Hochmauer, Hochpfad, Kirchenpfad, Klepperweg, Klosterberg, Langenacker, Lay, Metzelberg, Muehlpfad, Pfeilerbaum, Rueck, Sandgrub. Steinfels, Stiehl, Strelkamp, Tafel.*

Here in this district you find the typical Rhenish wine-taverns, where all the Rheingau wines may be tasted. The Rheingau is far too proud of its products to serve wines from any other region.

The wines grown on the Ruedesheimer Berg, particularly on the sites Schlossberg, Burgweg, and Bischofsberg Roseneck, are famed for their incomparable bouquet and their fruity taste.

The Ruedesheim wines have one characteristic which sets them apart from most others—in so-called 'good years' they are seldom at their best, and vice versa. There is a very simple explanation for this. The Ruedesheim sites like many on the Moselle, are on steep slopes; consequently, the moisture in their soil is apt to leave the higher regions comparatively quickly. The vineyards have little natural moisture, so, in hot summers, the warmth is not offset by sufficient water to feed the ripening grapes; this in turn retards the development of their sugar content. The 1921 and 1949 Ruedesheim wines from the best sites were too dry.

The war brought considerable damage to Ruedesheim vineyards. Surveys in the region have shown that about one quarter of the vine-lands were destroyed by bombing. The R.A.F. certainly did its work well on this important target, where many observation posts and anti-aircraft guns had been set up.

That the destruction was very far-reaching in its effect, is shown by the case of one vineyard-owner who needed 650 tons of earth to repair his thirteen bomb-craters. He employed five workmen eight hours a day for six months to put his vineyard in working order again. The loss of crops in five years must be somewhere in the region of 1600 half-Stuck—1,280,000 bottles.

With *Assmannshausen* still belonging to the Rheingau, we come to the *Middle Rhine* which stretches from here to Coblenz. Assmannshausen produces the best-known Red Hock.

Red Hocks

These observations would not be complete without a reference to red hocks, and in this connection I should like to borrow Professor Saintsbury's expressed opinion as contained in his *Notes on a Cellar-Book*. He writes :

> For the red hocks, however, I must put in a word, both in justice to them and in charity to my fellow-creatures. They— not merely Assmannshauser, which certainly is the best, but Walporzheimer, Ober-Ingelheimer and others—are specifics for insomnia after a fashion which seems to be very little known, even among the faculty. Many years ago, when I was doing night-work for the press, and even after I had given that up, when I was rather unusually hard run at day-work, I found sleep on the off-nights as well as the others in the former case, and often in the latter, not easy to obtain. I was not such a fool as to take drugs, and I found hot grog or (what is not in itself inefficacious) strong beer, conducive to an uncomfortable mouth, etc., in the morning when taken only a few hours before. But a large claret glass or small tumbler of red hock did the trick admirably, and without deferred discomfort.
>
> In good vintages the wines show a soft and delicate flavour, and though the red grapes ripen earlier than the white ones, under no circumstances can they be compared with the French growths. It is, therefore, easily understandable that there is no export of these wines; they are consumed within Germany, whereas foreign countries will in any case look for the fine red wines of Bordeaux or Burgundy, and not for Assmannshausen or any other German red wine, as they would have to pay the same duty.

The red-wine grape most favoured in Germany is the Blue Burgundy (*Spaetburgunder*). Its wine is dark, strong and finely spiced. It flourishes on the Rhine, on the Ahr, and above all in Baden. Next in favour comes the Mueller-vine (*Black-Schwarz-Riesling*) in Wuerttemberg.

38. Road sign over an old Roman milestone.

WINE JOURNEY

39 & 42 (*Opposite*).
Modern road signs.

40. Deidesheim and its vineyards.

41. The Wine Gate at Schweigen (French frontier), start of the Weinstrasse.

42.

44. Wachenheim.

43. (*Opposite*). Landscape in the Upper Haardt (near Leinsweiler).

46. (*Below*). Bad Duerkheim.

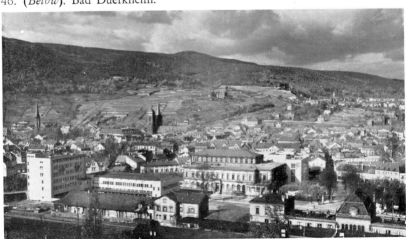

47. The Feigengasse (fig lane) in Deidesheim.

45. (*Opposite*). Vineyards in terraces near Bad Duerkheim.

48. Forster Kirchenstueck—the best vineyard of the Palatinate.

RHINEHESSIA

49. Vineyards reaching down to the river (between Nierstein and Nackenheim).

50. Bodenheim and its vineyards.

51. Oppenheim, St. Catherine's church and vineyards.

52. The Rhine at Nierstein.

53. Liebfrauen Church at Worms.

NAHE.

54. Vineyard site Rotenfels.

55. Bad Muenster a/St. and Ebernberg vineyards.

57. Bingen and the Scharlachberg vineyards and the Nahe, seen from the Ruedesheimer Berg vineyard and castle Ehrenfels.

56. (*Opposite.*) Norheimer Hinterfels and Niederhaeuser Steyer, two good sites.

58. Bad Kreuznach.

Lesser red wines are produced from the Blue Portuguese grape in the Palatinate (the Palatinate is the biggest red wine region in Germany), in Rhinehessia and in Wuerttemberg; and from the Limberger vine and the Trollinger (originating in the Tyrol) in Wuerttemberg. The last-named produces a somewhat sour table-wine. Then there is the *Affenthaler,* which is produced near Buehl in Baden.

Red wines in Germany—like the French red wines from Bordeaux and Burgundy—are obtained by fermentation of the grape *mash.* Under the German Wine Law it is permissible to add to a German red wine a quantity of foreign red wine not exceeding 25 per cent. of the total volume. This licence constitutes a great commercial advantage to growers and wine-merchants in Germany, as—with the exception of Wuerttemberg and Baden—practically no region producing German red wines would otherwise be able to condition its products for a ready sale.

The German red wine region *par excellence* is the *Ahr Valley,* which is also the most northerly wine region in the world. The wine produced there is called Ahr Burgundy. Owing to the lack of foreign wines in Germany, the Ahr products have an almost clear field and the chance to reign supreme. It seems doubtful, however, whether they will be able to maintain this position, even inside the country. The foreign consumer is certain to prefer a genuine Burgundy to the Walporzheimer.

Moreover, the cultivation of red wine on the Ahr is on the wane. The growers are of the opinion that the vineyards on the Ahr are 'Burgundy-weary', an opinion based on the discovery that in many places new cuttings lacked vigour in their development, while other species—when planted in vineyards earlier devoted to Burgundy vines—bore good fruit. Just as a farmer rotates his crops, so the vine-grower must from time to time change the species of vines in his vineyards. As a result of these considerations, the growers on the Ahr have begun to plant grapes which produce white wines. At the present day, red and white wines are being grown in about equal proportions. There is no need to go into detail about these white wines whose origins are nearer to the North Pole than any others.

Next on our list comes *Assmannshausen,* the city of Rhenish red wines (sites: *Hoellenberg, Hinterkirch, Eckerstein, Steil, Frankenthal, Bohren, Bomberg*).

Assmannshausen red wines are all derived from the 'Late Burgundy' vine. It is planted over an area of 28 hectares, mostly the property of the State Domain. In this connection it may be noted that the entire viticultural region of the Rheingau (of which the

7

Assmannshausen red wine vineyards form a part) covers 2,500 hectares, one sixtieth of the whole German viticultural area.

As the best red wine produced in Germany, the Assmannshauser has been praised in many writings. It is no Burgundy—despite the fact that it comes from a 'Burgundy' grape—but a Rhine wine with some of the qualities of a Burgundy. The difference is no doubt due to the difference in soil. The slate hills of the Rhine produce something less fine than the French Burgundy but possibly for the same reason rather stronger.

Here is a quotation from an Assmannshausen propaganda brochure concerning the local red wine:

> The fact that nothing but the Assmannshausen Burgundy grape can produce such full and noble 'quality' red wines has always aroused the envy of other German red wine districts. Efforts were therefore made to transplant the Assmannshausen late Burgundy vines to Baden, to Wuerttemberg, to the Main, to the Ahr, and elsewhere, and by this means to cultivate a wine of equal value. But the results were disappointing from the very first. It was clearly recognized on all sides that the failure could only have been avoided if the Assmannshausen soil had been transplanted together with the grape. Yes, indeed! Therein alone lies the secret. The nature of the soil is the deciding factor.
>
> The strong native vineyard soil consists of laminary efflorescent layers of Taunus phyllite slate, in colours ranging from bluish-red to violet. It is extremely favourable to the growth of the 'Late Burgundy' vine, which, brought from France, probably by Cistercian monks, has proved itself to be the best grape for the production of red wine. The Assmannshausen variety, which is a smooth noble red wine, has a slight characteristic flavour of almonds, a mild and velvety, delicate pungency, and is fully and harmoniously rounded. Its colour varies—according to the maturity of the grapes—from fiery red to a dark garnet hue.

Unfortunately, what Assmannshausen has to say of its soil, the Burgundy growers can say rightly of their soil and climate. So the Assmannshauser is a red wine, but no Burgundy.

The Assmannshausen sold pre-war in London at 660/- per dozen bottles (which then included only 12/- duty) was the most interesting wine I ever tasted. It was the 1934 Assmannshauser Hoellenberg Spaetburgunder Rot-Weiss, Feinste Trockenbeerenauslese, Estate Bottling Prussian Domain. This is a wine resulting from a very special kind of Beerenauslese of the late Burgundy grape. The grape-gatherers of Assmannshausen—in good vintages—have a sickle-shaped enamel container hanging from their punnets; into these containers they put the selected sleepy berries, some of which have already shrunk and dried out to a raisin-like consistency. This is done because in these raisin-berries the beautiful blue dye in the grapeskin has been destroyed by the fungus (Botrytis cinerea) and the employment of these otherwise valuable berries in the manufacture of the red wine would be detrimental to its natural ruby-red colour. Now, whereas in preparing red wines, the grape mash is allowed to ferment in order that the grape-juice (colourless even in blue-skinned berries) may be enabled to absorb the blue dye from the skins, the sleepy raisin-berries are pressed immediately. The juice gained by this process—coloured, rather sticky grape-juice—is then fermented on the lines of the white wine process. If these raisin-berries were to be fermented with the rest in the mash, the must or wine would take on an unpleasant mouldy taste. As it is, they produce a white wine, pressed from the noblest red-wine grapes; the juice having absorbed a certain amount of the skin-dye, the wine has a yellowish, brownish or reddish tinge according to its quality.

The 1934 wine, as well as later vintages—1938 and the 1950, are the most exceptional wines I have ever met.

I once gave this wine after lunch, instead of port. A wine shipper who was present considered it unorthodox to give hock as an after-dinner wine. For comparison therefore, a decanted bottle of 1908 Vintage Port was sent for. All present agreed that the Assmanns-hauser, with its low alcoholic strength, was to be preferred for after-lunch consumption.

There is no reason why the French wine-growers in Burgundy and Bordeaux should not adopt the same method and give the world something new and even finer in quality than the Rot-Weiss (Red-white) Assmannshauser.

This red-white wine must not be confused with the *Schiller Wine.* Schiller wine is the name given to a wine pressed from a mixture of red and white grapes. The name has nothing to do with the poet Schiller, but is derived from the red-white (merging into pink) radiance or 'shimmer' of the wine. (The German verb for 'shimmer' is 'schillern').

This species of wine was developed mainly during the worst crisis ever suffered by German viticulture—after the Thirty Years' War. During that period the many devastated vineyards were hastily replanted with any kind of vine likely to afford a good crop, whether it was a red-wine or a white-wine grape. Even nowadays the Swabians are very fond of their 'Schiller', but its production has been drastically reduced. In Wuerttemberg as elsewhere there is a very strong tendency—wholly admirable from the viticultural point of view—to keep grape-strains and wines pure by selective planting, selective harvesting and selective wine-production. This tendency will no doubt lead to a still greater improvement in the quality of German wines.

BEST-KNOWN GERMAN RED WINES

Ahr : Walporzheimer Honigberg, Ahrweiler Daubhaus, Neuen-ahrer Sonnenberg.

Rhinehessia : Ingelheimer (Hundsweg, Langenberg, Hirschtal, Bein, Hoellenweg, Steinacker, and Sonnenberg).

Palatinate : Duerkheimer Feuerberg, Forster Neuberg, Kallstadt and Herxheim. (According to a document in the Speyer Museum dated 1597, the 'Red Traminer' from Rhodt in the Oberhaardt was at that time considered to be the best wine 'Growing on the long chain of hills from Bale to Cologne').

Rheingau : Assmannshaeuser Hoellenberg.

Wuerttemberg : Brackenheim, Schwaigern.

Baden : Oberrotweiler Kirchberg, Ortenberg, Schlossberg.

Franconia : Klingenberg am Main.

Mittelrhein

After this short digression we return to the Middle Rhine—the district extending along the left bank of the Rhine from Binger-brueck to Rolandseck, and on the right bank from Caub to Koenigs-winter. *Lorch* and *Lorchhausen*—the places immediately following Assmannshausen— really belong to the Rheingau, but as the character of their wines has nothing in common with the products of the Rheingau, we need have no hesitation in including them in our survey of the Middle Rhine. There cannot be many river valleys in existence whose natural beauty rivals that of this stretch of the Rhine. This is where the 'beautiful Rhine' really begins, and anyone singing the praises of the Rhine is almost sure to be thinking of the Rhine valley from Bingen to Bonn. But unfortunately the same cannot be said of the wines of the Middle Rhine. The surface structure and the geological composition of the soil differ from that of the Rheingau. The vines grow on quartzite and devonian slate and at best produce wines of medium quality. These are either drunk locally, or else they find their way into the sparkling wine factories, where they are welcome for their steely taste.

The main locality on the Middle Rhine is (for our purposes) Bacharach on the left bank. At one time there was a popular saying :

'At Wuerzburg on Stein, and at Bach'rach on Rhine, you will find the best wine'.

That alone would show that in earlier days the Bacharach wine was famous. But the town of Bacharach owes this reputation less to its good vineyards than to the circumstance that it was a reloading station for the big ships. Only little ships could pass through the so-called Binger Loch ('Bingen Hole'). And so it came about that the Bacharach stocks were the general repository for the Rhine wines from Rhinehessia, the Rheingau, and the Rhenish Palatinate—and these wines were then sent into the world as *Bacharacher*.

Closely connected with Bacharach—in fact, always mentioned in one breath as it were with that city—are *Steeg, Oberdiebach* and Enghoell. Their ' Four Valley Wines ' are among the best produced by the Middle Rhine. That these wines used to find favour even with very pampered drinkers, is shown by the story told about the Emperor Wenzel (deprived of his throne at Koenigstuhl in Rhense in the year 1400) who is said to have estimated the value of the Freedom of the City of Nuremberg at about 4 casks of Bacharach Muscatel.

City of Bacharach. Sites :
Posten, Untere Wolfshoenlo, Hahn, Leimbach, Dell, Muehlchen, Bill, Bombach, Altes Kloster, Schlossberg.
Community of Steeg : St. Jost, Flur.
Community of Oberdiebach : Fuerstenberg, Bischofshub, Mittelberg.
Community of Manubach : Reetz, Langgoon, Grube.

Next—on the right bank of the Rhine—comes *Caub* with the sites : Bluechertal, Rauschelay, Kupferfloez, Silbernagel, Backofen, Schuetzeneck, Schlossberg, Herrenberg, Pfalzgrafenstein, Sonnenberg.

The late Dr. C. Spielmann, the Municipal archivist at Wiesbaden, compiled a description of the wine-market toll-book of the town of Caub in the year 1544 to 1677. This, it appears, stated that at that time wine-merchants from the Netherlands came with their ships to Caub and there bought up the entire stock of locally produced wine. This they then re-sold to North Germany, the Netherlands and England.

As a formidable stream the Rhine races past Boppard, the city with a royal Court of its own. The waves are then broken on the Altenburg, where the river turns sharply to the east, forming (in the Boppard Hamm) its biggest bend north of Bingen. Looking down from the *Schuetzen* we can survey 'wine-soaked' Hamm, which—more than 5 kilometres long and sited due south all the way —is (next to the Rheingau) the best situated tract of wine country on the Middle Rhine. Strong Riesling wines with a fine bouquet

flourish here on the upper Coblenz levels. *Sites*: *Ewigbach, Gelberspfad, Hohes, Ufer, Fesserlei, Giebel im Oberhamm, Feuerlei and Liesborn, Mandelstein, Lachespfad, Kerlerlei, Hetz, Rodenberg, Ohlenberg, Rabenlei,* and *Weisse Wack im Niederhamm.*

Kloster Eberbach in the Rheingau, whose wines are world famous, used to possess more than 64,000 vines in the Boppard Hamm. The 'Eberbacherhof'—the memory of which is kept alive by the picturesque 'Ebertor' on the Rhine—attended to the cultivation of the vines, and pressed and matured the wines in its own cellars (which incidentally are still extant).

Before we pass on to the Moselle which we are now about to reach at Koblenz, it should be noted that the Middle Rhine winelands extend farther to the north; here they comprise—in particular —Linz, with its sites : Auf der Rheinhoelle, In der Rheinhoelle, Im Hammer Thal, Im Langenhaelschen, Auf dem Rabennest, In der Aue; and finally Koenigswinter with its sites : Bocksacker, Drachenlay, Steingass, Kapellenberg, Herrenberg, Vitzenberg, Helte, Goldenfuesschen, Kreuzbruennchen.

Moselle Wines

The collective designation 'Moselle includes—besides the wines of the Moselle proper—those of the Moselle tributaries, the Saar and the Ruwer.

The Rhine provides us with wines which may be described as mighty, massive, weighty, and full. His daughter, Mosella, supplements his gifts with wines which vary in character according to their place of origin. These wines had a changing fate on foreign markets.

Unfortunately, particularly after the war, many natural wines (especially of the 1946 vintage) were shipped, which had better remained in their country of origin, for a scarcity of sugar had prevented the growers from supplementing the lack of sugar of the grapes, and many lovers of Moselle got very suspicious of them. The vintages 1947, 1948, and especially 1949, made up for it, and these wines have now come back to fashion.

The Moselle valley from Trier to Coblenz is a very long and narrow strip of land—100 kilometres in length, but when measured across from the vine-covered slopes on one side of the valley to those on the other, the average width works out at no more than seven and a half kilometres. The whole area therefore comprises about 750 square kilometres.

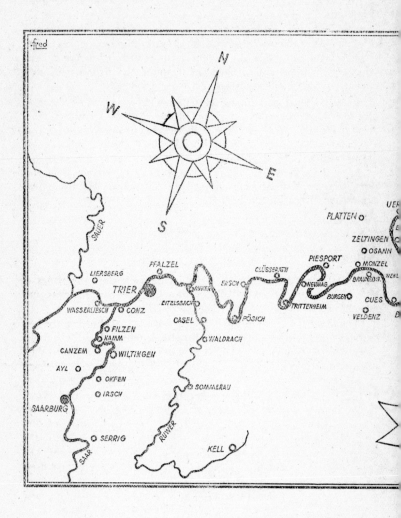

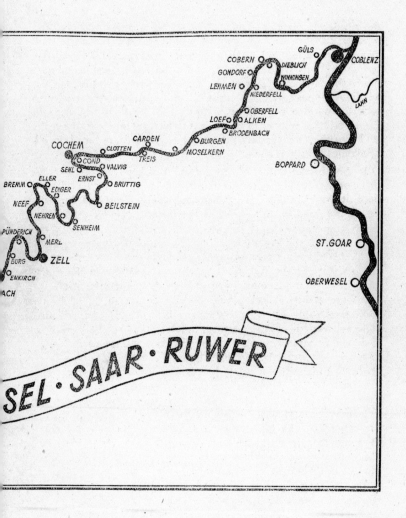

But the Moselle, once it has joined up with the Saar near Trier, winds in and out so much that the distance from Trier to Coblenz —100 kilometres as the crow flies—is just about doubled, giving that much more space for vine-cultivation. To this must be added the vineyards of the Saar and the Ruwer. On the strip of land just described, there are at least 200 inhabited places—towns, hamlets, villages, parishes, castles, monasteries, 176 communities grow wine. The general direction of the river's flow is toward the north-east, but some of its windings are at such an acute angle that in some places the flow is actually in the opposite direction. Most of these windings are very short; in nearly all cases the river very soon turns back to continue its original course. The windings result in the formation of a number of peninsulas, which jut out from the mainland into the river; mostly these tongues of land are broad-tipped, sometimes being very long.

If the Moselle from Trier to Coblenz had kept to a straight line in a north-easterly direction instead of indulging in all these fluctuations, it would have had a left bank facing south-east and thus continuously turned to the sun, while its right bank would have faced north-west and been just as consistently deprived of all sunshine. But owing to the multitude of curves, the banks of the river on both sides show the greatest possible variety in their relation to the sun, so that climatic conditions on the riverside and in the valleys vary from point to point, often at very short intervals. Here you may have a little hillock whose slopes face due south, where the sun's rays caught in rock crevices, are thrown back, their intensive collected warmth of the greatest possible benefit to the vines. On such slopes vines are planted on all available space, and not a corner is left free. At one time these favoured hillocks may be on the right bank, while the next is found on the left. The best wines are derived from slopes such as these which face due south. There are other rocky promontories with slopes facing south-east and east, or south-west and west, which, in the course of a year's changes are exposed to the sun's rays in all sorts of crannies and crevices. It is here that the medium grades of wine are obtained. And finally there are the slopes, which, turned away from the south, get no sun at all. They are cold, and useless for vine-growing purposes.

Owing to this curious structure, the inhabitants of the region usually have their villages and dwellings on one side of the river and their vineyards on the other. This has given rise to a complicated system of property-ownership on both banks and also explains the very large number of bridges over the Moselle. Nearly all these bridges were destroyed by the Nazis in their retreat, but have since been replaced. I happened to be present when the new bridge at

Zeltingen was inaugurated (4-6 June, 1948). Till then Zeltingen had been practically cut off from the world; for, though most of the Moselle hamlets have at least a ferry to take them across the river, Zeltingen has none and was dependent on the neighbouring community of Rachtig. Incidentally, these ferries are really flat-bottomed boats, rather like landing crafts.

The slopes bordering the Moselle are much higher than those on the Rhine, or for that matter, on any other German river. Up and up go the steps, innumerable are the terraces, one above the other, and even the topmost levels are covered with vines. This means hard work for the wine-grower.

For one thing, the Moselle wine-grower has a task peculiar to this region. Throughout the whole winter he has to prise slabs of slate out of the rocks, chop them up small and distribute the pieces in the vineyards—right up to the top level. These slates not only give the Moselle wines their basic taste, but the slabs hewn from the rock have a certain vital energy which they communicate to the vines. They help to keep the soil moist and act as fertilizing agents when they disintegrate. But of course their disintegration means that they have to be constantly replaced. Their usefulness does not end there. In the summer time—on hot days—the slate stores up the heat of the sun during the day, and when evening comes, the warmth is radiated back on to the grapes, so that even by night, the vines—through the action of the slate—indirectly get the benefit of the 'sunshine' they need to complete the maturing process.

Another hard task for the Moselle wine-growers is the transportation of loads of fertilizer from the riverside to all the vineyards, including those at the top of the long slopes.

It seems likely that within a reasonable time these tasks will be alleviated. Plans have been mooted to build funicular railways modelled on the Swiss ski-lifts—some indeed have already been constructed, notably in Enkirch—which by connecting the valley with the mountain paths will make both the slate distribution and the transportation of fertilizer a much less strenuous task.

On the Moselle they cultivate nothing but vines, market nothing but the wines they produce. They have hardly any corn-fields. In so far as they have meadows or keep cattle, it is only in the interest of their viticulture.

Except on the Upper Moselle, the only kind of grape grown is the Riesling, even though this species has only been cultivated there since the 16th century. Its triumphant progress on the Moselle, to the final exclusion of all other species, is due on the one hand to the much-appreciated taste which it imparts to its wines and its allegedly

health-giving properties—it is jokingly known as 'Riesling tea'—
and on the other to the reliability of its yield.

On the whole the climate is favourable to grape-growing, with a
good average temperature and good atmospheric conditions. Apart
from evaporation from the river, the vines obtain moisture from a
varying number of rainfalls, and warmth from the heat-absorbing
action of the slate-stone.

In addition, in those vineyards where quality wines are produced,
the vines are mostly kept close to the ground, in order that the
grapes may ripen earlier and more evenly.

To ensure that the Riesling grapes reach full maturity even in
poor seasons, the grape-harvest is delayed as long as possible—till
October or even November. The grapes are not left on the vines—
as in the Rheingau—until they reach 'Edelfaeule', but only till they
have reached full maturity and are then pressed immediately in
order to preserve the effervescent and racy qualities of the wine and
its golden-green colour.

The vine country falls naturally into three parts, based on the
differences in soil and the resulting differences and peculiarities of
the vines cultivated thereon; the Lower-Moselle, the Middle Moselle,
the Upper-Moselle.

The region of the Middle Moselle produces a wine which has the
lowest alcohol content (about 7 per cent., app. 12-13°) of any German, or indeed any European wine; but at the same time it boasts
the greatest wealth in 'bouquet' substances and a pleasant refreshing
acidity. The praises of the Moselle wines have been sung for many
centuries, as a simple reference to Ausonius' 'Mosella' will recall. A
quotation will serve to illuminate the character of the Moselle:

> Every wine grown in each small hamlet has its own jealously
> preserved point of honour. All these wines may resemble
> each other in that they have been grown on the same steely
> slate ground, a fact that is immediately perceptible by the
> tongue (the taste one knew as a schoolboy when one licked
> one's slate); but each individual sample of liquor with a
> separate name and from a separate site shows some charac-
> teristic that is inimitable elsewhere. Something in each sample
> rejoices in its own recognizable peculiarity, ranging from
> something frankly rustic to the finest shades of aristocratic
> heredity and hedonism. The wine does not make you feel
> heated—it is cool and pleasant to drink. It is neither heavy,
> nor has it ill effects. It is light, volatile, fine, and clear: like
> fresh agreeable music which remains in the memory without
> troubling mind or body, it hardly affects you at all. That is
> a point of honour with the wine, that is balsam for the shat-
> tered nerves of modern man.

And thus it has come about that not only the wine-drinker, but
the doctor, too, has learned to prize the qualities of this wine:
Doctors, in a word, take Moselle wines seriously. They attach importance to them as helping to preserve good health in those who
enjoy it and to improve the condition of those who are sick. It has
for instance been ascertained that cases of calculus are practically
unknown on the Moselle and that Moselle wines have a specific curative influence on cases of renal, urinary, or biliary calculus (commonly known as kidney-stones, bladder-stones and gallstones). Even
Ausonius stressed that *vinum mosellanum sanum est*. Among many
medical treatises dealing with this subject, Henderson's *History of
Wines* (1824) deserves mention. He writes that the lighter Rhine
wines and the Moselle wines are far more cooling in their effects
than those earlier mentioned (wines imported into England from
other districts and countries), and are often prescribed in their own
country for promoting urination. 'They have proved very effective
for many kinds of fevers in which the patient had a weak pulse
and debilitated nerves. They can be prescribed with more confi-
dence than most other kinds of wine, as they contain but little
alcohol, the action of what little alcohol there is being weakened by
the presence of free acids. They are also said to be effective in
reducing a dispose tissue.'

At one time no ship set sail without a store of Moselle wines
as the best and safest cure for scurvy.

Moselle wines have always been considered an asset at any
dinner-table, and today they are to be found on any and every
wine-list.

Lower Moselle

On the Lower Moselle from Bullay to Coblenz we find that ferrous combinations in the crumbling yellow efflorescent soil (which
in some parts forms a layer of rubble $1\frac{1}{2}$ to 2 yards deep) have given
it a reddish or a yellowish-brown tone. The soil dries out quickly
and the layer of yellow, grey, or bluish dark-grey rubble which
covers it is very thin. Moreover, it has to be supported by numerous
buttresses, being very liable to slip on the steep slopes. The wines
produced in this district are of a poorer quality than those from the
Middle Moselle.

The Silurian stratum is of hard slate with large fragments of
rock. Its disintegration is slow, on account of its high content of
silicic acid. The slopes are poorly nourished along here. Worthy
of mention here are only: *Winningen,* with its sites Hamm and

Uhlen (of which Uhlen belongs partly to Cobern); and (farther up the Moselle) *Pommern* (with sites Kern, Goldberg, Kapellenberg, Sonnenuhr); *Cond; Cochem; Valwig* (sites: Hahneberg, Huttenberg).

Notable among the sites of the locality *Bremm* are: Calmont (part of which belongs to *Eller*). Calmont is the steepest vineyard site I have ever seen, and the most laborious to cultivate. It is probably the steepest in the world. Calmont also furnished the background 'scenery' for Clara Viebig's novel *Die Goldenen Berge* (The Golden Mountains); Sites: Kirchberg, Kreuzweg, Sternberg, Frauenberg (part of which belongs to *Neef*); and Vogelsang.

Beyond *Alf* and *Bullay* comes the region of the *Middle Moselle*.

Middle Moselle

Here we find wines that are aristocratic and spicy and have an exquisite bouquet.

Best known among Moselle wines is the Berncasteler Doctor which became world-famous after it had been warmly recommended by King Edward VII's personal physician. The vineyard site is not very large and is moreover cut up into three estates (owned respectively by Dr. Thanisch and Messrs. Deinhard and Lauerburg. In a good year the site will produce no more than from 1,500 to 2,000 dozen bottles, so that it is easy to understand why very high fancy prices—one might almost call them monopoly prices—are paid for them. Nevertheless for the last thirteen years it has been the wines from the Wehlener Sonnenuhr that have attained the highest prices at most auctions. Sold on the value of the wine alone—despite the fact that the *Bernkasteler Doktor* has by far the greatest 'name'— the wines from the Wehlener Sonnenuhr have often attained prices more than 20 per cent. higher than those achieved by the famous Doktor. Inside Germany the Wehlener Sonnenuhr is accounted easily the best of all Moselle wines. Fifty to seventy years ago it was the *Brauneberger Brauneberg*. So even vineyards have their changes of fortune!

All the wine communities of this region are worthy of mention, but we must content ourselves here with naming the best among so many that are good, namely:

On the right bank of the river

Zell, Enkirch, Trarbach, Erden, Zeltingen, Graach, Berncastel, Muelheim, Brauneberg, Neumagen, Dhron (Inland, belongs to Neumagen), Leiwen.

On the left bank of the river

Traben, Kroev, Uerzig, Wehlen, Cues, Lieser, Piesport, Trittenheim.

The large-scale wine-growers on the Middle Moselle have combined to form two associations—the Large Ring, and the Small Ring. The largest owners are the State and the Church—a remnant of the days of feudal and ecclesiastical power. There are the State Domain and the Bischofl. Seminar (Episcopal Seminary), the Hohe Domkirche (Cathedral), the Priester Seminar (Priests' Seminary)—all situated in Trier, but owning land in many communities. Then there are a large number of lay enterprises, among which may be mentioned the wine estates of Dr. Thanisch in Berncastel; of Zacharias Bergweiler-Pruem (successors to), Johann Josef Pruem, Peter Pruem and S. A. Pruem in Wehlen.

The Hunsrueck mountains crowd so far into the valleys along the curving stretches of the river Moselle that little space is left for habitation and cultivation. Whenever a community grew up there, it could only manage to straggle along two or three parallel roads. This applies for instance to the little town of *Zell im Hamm* (as that curve of the Moselle has been called from time immemorial). Zell (Lat. *cella*) was a Roman settlement. This has been proved by various objects dug from its soil and now housed in museums at Bonn and Wiesbaden, and is also attested by a Roman sarcophagus erected in the upper part of Zell itself (the part known as Brandenburg).

Sites: *Zeller Schwarze Katz, Burglay, Mertes Garten, Johanniskelter, Eulenberg, Nussberg, Langer Riemen, Collis, Jungfernberg, Altenkehr, Layergass, Auf Kreuz, Geisberg, Domherrnberg, Klapertchen.* Although the Zell wines have never been in the top class, *Zeller Schwarze Katz* is to be found on all German wine lists. Everyone knows the label showing a black cat on a barrel. There is not so much produced in the whole of Zell as is sold under the 'Black Cat' label. The name (Schwarze Katz—Black Cat) is nowadays nothing more than a generic title, and in my opinion a name under which often a better species of wine is sold than that which originally gave it its designation.

Reil, with its sites Stein, Falklay, Weingrube, and Sorrentberg produces robust steely wines.

Enkirch. The name is derived from the Latin *ancora* (possibly connected with the Greek *agkura*) and means 'anchor'. People began to settle here—below the strongest rapids—as it was the landing-place for Moselle boatmen who were being towed up the river; it was here that they would make their preparations for overcoming the rapids. Enkirch has the largest cultivated vineyard acreage (165 hectares) of any single locality, and in good years produces 1,200 to 1,500 'Fuder'. The only estates which exceed this quantity are those belonging to more than one community with such double names as: Berncastel-Cues, Traben-Trarbach, or Zeltingen-Rachtig.

The most famous of its sites is the *Enkircher Steffensberg* with its subsidiary sites; then comes the *Herrenberg* (with its subsidiaries), and next the *Edelberg*.

Among those who have sung the praises of Enkirch, the 'Anker Inn', and above all of Enkirch wines is the Danzig poet and journalist Johannes Trojan (Born 1837) who, towards the end of his life, was Editor-in-Chief of the Berlin journal *Kladderadatsch*.

KROEV. This ancient wine-village, situated at the foot of a wide range of vineyard-covered slopes, close to the motor highway through the Middle Moselle, has a colourful past. Here we find ancient timbered buildings, picturesque courtyards and quaint corners, besides a really beautiful baroque church. The sites are named: Steffensberg, Kirchlay, Paradies, Bockskopf, Nacktarsch. This last name has indelicate implications, but—as must be regretfully recorded—that fact has apparently added to its popularity. It is to be found on every wine list in Germany.

UERZIG lies on a bend of the Moselle river. It is open to the south, and on its other three sides is cut off and completely sheltered by mountain ridges. On this spot, clay and coloured sandstone from the Eifel, breaking through the slate strata, give the rocks a peculiar red colour and the local wine a characteristic flavour. Uerzig is one of the earliest documented wine-producing communities on the Moselle. In the year 690 the daughter of King Dagobert of the Franconians owned a wine estate there. The name—*Ursiacum*—is of Celtic-Latin origin. Its best sites are: *Kranklay, Urlay, Michelslay, Wuerzgarten, Urglueck, Goldwingert, Schwarzlay*. They are situated around a picturesque group of rocks, crowned by a mountain-top, which is one of the most beautiful spots on the Moselle. This is attested by one Von Stramberg who, in 1837, wrote a description of the Moselle. He called Uerzig 'one of the classic places of Germany' on account of its particularly charming situation and the good quality and unique character of its wines. These wines have a bouquet and spiciness which I find astonishing in view of the fact that they are lighter than those of neighbouring communities.

Two sets of castle ruins show where in medieval times certain nobles had entrenched themselves on the forbidding rocks. The one was owned by the well-known family of the Ritter von der Leyen, the other belonged to the Von Urleys, the ancestors of the

famous Dutch painter Bernaert van Orley (1492-1542). In the year
1066, a sensational political murder was perpetrated on the rocky
fastness that belonged to the Urley family: Konrad, Archbishop-
Designate of Trier, was thrown from the rocks by his opponents.

Next to and below the Uerzig vineyards we find the famous Erden
plantations; most of these, however, are owned by inhabitants of
Uerzig. The sites here are: Treppchen, Praelat, Herrenberg, Busslay, Kammer, Hoetlay. The Erden sites are very sunny, the wines
full and spicy, with a pleasant, slightly earthy taste.

And this brings us to the Moselle bend *par excellence,* on which
are situated the best-known of all Moselle wine-growing localities.
First and foremost there is *Zeltingen* with its modern bridge joining
the Eifel and the Hunsrueck. Here—beginning far below the place
itself—is a veritable parade of vines, stretching farther than the eye
can see, well beyond Zeltingen up the river, merging with those of
neighbouring communities till they reach Berncastel, and forming
the largest unbroken vineyard area in all Germany. To Zeltingen
itself belongs the biggest stretch; in a good year its produce amounts
to over 2,000 'Fuder' of wine. The long viticultural tradition of the
place and its good slaty soil have given Zeltingen wines their reputation and maintained it. Usually they are the cheapest on the wine
list, placed among the smaller, lighter wines of the Middle Moselle,
and consequently many drinkers of Moselle look on Zeltingen products as nothing more than cheap table wines. They are quite
wrong, however, because Zeltingen wines are produced in a wide
range of qualities, from the simplest to the very best; from the light
and volatile to the full and heavy with plenty of body and vigour—
wines in fact for everyday use, but also wines to be brought forth
as special delicacies on festive occasions.

KIRCHENPFAD. Simple, wholesome wines, not exciting, but
thoroughly dependable. Good foundation, harmonious.

STEPHANSLAY lies broadly across the lower end of the village.
Its wines are very light and volatile.

STEINMAUER dominates the middle of the village, seeming to
tower over it from an eminence. Similarly the wine gives an impression of power—it has a strong persistent flavour.

HIMMELREICH. This lies above the village in the best position.
The soil is ideal—pure slate—exactly what the vines need. It produces finest wines of great elegance and with a rich spicy bouquet.

SCHLOSSBERG. High class wines, weighty, heavy and yet aristocratic. We have now reached the elite among Moselle wines.

8

SONNENUHR (Sundial. *Zeltinger Sonnenuhr*, a wine that has attained perfection. Nobly mature, full and fruity.

WEHLEN (with Machern). Sites: Sonnenuhr, Nonnenberg, Ley, Feinter, Rosenberg, Michelsberg, Klosterberg, Klosterlay. Wehlen is situated on the left bank of the Moselle in a grove of fruit-trees. It is over a thousand years since the inhabitants of this little community first started to plant vines. The Wehlen wine rejoices in a splendid maturity and a spicy bouquet, due in part to intensive cultivation for quality, but particularly to the nutritive durable soil and the favourable sunny aspect of the sites. The best of the sites (and in my opinion the best site on the Moselle) is the *Wehlener Sonnenuhr;* but the other sites too produce spicy 'quality' wines of great value.

TRABEN. On the right bank of the Moselle. On the sites at the foot of the *Grafenburg—Schlossberg, Langfuhl, Halsberg, Huehnerberg*—good wines are produced. These Trabach wines are firm, steely, and have an agreeable bouquet. But the Traben wines produced on the sites *Steinbacher, Bergpaechter, Rickelsberg, Backhaus, Steffensberg, Wuerzgarten,* and *Geiersberg* mature too early and do not keep well.

GRAACH. This produces weighty, full, heavy wines that keep well but are coarser than those of the surrounding communities. Sites: *Muenzlay, Picoter, Lilienpfad, Stablay, Goldwingert, Kirchlay, Abtsberg, Bistum, and above all Domprobst and Himmelreich.*

The estate known as Josephshof lies between Graach and Wehlen in the heart of the Middle Moselle. It belongs to the Reichsgraf von Kesselstatt.

BERNCASTEL-CUES. The viticultural area of the town includes that part of it known as Cues, on the left bank of the river. It is among the most valuable vineyard districts on the Moselle and produces wines of superb quality. Sites (on the Berncastel side): *Doktor, Olk, Lay, Rosenberg, Schwanen, Pfalzgraben, Badstube, Amorpfad, Johannisbruennchen, Schlossberg, Held, Teurenkauf, Matheisbildchen.* The name of the site 'Bernkasteler Doktor' is attributed to a legend. Archbishop boemund II, Elector of Trier 1351-1362 (so runs the tale), lord of large tracts of vinelands on the Moselle and the Rhine, and owner of a castle situated on the windy heights above Berncastel, was addicted to spending much of his time in this favoured spot. One day he fell ill there. He was grievously sick and his doctors plied him with medicines in vain. As he lay on what was thought to be his deathbed, a flask of wine was brought to him from one of the best sites in the neighbourhood. He drank, and a miracle was wrought. The dying prelate recovered and in gratitude bestowed on the wine—and the site—the appellation 'Bernkasteler Doktor'.

> Ye who are sick and sorrowful,
> Arouse yourselves and take a pull
> of Wine—the finest 'Doctor'.
> It's better than the best of pills,
> For 'Doctor' Wine can cure all ills—
> A great and kindly doctor!
> For cheering draughts so justly famed,
> its native hill is proudly named
> (just like the wine) 'The Doctor'.

Berncastel wines often show the same peculiarity as those from Bingen, viz., a smoky flavour.

On the Cues side the sites are: *Weisenstein, Herrenberg, Lay, Rosenberg, Koenigstuhl.*

The tourist visiting Berncastel-Cues is greeted by a marvellous sight. From where he stands he has a view—both up and down the river—of unending rows of vines. Literally millions of the best Rieslings display their wealth to the beholder from this enchanted spot, while, crowning the vine-covered sun-drenched hillside, the ancient oaks of the Hunsrueck mountains give their dignified blessing to the scene. The town itself has a romantic note, which renders it unique among the small towns of the Moselle. Its centre is the market square on which many medieval streets and alleys converge, and whose most striking feature is a magnificent Renaissance town-hall. Built in 1608, it is surrounded by framework houses of even greater age with pointed gables and wood-carvings of great artistic value. Another interesting feature is St. Michael's Fountain splashing merrily in the centre of the square. On the first Sunday in September this has a special function. On that day the citizens of Berncastel-Cues, together with many guests from near and far, celebrate the local wine festival, and the fountain gushes forth wine for their delight. Altogether it is a cheerful festival. Gaily festooned boats carrying laughing nymphs ply up and down the river, while from its site on the right bank St. Michael's Tower watches over the whole area as it has done for the past thousand years. At night the festive scene is illuminated by the floodlit ruins of Landshut Castle on the summit of the Schlossberg.

LIESER, a locality with a population of 1,500, lies on the river Moselle at the mouth of the little stream known as the Lieserbach. Sites: *Lieserer Niederberg with its subdivisions Held, Hutlay, Suessenberg, Die Pichtern, Baerlay, Mariengrube; Lieserer Schlossberg with its subdivisions Rosenberg, Lay; Lieserer, Paulsberg and Kirchberg.* Lieser wines are justly famed for their wholesome qualities, their excellent flavour and stimulating 'prickle'. On the Lieserbach, a little way above the Moselle, lies MARING-NOVIAND, with its sites: *Maringer Sonnenuhr, Maringer Honisberg, Maringer Rosenberg, Maringer Roemerpfad, Maringer Schwarzlay.*

Next comes BRAUNEBERG (*Sites*: *Brauneberg, Hasenlaeufer, Falkenberg, Juffer, Buergerslay*). Till 1925 the place was called Dusemond, the name being a popular distortion of the Latin *dulcis mons* (sweet mountain). The Romans who planted vines on the Moselle bestowed this name on the place because of the excellence of the Brauneberg wines. In the year 1806, when Moselle vineyard sites were divided into classes according to the quality of their products, Brauneberg was the only name in the first class. The list can still be seen in the Landrat's office at Berncastel.

Brauneberg wines frequently have a strong but pleasing earthy taste which gives them a fullness commended by many consumers, particularly by those partial to the combination of the specific Moselle bouquet with a heavy wine.

Nestling among steep vineyard slopes, in a graceful bend of the Moselle lies PIESPORT with its sites: *Piesport Grafenberg, Standel, Schleif, Falkenberg, Hubertuslay, Lay'chen, Weer, Goldtroepfchen, Treppchen, Pichter, Taubengarten, Hohlweid, Gunterslay.*

Of these sites, the following belong in part to another community and are therefore used as collective site designations: Piesporter Grafenberg, Schleif, Taubengarten, Hohlweid, Pichter. Piesport wines are liable to have a slight tarry flavour which gives them an agreeable fullness.

NEUMAGEN. This is the oldest wine-growing locality in Germany, the place in which the oldest evidence of German viticulture was discovered, including 'The Wine-Ship', which is more famous than any other. The Roman poet Ausonius sang the praises of this spot —under the name 'Nociomagus'—in a long poem entitled *Mosella*. Its best-known and best sites are: *Engelgrube, Rosengaertchen,* and *Laudamusberg.* Other sites: *Auf dem Treppchen, Auf der Birk, Berggrube, Grosslay, Hambuch, Held, Hengelberg, Leyenberg, Pichter, Schering, Thierbach, Wispelt, Bock, Falkenberg, Geissberg, Paradies, Pfaffenberg, Sonnenuhr.* The peculiarities of the Neumagen wines are a flavour of bitter almonds and often a suggestion of the taste of black currants.

DHRON lies on the Moselle at the mouth of the pretty little stream called Dhronbach. The Roman poet Venantius Fortunatus

extolled the place in verse. Sites: *Dhroner Hofberg*. This takes
its name from the court (at the foot of the hill) which was formerly
part of the property of the Tholey Monastery (Saar). Its wines are
aristocratic, have a noble bouquet and unusual spiciness; *Dhroner
Saengerei; Dhroner Roterd*, which derives its name (meaning 'red
earth') from a vein of reddish sand which here traverses the slaty
soil.   Stramberg says of Dhron wines that they have 'the most
agreeable bouquet'.

NIEDEREMMEL. Here, too, Roman remains have been found. It is
the starting-point of the famous Roman road to Bingen. Its vineyards are all on the left bank of the Moselle, and all its sites are
Piesporter. Within the Niederemmel precincts lie the famous Piesport sites of Taubengarten, Hohlweid, Guenthersley, and Lay. Hohlweid includes the district of Aurenkomp, a name derived from the
Latin and meaning 'gold beaker' or 'Gold mine'.

Then come: TRITTENHEIM wih its rather light but firm wines
(*Sites*: *Laurentinusberg, Neuberg, Altaerchen, Falkenberg, Fisswin-
gert*); LEIWEN (Sites: *Steinmaeurchen, Klostergarten*) with wines
more rounded than those of Trittenheim; and finally LONGUICH
with its sites *Probstberg, Hirschberg* and *Herrenberg*, which produces amiable, delicate wines of medium quality. And herewith
we take our leave of the Middle Moselle, to which we shall return
later for the purpose of visiting its two tributary valleys, those of
the Saar and the Ruwer.

Upper Moselle

The vines of the Upper Moselle—like those of Champagne—are
rooted in shell-limestone. The wines they produce are 'small' wines,
mostly sour and—on account of their meagre alcohol content—not
suited for consumption in their pure form. As a rule they find their
way into cheap blends or manufacture of Sparkling Moselle.

The frontier delimitation of the autonomous Saar district has
cut off the communities of Weis-Nenning, Besch, and Perl from the
Upper Moselle wine-growing region. The territory of the 'Saar'
does not include a single vineyard devoted to the cultivation of
Saar wines, so that the three communities of the Upper Moselle
represent the modest viticultural efforts of the whole of the Saar
territory. ('Moselle Viticulture in the Saar').

In the 'Three-Country-Corner' (Germany, Luxembourg, France)
the vineyards sustained heavy losses during the war. But the
general economic situation, in particular the wine market in the Saar,

has encouraged the growers to devote themselves with greater intensity to cultivating their plantations. The restoration of the destroyed vineyards is being conducted at top speed, while those that escaped damage are being tended devoutly. In its climate, the region of the Upper Moselle is extremely favourable, so it is reasonable to expect that the efforts of the growers will meet with success. They plant the *Sylvaner, Rulaender* and *Auxerrois* grapes, and all these wines enjoy popularity on the Upper Moselle, for though they do not yield such large quantities as the *Elbling*, they are qualitatively far better. In the Saar itself the newly acquired territory on the Upper Moselle is known as the Riviera of the Saar, because many foreign tourists make for this part of the country, and the demand for Moselle wines apparently plays a part in their choice.

Saar

The younger Saar wines in comparison with others may be designated as the tomboy of this wine family, being steely, elegant, and volatile with a delicate bouquet; while the youngest scion of the Moselle—the product of the Ruwer—is racy, steely and fragrant.

The vine-plantation area comprises 1,000 hectares and stretches from Saarburg to Konz. In the lower reaches of the Saar the soil is slaty, while above Saarburg it consists of shell-limestone. The commonest grape species planted here is the Riesling. Owing to the comparatively high situation of the vineyards (over 600 feet) and the harsh winds coming from Lorraine and Hunsrueck, the average wine produced in this region is of no more than medium quality, but in a good year Saar wines are nevertheless in fairly great demand on account of their distinctive bouquet and flavour, their superior race and elegance. The 1949 vintage attained an unexampled maturity, and were the best wines ever made there. But May frosts destroyed two-thirds of the crop, so that only a small quantity of this desirable wine was produced.

The Domains of SERRIG and OCKFEN own very good sites and produce wines that are much sought after, such as the Ockfener Bockstein. Also popular are those produced by Apollinar Josef Koch in Wiltingen.

The best sites in the Saar are Ayler *'Kupp'*, *'Herrenberg'* and *'Neuberg'*. Others worthy of mention are: Ayler *Neuenlage, Rauberg, Scheidterberg, Katzenberg, Koepp.* The largest wine-growing locality in the Saar is WILTINGEN, with its sites: *Scharzhofberg, Scharzberg, Gottesfuss, Klosterberg, Rosenberg, Kupp, Schlossberg, braune Kupp, Wawerner Ritterpfad.* Then come: CANZEM, *with sites Altenberg, Hoerecker, Kelter- and Wolfsberg, Herrenberg, Sonnenberg, Kleberberg, Karlberg, Pulchen, Urbelt, Schwey, Vogelberg;* and OBEREMMEL. This last lies in a side-valley of the Saar near Wiltingen and produces good wines. *Its sites are: Agritiusberg, Rauler, Huette, Junkerberg.*

Ruwer

On the narrow slopes of a slate-strewn valley of the Ruwer and in a little valley in which the State Domain *AVELSBACH* produces dry wines, we find about 200 hectares of vineyards planted with the Riesling grape. The accusation of acidity usually levied against Ruwer products is perfectly justified and they are in consequence less popular than Moselle wines. But in good years like 1921, 1934, 1949, they rank with the finest. These vintages have a volatile elegant bouquet reminiscent of blackcurrants combined with a touch of 'earthiness'.

CASEL. Sites: *Nieschen, Taubenberg* and *Hitzlay Koenig-Johann-Berg.* (A site of historical interest. Close by is the hermitage in which John, the blind King of Bohemia who fell in the Battle of Crecy on August 26th, 1346, was buried). His grave is now—since 1947—in the Cathedral of Luxembourg, a sort of National Memorial.

Other wine localities in the Ruwer region are: EITELSBACH with its world-famous Karthaeuserhofberg (Carthusian Castle Hill), wine-grower Rautenstrauch; MERTESDORF, WALDRACH, MOR-SCHEID; and lastly Maximin-Gruenhaeuser Herrenberger whose 1933 vintage holds an unforgettable memory for me. When fire-watching with two friends we consumed a bottle of it and were singing its praises and commenting on its marvellous development when the sirens gave the alarm. That night I lost my whole store of Original Bottlings, including several cases of the wine we had been drinking.

Viticulture in South Germany

When discussing with Director Goedecke (in the Domain of Niederhausen) some questions of viticulture on the Nahe, I expressed my amazement at its extraordinary development in the course of the past twenty years. He replied that I should be still more amazed if I were to study viticultural developments in Southern Germany, particularly in Wuerttemberg. I must confess that though I had certainly tasted these wines in the course of my travels, as I make a habit of trying the local products wherever I go, they had made no impression on me, I could only remember that, after drinking the Markgraefler (Baden) I felt weak at the knees and that after the luncheon at which I had partaken of it I abandoned any plans I had made for the rest of that day. I remember too that these wines were cheap and that as students in Heidelberg we had mixed many of our 'Bowlen' (cups) with the help of these cheap, sour wines and large quantities of sugar. Still, I had observed the astonishing development of Alsatian wines and had learnt to enjoy and admire them. So, why should not the South German wines from the right bank of the Rhine at the same geographical level and grown on a soil of a very similar nature, be equally capable of attaining world-fame? And with this in mind, I made a wine excursion into South Germany, having taken the precaution of acquiring as much information as possible beforehand.

Having been badly hit by the phylloxera pest, the wine-growers in this region are about to re-organize their plantations by planting vines which are impervious to this noxious insect. The vineyard area has decreased considerably, partly on account of the phylloxera depredations and partly as a result of war and post-war conditions. It is now only about 60 per cent. of what it was in 1937.

A glance at the viticultural map will show that South German vineyards cover a considerable area. But, apart from the decrease caused by the war and the phylloxera, it must be noted that the local consumption is high and that there is an immense tourist traffic from other parts of Germany and from abroad. These visitors consume most of the local wines served in the hotels and restaurants of the southern wine area. There is therefore at present no question of marketing these wines elsewhere and in particular there are none available for export. They must nevertheless be mentioned in this survey for the sake of completing the overall picture.

The region—like Alsace—produces a great many different kinds of wine, some of which bear names other than those used for similar Alsatian products. In South Germany we find the *Elbling* white wines (sometimes known as Raeuschling); Gutedel; Rulaender; Sylvaner; Mueller-Thurgau; Traminer (sometimes called Clevner); Muscatel; White Burgundy, and Riesling. Also the red wines: Trollinger, Schwarzriesling (Mueller-Rebe), Limburger, and Spaet (late) Burgundy. All these wines have qualities characteristic of the district.

A few words about the region itself and its individual products.

Politically speaking, the region comprises Bavaria, Baden, Wuerttemberg and Hessia. But the law groups the wines from these parts rather differently, viz., as follows:

The designation *Wuerttemberg* is used to denote wines originating in Wuerttemberg wine-growing communities with the exception of those produced near Lake Constance.

The designation *Lake Constance* (Bodensee): for wines from those parts of Baden, Wuerttemberg, and Bavaria that are adjacent to the Lake.

The designation *Bergstrasse*: (a) for wines from those parts of Baden situated on or near the Bergstrasse from Wiesloch to Weinheim; and (b) for wines from the wine-growing communities of the Hessian Province of Starkenburg.

Baden is used to denote wines from Baden's wine-growing communities except those around Lake Constance and those in the neighbourhood of the Bergstrasse.

Wuerttemberg

The centre of Wuerttemberg viticulture is the Training and Research Station of Weinsberg near Heilbronn. Numerous vineyards have been newly planted there (since 1946). There is even a rain-producing plant and this may become a model for the whole German viticulture, for it ensures good yields and good quality even in seasons with meagre rainfalls. The wine-growers of Ruedesheim on the Rhine will certainly give a warm welcome to this invention, as their greatest enemy is a dry, sunny summer, when

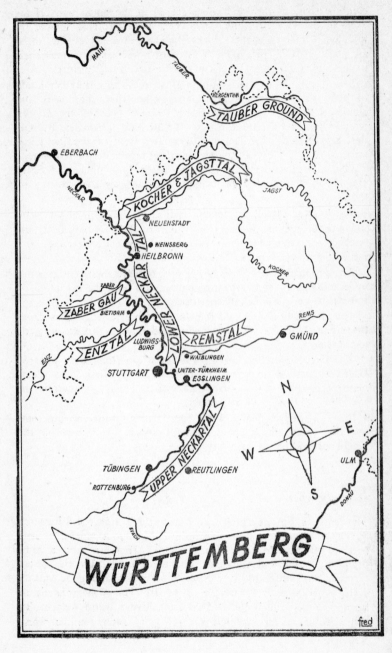

the dehydrated soil is incapable of feeding the grapes sufficient water to make their sugar.

Formerly the products of Wuerttemberg vines were little known outside the State borders, owing mainly to the fact that they barely sufficed for the needs of the local consumers. Moreover, until a short time ago, the quality of these wines was not high enough to tempt external buyers.

But of late years Wuerttemberg vineyards and Wuerttemberg cellars have improved to such a degree that their wines have emerged from their former obscurity and are now highly prized, sometimes attaining higher prices than those from other localities. They have also received publicity of a welcome and effective kind. The present President of the West German Federal Republic, Dr. Theodor Heuss, obtained his doctorate—45 years ago—with a thesis on *Viticulture and Wine-Growers in Heilbronn on the Neckar*. In this he surveys the history and development of Wuerttemberg viticulture from the 8th century. The thesis has been re-printed and —owing to the personality of its author—has contributed in no inconsiderable degree to the popularity of Wuerttemberg wines.

In many ways—due to special conditions—Wuerttemberg is unique among German wine-growing regions. For one thing its climate is poor; for another its soil consists mainly of shell-limestone, red marl, and bituminous marl. And these soils do not suit every kind of grape. Similarly the sites have to be carefully chosen to suit the various species. And so, for one reason or another, each little plot in the various wine-producing districts of Wuerttemberg is known for its own particular kind of wine which in many cases is brought to a high state of perfection. There is for example, the Sylvaner in the Kocher Valley and the Tauber Valley; the Black Riesling in the Lauffen region on the Neckar; the Trollinger and the Limberger in the Heilbronn district; the Riesling in the Rems Valley and on the slopes of the Burgberg and the Schemelberg near Weinsberg.

Except perhaps Baden, no German wine-region can point to such a large variety of grape-species under cultivation as Wuerttemberg, which caters both for white and red wines. The most important kinds are Gutedel, Mueller-Thurgau, Traminer, Rulaender, Sylvaner, and above all Riesling, the pride and joy of any wine-grower's heart.

In the course of the last 100 years the viticultural area under cultivation has decreased by 61 per cent., while the value of the yield has more than doubled during the same period.

Passing through Wuerttemberg's wine-districts, the traveller cannot fail to notice little houses built in the midst of the vineyards—a sight peculiar to this part of the country. They are used by the wine-growers as a resting-place after the day's work where they can take their glasses of wine in ease and comfort.

There are only very few large wine estates in Wuerttemberg—most plantations are on a small scale and have been owned by the same families for generations. (In the municipality of Heilbronn, for instance, there exist 7,950 different vineyard-holdings, making up 445 hectares in all, of which 261 are in cultivation). The Wuerttemberg vineyard-owner does not depend on his vines alone for a living—he has other lands under cultivation, very often orchards. These 'side-lines' help him over bad times in the vineyard—poor harvests, disappointing quality of the yield and so forth—or unfavourable market conditions.

The good cellarage conditions and the consequent superior quality of Wuerttemberg wines is mainly due to the highly developed co-operative system that prevails there. A wine-growers' Co-operative with (in some cases) first-class modern equipment for presses and cellars is to be found in practically every wine-growing locality worth mentioning and these local Co-operatives combine to form the Central State Association of Wuerttemberg Wine-growers' Associations, at Stuttgart. The central organization has a cellerage plant with long rows of steel tanks which is a unique sight. There are 119 of these tanks, each holding 7,000 litres.

The few large wine estates—mostly owned by very old Wuerttemberg families which have always made it their business to produce high-grade wines—play quite a considerable part in promoting the constant improvement of Wuerttemberg wines.

The Weinsberg Institute, to which reference has already been made, is also an active force in this respect. It is a Government institution with a property area of 33 hectares—including new plantations and agricultural lands—which overlaps several municipal and site boundaries (Weinsberg, Talheim, Gundelheim, Burg Wildeck). It has manifold viticultural and cellarage facilities which, together with the ripe experience of its workers and the results of numerous experiments, enable it to produce wines which serve as examples of what Wuerttemberg can and should bring forth. It is one of the few establishments in Germany which markets only bottled wines and then not before they are fit to drink, i.e., until they have acquired at least a degree of 'bottle maturity'.

The centre of Wuerttemberg's viticulture is Stuttgart, which is also the seat of the Winegrowers' Central Organization. Small wonder! The city of Stuttgart is a child of the Neckar, and it is in the valley and side-valleys of this river—and beyond them in the valleys of the Rems, Enz, Kocher and Jagst—that most of the Wuerttemberg wine is grown.

The following are important wine centres: Untertuerkheim, Fellbach, Heilbronn, Mundelsheim, Weinsberg, Walheim, Neckarulm, Reutlingen, Eberstadt, Feuerbach, Grimsbach.

Baden

In Baden we find mainly small agricultural holdings, parts of which are laid out as vineyards. Large wine estates are rare. The small (vine-) growers have formed themselves into wine-growers' associations which develop the wines and market them.

The best-known sites in this region are: *Lake Constance* (Bodensee). *Meersburg.*

The winelands on Lake Constance are the most southerly in Germany and are situated higher up then any others. For many centuries the whole industrial life of the population was centred on viticulture. That is no longer the case today, but even now it ranks high among the local vocations.

Renowned for their wines in this district are: Meersburg, Hagnau, Immenstaad, and the Island of Reichenau. The best-known wines from Lake Constance are the so-called *Weissherbste,* which are white wines slightly tinged with red; they are produced from the grape called the blue Spaetburgunder (late Burgundy, pinot noir), Rulaender (pinot gris), and Traminer, also grown on good sites in Meersburg. The wines are mild, in good years sweet and full like those from southern climes. The Lake, which stores up warmth, and the warm 'foehn' (South wind) help to bring the grapes to full maturity. The Baden Domain in Meersburg—like the Domain in other districts—does all in its power to further constant improvement in the quality of the local products.

An extensive unbroken viticultural area reaches from the south side of Bale to Freiburg. It is called the *Markgrafschaft.* On the deep fertile soil found here at the edge of the Black Forest the Gutedel grape (Chasselas) flourishes—its territory in fact crosses the frontier to the south extends into the Swiss viticultural area. Wines made from Gutedel grapes are light and fresh, have a delicate unobtrusive bouquet and low acidity. The most important communities sites are: Haltinger Stiege, Otlinger Pflanzer, Fischeninger and Weingarten; Efringe-Kirchener Weingarten; Schliengener Sonnenstueck; Auggener Letten; Laufener Altenberg; Schallstadter Batzenberg; Kirchhofener Kirchberg; Ehrenstettener Oelberg; Ebringener Sommerberg.

On the massif of the *Kaiserstuhl',* a kind of island of volcanic origin to the west of Freiburg Bay, we find the Baden speciality known as the Rulaender (grey Burgundy) grape. Its wines are heavy, rich in alcohol, and of medium acidity. Other quality wines in the Kaiserstuhl region are Traminer, Riesling, and Sylvaner. Red wines too are produced in this neighbourhood.

The most important communities here are:—

Achkarren, Bahlingen, Bickensohl, Bischoffingen, Burkheim, Eichstetten, Ihringen, Königschaffhausen, Oberbergen, Oberrotweil, Wasenweiler.

In the Middle Baden viticultural area—i.e., the region around Offenburg known as *Ortenau*—mainly high-grade wines are produced. Riesling is cultivated here, but known under the name of *Klingelberger,* so are Traminer (Clevner) and Rulaender. The meagre, dusty soil of the hard granite surroundings results in small quantites of good quality wines.

The most important communities here are:—

Durbach, Fessenbach, Ortenberg, Waldulm, Zell-Weierbach.

In the neighbourhood of Buehl—well-known for its rich stone-fruit harvests—we find extensive Riesling plantations. It is here that the so-called *Mauerweine* are bottled in 'Boxbeutel' (for 'Boxbeutel' cf. sub Franconian wines supra).

Most important communities and sites: (Kappelrodecker Dasenstein; Waldulmer Russhalte; Buehlertaler; Neuweierer Altenberg; Varnhalter Klosterberg; Klingelberg).

Having passed through this country we see before us the outline of the Palatinate hills, and beyond them lie the extensive winelands that accompany the Rhine on its further course. We have, in other words, passed Durlacher Turmberg and have entered northern Baden territory. Here the vineyards lie scattered over the landscape, coloured beauty-spots which lead us on to the neighbouring wine-country. New vineyards become visible everywhere. They may be noted on the Eichelberg, may be seen sheltering under the Ravensburg near Sulzfeld, on the red marl of the large wine-growing community of Wiesloch, and on many venerable spots of the Kraichgau hill country, of the fable-ridden Neckar Valley right up to the river of Castle Hornberg—of Goetz von Berlichingen fame. Finally, we find the last off-shoots of Baden viticulture in the Tauber and Main valleys as the remainder of what was till a few centuries ago an important wine-growing region.

In the midst of this South German wine-country stands Heidelberg with its castle. Inside the castle—in the Koenigssaal (King's Hall) of the Women's apartments—the guide points out to travellers an

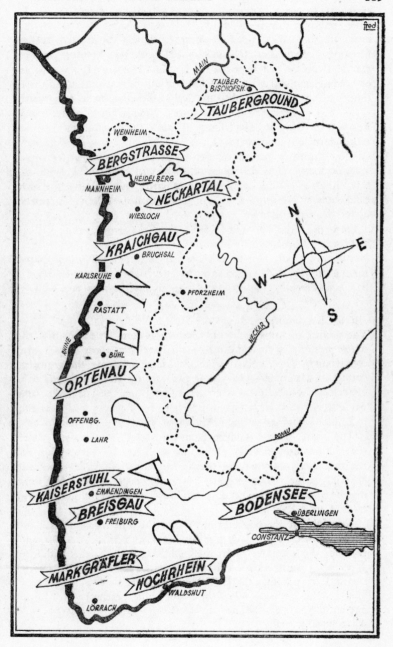

extremely practical apparatus—namely a pump by means of which wine used to be drawn up out of the 'Great Cask' which stood underneath the hall. This famous 'Great Cask' was constructed by the Electoral Cellarmaster Johann Jakob Engler the Younger in the year 1751 on the orders of the Elector Karl Theodor. It was capable of holding 220,000 litres (300.000 bottles). It was only filled three times and has long ago become leaky. Scheffel made the thirsty Court Fool—the dwarf Perkeo—into a famous figure of fun. But nearly everybody in Heidelberg is both thirsty and inclined to make merry on good wines.

Wine formerly played its part even in the examination for a legal doctorate. The first question to be answered by the candidate was, 'Red or white ?'. while a jug of water was available for such candidates as preferred a cooling rather than an alcoholic beverage under the circumstances.

Once the examination was safely and successfully over, the reward was a fruit cup enjoyed in a boat on the Neckar by torch-light. Never have I tasted anything more delicious than the one prepared for me on just such an occasion by the friends whom for years I had been teaching the secrets of making the perfect 'cup'.

BOWLE ('Cups')

The mixing of 'cups' is an old German custom, little-known in the more westerly wine-countries—a characteristic form of German conviviality. These mixed wine drinks are not only the crowning feature of a summer evening for parties on a Rhine steamer, on a Heidelberg terrace, or at a garden festival, but they have the same gay effect if they are adopted over here for a nice summer evening in Frinton, Torquay or any other bright spot.

The name 'Bowle' is taken from the vessel (the bowl) in which these drinks are brewed. The wines used for the purpose are not the best qualities—they are mostly ordinary light table wines and sparkling wines. The recipe is left to the taste of the mixer, who may be inclined to concoct a strong brew, or more cautiously restrict himself to a light mixture.

Manifold are the possibilities open to the host regaling his guests with a Bowle. He can change his beverage with the seasons until far into the autumn. From the middle of May to the middle of June the favourite Bowle is based on the fragrant woodruff (Waldmeister); then comes the Bowle based on strawberries, followed in July by the Pfirsichbowle (cup made with peaches). Nor is the present-day mixer confined to fruits in season—preserved fruits serve equally well.

59. Vineyard Ruedesheimer Berg.

RHEINGAU.

60. Kloster Eberbach with entrance gate to Klosterpforten-restaurant.

62. (*Opposite*). Schloss Johannisberg.

61. Vineyards of Ruedesheim.

63. The vineyards of Oestrich and Hallgarten, with Oestrich village in the foreground and the Hallgarter Zange in the background.

64. Assmannshausen (with Hotel Krone).

RED HOCK DISTRICTS.

65. Ober Ingelheim (Rhinehessia).

66. Altenahr.

67. Walporzheim (Ahr).

68. Vineyards near Caub.

MIDDLE RHINE.

69. Castle Maus and St. Goar.

70. Oberwesel.

71. Vineyards near Oberwesel.

72. Near Bacharach.

73. The old town wall and gate.

MOSELLE.

74. (*Opposite above*). Bernkastel Kues.

75. (*Opposite left*). Bernkastel market square.

76. (*Opposite right*). The Moselle's best site : Wehlener Sonnenuhr (sundial).

Bernkastel-Kues

77. One of the many river bends (near Traben-Tharbach).

79. (*Opposite top*).
The oldest
wine-growing
community of the
Moselle : Neumagen
and its vineyards.

BADEN

78. (*Left*). Meersburg
(Bodensee).

80. (*Opposite middle*).
Reichenau (Bodensee).

81. (*Opposite bottom*).
Vineyards in the
Buehl valley.

WUERTTEMBERG AND FRANCONIA

85. Esslingen (Neckar).

82. (*Opposite*).
The Weibertreu
(near Heilbronn).

83. (*Opposite*). Fortress
Marienberg near Wuerzburg
and site 'Innere Leiste.'

84. (*Opposite*). Vineyards
Fuckenhausen (between
Ochsenfurt and Marktbreit).

86. Castle Hornberg (Lower
Neckar).

87. & 88. The largest cask in use : as a restaurant (Bad Duerckheim).

89. Road of Weinstuben and hotels in Bacharach (Middle Rhine).

90. & 91 (*next page*). The Bauernschaenke in Assmannshausen.

This is how it is done: the fruit on which the Bowle is based is put into the bottom of the vessel and sugared. The sugaring is an art in itself. It must not be overdone, as too much sugar would completely neutralize the acids contained in the fruit. True harmony between sweet and sour must be striven for and attained. Then come one or two glasses of a good brandy to draw out the full aroma of the prepared fruits. Last comes the wine. When that has been poured on to the brandy-soaked fruits, the brew must be allowed to stand and 'draw' for a while. It is very important that the 'cup' should be drunk in a cold or at least cool condition. Nothing spoils the taste more than if it is served warm and allowed to become flat. Just before serving, a little sparkling Hock or Moselle should be added if possible—this puts the finishing touch to the beverage.

FRUIT 'BOWLE'

If a fresh pineapple is available, it should be peeled, cut into slices and then into little squares, and sugared; or 10 ripe Apricots are peeled and cut up; or 8-10 ripe and soft peaches are peeled and cut into quarters or eights; or any other fruit to the same quantity in weight (such as strawberries, which make a most delicious bowle). then sugar is added, the quantity varied in accordance with the degree of ripeness of the fruit (5 oz. of sugar to 15 oz. of fruit). Then a bottle of wine is poured on to it, and the mixture allowed to 'draw' for about two hours. After that, the full quantity of wine should be added—up to six bottles according to the quantity of fruit—and finally sparkling Hock. If tinned fruits are used, then the 'Bowle' can be started with their juice, but in that case a small measure of brandy improves the taste.

KALTE ENTE

For the beverage known as Kalte Ente (lit. cold duck), take two bottles of a light Rhenish or Palatinate wine and one bottle of sparkling Hock. Pour the wine over slices of lemon which are removed after a short time. If possible, add a glass of curacao, and sugar according to taste. The proportion of sparking Hock can be increased if desired.

Bergstrasse

From Heidelberg we turn to the Bergstrasse, which is partly Rhine-hessian, partly Baden territory. The wines of Zwingenberg, Auer-bach, Bensheim, Heppenheim are comparable to the lesser

9

Rhinehessian wines. They are bottled in the first spring following
the grape harvest and are drunk by the thousands who flock to the
Bergstrasse in May to admire the blossoming fruit-trees.

Franconian Wines (Steinwines)

The study of Franconian wines takes us eastward along the Main
towards Aschaffenburg.

The earliest documents relating to the plantation of vines in
Franconia go back to the 7th century, and the first planters in this
region were women, the nuns of the Benedictine Convents of
Ochsenfurt and Kitzingen. According to the local sagas they must
have been very lively ladies—apparently when they went for walks,
they were followed by one of the servants of the convent carrying
—not their prayer-books but skins filled with wine!

The whole wine-region comprises 221 communities with altogether
about 4,000 hectares, shared by approximately 10,000 growers. The
wines would deserve mention, if for no other reason, because
Goethe preferred Franconian wines to all others.

Quite apart from the great hospitality shown to guests in his
home, Goethe's domestic wine consumption was anything but inconsiderable. Even when he was taking the cure in Carlsbad,
he would order a whole barrel (about 60 litres) of Franconian table-
wine, which means that he expected to drink about 2 litres a day
when undergoing his cure. His genuine last words (in the presence
of the Director of Buildings Coudray, on 22 March, 1832) are said
to have been : 'You haven't put any sugar in my wine?'

I have found that the proper occasions for drinking these so-called
Stein wines are those where the text-books suggest Chablis. Stein
wines are finer and stronger, firm and nutty. It is always said that
a Chablis can only be properly understood and enjoyed when drunk
on its ground, but that does not apply to Stein wines. The latter
travel well and deserve to be more widely known.

The Sylvaner vine, which is more intensively cultivated in Franconia than any other, produces wines with qualities varying according
to the site. They may have an exquisite bouquet, or a juicy freshness, or again they may be racy and invigorating, or pleasantly full-
bodied.

The late Dr. Kittel of Wuerzberg, who was fond of singing the
praises of Franconian wines, stated that the scientific treatise written
in the year 1179 by St. Hildegard, Abbess of Bingen, mentioned the
healing properties of Franconian wine. An opportunity of testing

these qualities arose in the 17th century when the Black Death was rampant in Franconia whither it had come, from the East—the Bohemian Forest—bringing death and destruction in its train. A worthy Canon of Wuerzberg, attacked by the plague and apparently dying, was anxious (so runs the tale) to have one last taste of his beloved Stein wine. He drank it—with miraculous effect. For two nights and two days he slept. Then he sprang out of bed—completely cured. The story of the miracle spread with incredible speed, and the whole of Franconia joyfully undertook the same cure as the Canon. Those who were sick drank to get well, those who were well, as a protective measure—apparently with excellent results.

Many wine historians have pointed out that Franconia produces a large number of rare wines. There are very considerable differences between, for instance, the great first-grade products of Wuerzberg, Stein and Leisten. And as to the other Franconian wines, there are: the fine, racy Steigerwaelder; the rich, succulent Eschendorfer; the elegant wines from the neighbourhood of Kitzingen; the delicate Saale products; the aromatic Kallmuth; the pungent wine from the Tauber and Lower Main; the spirituous Hoersteiner; and many others with varying characteristics. And of course each year the vintages differ, even from the same localities.

Franconian wines are traditionally bottled in a peculiarly shaped flask, known as a *Boxbeutel* the origin of which is obscure. Possibly a glass-blower may once have turned out the strange shape, either accidentally or intentionally, or maybe the Low German 'Bockesbeutel' (a bag in which prayer-books or other volumes were transported) had something to do with the original invention, and its name. It must be remembered too that there is a grape called 'Bocksbeutel', possibly a reference to its shape.

Dr. Kittel ascribes the origin of the name directly to the bag-like shape (Beutel) of one of the internal organs of a goat's anatomy (Bock), which the characteristic Franconian flask resembles. Probably he is right.

The Boxbeutel is almost exclusively reserved for Franconian wines, but is also used for certain high-grade Baden wines—the so-called 'Mauer' wines from Neuweier. It is an old custom that these too should be sold in boxbeutel.

Franconian growers have a far harder task than those in other districts. Their vineyards are situated on slopes so steep that newcomers to the work can barely stand or walk on them.

The soil within the Franconian region is as varied as the qualities of the wine. In the eastern parts the vineyards are planted on red marl (a clayey soil); in the Main triangle, i.e., the part bounded by

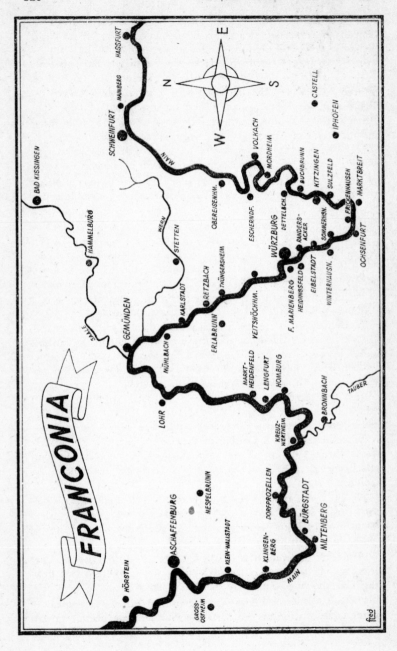

Schweinfurt, Ochsenfurt, and Gemuenden, the vines are grown on efflorescent shell-lime soil; in the territory of the Lower Main on variegated sandstone; in the Alzenau lands on primitive rock. From Bamberg westwards to Zeil and to the south through the Steigerwald to the Aischgrund, vines are planted on loamy red marl, here frequently intercalated with gypsum (for example at Iphofen). It is this soil, usually heavy and water-laden, that—particularly in hot seasons—produces good mature wines, the reason being that its capacity for retaining moisture is very great and hardly ever fails, even in a very dry year. As already mentioned, shell-lime soil is found in the country delimited by a line drawn south from Schweinfurt to Markbreit and Ochsenfurth and then turning north towards Gemuenden. The same soil is met in the side-valleys of the Werrn, the Saale, and the Tauber; usually it is heavy and efflorescent. Wherever the steep slopes are well-wooded, so that the trees supply moisture even in dry seasons, the vines are likely to flourish. But when there are no trees, the soil is liable to be sucked dry in hot years and consequently the vines suffer.

North of Aschaffenburg, in the district of Alzenau, it is mainly the Riesling vine that flourishes on the primitive rock soil of Hoerstein, Wasserlos, and Michelbach. The extremely well-ventilated soil is of volcanic origin and consists principally of weathered potash-mica slate. The wines are similar to those of the Rheingau.

Franconian viticulture is restricted to plots which are unsuitable for any other kind of plantation, i.e., to the warm southern, south-western, and western sites on the steep mountain slopes in the river valleys of the Main, the Franconian Saale, the Werrn, and the Tauber. Economic necessity drove the vine plantations from the valley and up into the steep hills.

Wuerzburg is the home *par excellence* of Franconian wines, and Wuerzburg's site 'Stein' has given to Franconian wines the name by which they are known in other countries—Stein wines. Under the German Wine Law, the name 'Stein Wine' is reserved for wines from the Wuerzberg sites 'Stein and Steinacker' and may not be used for Franconian wines as a whole. Any wine bottled in a boxbeutel with nothing on the label but the word 'Stein' (or 'Stein Wine'), is assumed to be a Wuerzburg Stein wine and must conform to this expectation.

By way of footnote to the above, however, it should be mentioned that the appellation 'Stein Wine' is current in the Austrian wine districts around Gumpolds-Vurchen, in Nussberg, and in Soos. But here it means all wines grown on a stony (Stein-) ground and has nothing to do with the name of the place of origin.

In Wuerzburg we find the leading producers, viz., Bavarian Domain, the Buergberspital (Citizens' Hospital), and the Juliusspital (Julius Hospital). The Buergerspital dedicated to the Holy Ghost is a foundation endowed by the Wuerzberg citizen Johann von Steren in 1913 as a home for the aged and impoverished Wuerzberg citizens. The foundation had always included some vineyards, and these in course of time have been increased until they gradually grew into a large wine estate. The Buergerspital zum Heiligen Geist now owns about 100 hectares in vineyards which extend along the Main from Randersacker through Wuerzburg to Thuengersheim. Except for Ruedesheim on the Rhine, no German vineyards suffered quite so much from bomb damage as those in Wuerzburg.

The State wine estate in Lower Franconia (Bavarian Viticultural Domain) originated in the vineyards owned by the former Prince-Bishop in Wuerzburg. Apart from the vines grown on their own estate, these princes had enormous quantities of wine in their cellars which had been collected as tithes from the wine-growing population. When the rule by the Prince-Bishop came to an end, their large wine estate was made over to the Duchy of Wuerzburg, and in 1816 it was transferred to the Bavarian Crown as State property. With it went the one-time princely, later State Court cellars (Hofkellerei) in Wuerzburg, which from time immemorial had been linked to the estate. At present the State vineyards cover about 80 hectares, divided between the estates of Stein, Leisten, Randersacker, and Hoerstein.

The State Domain and the Hofkellerei have installed model plant and created admirable working arrangements both on their vineyards and in their cellarage systems.

The immense storage cellar in the residential castle at Wuerzberg —known as the most beautiful princely palace in Germany—must have been planned by the original architect with an eye to the future development of a promising wine. It is fully adequate for all requirements.

Only two kinds of vines are grown on the State winelands: the Riesling and the Sylvaner. The Riesling is not noted for production in any great quantity, but rather for the quality of its wines, which are aromatic, have a fine bouquet and bear eloquent witness to noble ancestry. The Sylvaner too is a noble wine; grown from sweet juicy grapes, it is rich and full, with a strong fruit flavour. The sunny slopes from which it originates have stamped it with an individual character.

As a rule, Franconian wines are marketed by auction. The prices achieved here (where the climate is more 'continental') vary even more than in the Rhineland. In particular, Franconian crops are frequently damaged by early frosts. This accounts for the fact that the yield may be anything from one to eight hectolitres per acre.

Classification and Vintages

Now that we have come to the end of our journey through the wine country of Western Germany—the Rhineland—let me say a few words about the classification and the vintages of wines.

In France, the *Chambre Syndicale des Courtiers* in Bordeaux have classified the wines of Bordeaux in order of merit—the red wines in five growths, the white wines in two. Nothing of the kind is possible respecting German wines. The French Chateau as a rule produces one *cuvée* only, the only notable exception being Mouton Rothschild, which prepares two *cuvées* and markets the lower quality under a special brand.

In a book called *A History and Description of Modern Wines* (London, 1851) I have found a classification which is worth reading. No such classification and no similar one can, however, be of any real use.

In Germany, the situation is quite different. German growers, large and small, stock their wines in individual casks as they come from the press. On the Moselle they usually use Fuders (960 litres) and half-Fuders; Stucks (1,200 litres), half-Stucks, and quarter-Stucks are customary in Rhinehessia and the Rheingau; while in the Palatinate they use Fuders of 1,000 litres capacity. The wines mature in the casks and keep their individuality at least as long as they remain in the wine-grower's cellar. For this reason wines from the same growers differ greatly in quality. The differences are due to various circumstances—the grapes may have been gathered in the early or the late harvest period; they may have been gathered with particular care, for instance by the selection of special bunches of the fruit, or even of specially ripe or over-ripe single berries, etc.

The Lagen are divided into a great many smallholdings of various sizes. Only a few Lagen are in the hands of one owner, the best examples of this being: Schloss Johannisberg (Fuerst von Metternich), Schloss Vollrads (Graf Matuschka-Greiffenclau), Josefs-hof (Reichsgraf v. Kesselstadt), Steinberger (State Domain). These subdivisions afford another reason for differences in wines from the same Lage. One owner may tend his vineyard more carefully than the other, may manure it at shorter intervals, and this makes for great differences in taste—quite apart from the different dates and selective methods of gathering the fruit already mentioned.

Some growers have for these reasons adopted a method of classi-fying their own wines by furnishing them with different labels, caps, or seals, and some use the word 'Cabinet' (or Kabinett) to designate wines which fetch a certain price (laid down by the individual grower).

Schloss Johannisberg was up to recently, an exception. These wines actually fell into five classes:

1. Wines which can be used exclusively for the manufacture of sparkling wines.

2. Wines sold in cask and bottled by the merchant simply as *Schloss Johannisberger*.

3. As under 2 above, but with special permission to the buyer to sell them as *Gewaechs Fuerst v. Metternich*.

4. As under 3 but with special permission to the foreign agent to affix the Schloss Johannisberger Cabinet label and to sell them as growth Fuerst v. Metternich. This concession has been made to the foreign agents on account of prohibitive duties for wines imported in bottles. Formerly 'Cabinet' wines, comprised only wine bottled at the Schloss and sold from there in bottles and this still applies to the German home trade, where the present range of Cabinet wines is as follows:—

Orange, Violet, White, Lilac, Sky Blue, Dark Blue, Gold Blue and Gold Seal (Prices to the wholesale trade in Germany range from 4.50 DM (9/6) to 50 DM (£4-5s.) per bottle.

5. Wines sold in cask or bottle by the Schloss, bottled at the Schloss—*Originalabfuellung Fuerst v. Metternich*. These wines are sub-divided—according to price—into three further classes with three different labels and capsules (green, white, pink).

As a matter of fact the recent change-over to fermentation and storage in large vessels may bring about a change in this classifica-tion. Schloss Johannisberg has in any case made a start with this method by using tanks of 5,000 litres each for the 1950 vintage, the State Domain in the Rheingau has at present nine tanks of 8,500 litres each, and one tank of 21,000 litres, the balance of the 1950 crop is still kept in casks of 600 litres.

The growers themselves are well aware how misleading it is for the consumer when two wines of the same name vary so greatly in all their characteristics, as I have shown above. The consumer should always protect himself when re-ordering by insisting on a supply from the same cask.

It has been suggested in some quarters that German growers should accept the French method. It would certainly deprive us of the Auslese, the Beeren- and Trockenbeerenauslese wines, but it would increase the average overall quality to a high degree. Those who are of this opinion hint specially at the Steinberger wines. If you taste the whole range, you will find that the 'Steinberger' is no more than a vin ordinaire—not worth drinking—because all that is best in the vineyard has gone into the Auslese, the Beerenauslese, and the Trockenbeerenauslese, and the latter is considered the best wine of the Rheingau. They argue what a grand wine the 'Steinberger' would be if all the vineyard products were to be used for one *cuvée,* and it would help to bring an exquisite wine within range of thousands instead of the few who can afford to buy the extract, the Trockenbeerenauslese. And what is true of the Steinberger, applies, of course, to all vineyards.

It is true that the price differences are sometimes colossal. At the auctions in January 1951, for example, the best cask of 1949 Steinberger (the ordinary Steinberger) cost 50 per cent. more than the cheapest. When bottled, they look exactly alike, therefore, the argument goes on, the unfortunate consumer who, having had and enjoyed one consignment of bottles from the best cask, may get his next consignment from the cheapest, and is due for a sad disappointment. Is it false pride on the part of the German grower when he boasts of the high price his best cask has attained, if at the same time, his other wines are the poorer for it? Whoever has tasted the Auslese, Beerenauslese and Trockenbeerenauslese wines cannot and will not agree with these arguments. These wines are the nectar of the gods, wines to be sipped on an occasion, and represent the finest nature can produce. It would be a loss should we ever be deprived of these enjoyments, and it is not likely that the growers will listen to such arguments. They may reduce the ordinary wines to one or two *cuvées,* but will never give up their endeavour to produce the best. The competitions arranged by Government bodies and Viticultural Associations will contribute to increase the growers' ambition still more.

To sum up :—

Only his own palate and purse can decide for any individual consumer what wine is the best for him. And if he is inexperienced, he cannot do better than follow the advice of his wine merchant who has tasted and selected the wines on his list with a view to satisfying his clients' needs. As already indicated, the only classification is by the taste and value of each single cask. There are of course specially favoured Lagen which enjoy suitable soil and much sunshine and therefore produce genuinely good wines. Knowledge of these factors will assist the consumer and help to avoid disappointment. The following are some of those favoured sites :—

PALATINATE :
 Forster Freundstück,
 Forster Kirchenstück,
 Forster Ungeheuer,
 Deidesheimer Leinhöhle,
 Deidesheimer Kieselberg.

RHEINHESSIA :
 Niersteiner Pettenthal,
 Niersteiner Fläschenhahl,
 Nackenheimer Rothenberg,
 Oppenheimer Sackträger.

RHEINGAU :
 Rauenthaler Baiken or Gehm,
 Erbacher Marcobrunn,
 Steinberger,
 Hallgartener Hendelberg,
 Johannisberg Schlossberg,
 Winkeler Hasensprung,
 Ruedesheimer Berg.

MOSELLE :
 Wehlener Sonnenuhr,
 Brauneberger Juffer,
 Bernkasteler Doktor,
 Uerziger Wuerzgarten,
 Graacher Himmelreich,
 Piesporter Goldtropfchen.

SAAR :
 Ockfener Bockstein,
 Ayler Kupp.

NAHE :
 Schloss Boeckelheimer
  Kupfergrube.

Furthermore, a Spaetlese—or Auslesewine is always apt to give full satisfaction on account of its special ripeness and fruitiness.

Some enthusiastic wine-drinkers—and not by any means the least knowledgeable—prefer old well-seasoned wines to any others. Nowadays such wines are difficult to find. Pre-war wines are scarce. In England, however, some leading wine-merchants still have 1934, 1935, and 1937, even some 1921 wines in stock. But as these stocks are small and the wines named are in any case the best that are to be found (they cost £1 per bottle even before the war), they are very dear today; added to the original price there is interest compound interest, and owner's risk to be taken into consideration.

Even the most fastidious taste should be satisfied with the 1943, the 1945, the 1947, the 1948—and with the 1949—vintages.

It has generally been considered that Moselle wines keep in a flourishing condition for seven years—but I have drunk much older Moselles which had lost nothing of their vigour. On the whole however I prefer younger wines with their freshness and delicate flavour—a two to three-year old Moselle, or a four to ten-year old Rhine wine should be able to fully satisfy even the most captious consumer.

Wines are living organisms and must be treated as such—i.e., account must be taken of their individual peculiarities. Rheingau, Rhinehessian and Palatinate wines often reach a ripe old age without deteriorating. But their development is partially dependent on the cellar temperature. It is a universal rule that chemical and biological development is hastened by a high, and slowed down by a low, temperature. If therefore a wine is housed in a warm cellar, it will mature more quickly, age more quickly and suffer deterioration earlier than if the cellar is cold. It is advisable to keep bottled wines in a cellar in which fluctuations of temperature are reduced to a minimum. For white wines the optimum temperature is about 50-54°F.—for red wines at least 64°F.

Bottled wines do not stay static in quality; they continue their development till it reaches its peak. Having reached this stage, the wines remain at their best for years, or even for decades, and then gradually deteriorate.

Great wines deteriorate very slowly. Some retain their good qualities for 30, 50, even for more years. The Museum of Bottled Wines in the Kurhaus, Wiesbaden, which was destroyed in the year 1945, showed Rheingau wines (*Original-* and *Hochgewaechse*) which were over 200 years old (the oldest was a 1706 vintage). In the autumn of 1941 the owner had tested his collection and re-arranged it according to the current value of the individual exhibits. He then published a little brochure of the results of his 'pdobe'. Here is an extract from his booklet:

> From the year 1859 onwards some of the wines have retained their original noble sweetness; together with the delicate acidity characteristic of Rheingau products and the bouquet which in the course of the years has been wonderfully enhanced, their present qualities combine to give the wines a flavour which may be designated as 'fluid' fruity and highly aristocratic'.

The collection included wines from all Rheingau communities.

um of Bottled Wines in Deidesheim, belonging to the
writer on wines and vineyard-owner Gehelmrat Dr.
nann-Jordan, is still in undisturbed existence. Here we
ders of every vintage since 1889. A few specimens (not
collection) go back to an 1811 Forster Ungeheuer Estate
The oldest estate-bottled wines are from the year 1706.
are a few such collections left in Germany; others were
destroyed during the war. The State Wine Cellars of Assmannshausen, Eltville, and Kloster Eberbach still exist and count among
their treasures wines which go back to the year 1893. The collections
of the State Wine Domains, Ruedesheim and Hochheim were on
the other hand destroyed to the last bottle.

Similarly involved in destruction was the Museum of Bottled
Wines at the Pfortenhaus Inn in Kloster Eberbach. Before the war
its wine-list included vintages going back to the year 1857. Some
estates and collectors have now begun to re-stock their collections,
in which the vintages 1945 to 1949 now have an honoured place
and are likely to rejoice the hearts of future generations. In the
whole history of German viticulture, there have never been so many
good years in succession, as the vintage chart will show (See Appendix). It should be noted however that vintage charts can only give
a general survey of the annual products and may be incorrect in
regard to some districts and Lagen. In some places good wines have
been produced in bad years, while poor wines may be brought forth
sporadically even in the best years.

In general the 1921 vintages can be described as 'excellent', the
1920 products as 'good'. In Ruedesheim (Rheingau) is was the other
way about. In other places too—particularly in the Palatinate—
some of the 1920 wines outshone by far those produced in the
'peak' year 1921. The 1939 wine was 'inferior' owing to frost
damage just before the grapes ripened. And yet some sheltered
Lagen produced wines of particular elegance and finesse in that
same season.

How incalculable wines may be was proved in the year 1890
which produced the so-called 'Ice-wines'. These constituted an
extraordinary phenomenon, because—despite all prophecies to the
contrary—they turned out to be exquisite. The ripe berries on the
vines had been frozen by an 'ice-rain', i.e., by a rainfall when the
temperature was below freezing point. The water in the berries
turned to ice and this left the remaining grape-juice more concentrated and proportionately richer in sugar content. The wines made
from this thick syrup were so sweet and fine as to be comparable
to outstanding Auslesen.

Some of the 1949 wines have similar qualities, as was proudly reported to me by Joh. Jos. Pruem of Wehlen and proved by him. His Wehlener Sonnenuhr feinste Auslese (Fuder No. 21 of the auction of 25th April, 1951) is a real 'Edelgewaechs'. He told me he had waited for years for the opportunity to make an 'ice-wine'. In the year 1949 he was successful in postponing his harvest long enough to do so. Schloss Johannisberg produced in 1950 one cask of ice-wine by pure accident.

For the ordinary consumer 'Museum' wines are of no great interest. For the last 20 years I have been laying aside a few bottles of certain good wines, in order to observe their development over a long period and to test their durability and the age to which they can attain. But sometimes, moved by curiosity—or because I was particularly fond of some particular wine—I have raided these stores until all the 'museum relics' of the vintage in question were consumed. On the whole it is certainly better to drink wines before they reach their peak, rather than when they have begun to decline and risk having waited too long.

Stored wines must be examined from time to time, and in particular it must be ascertained whether the corks of the bottles are still intact. Unfortunately, the good quality corks used in England, particularly for vintage ports, are not used in Germany. The better German wines ought to be corked in the same way. Cork crumbles with age, so bottle-corks must be renewed after 10-15 years. Many a good wine—and only the superior qualities can in any case be preserved so long—has been ruined because the corks were not replaced in time.

Vintages

The fact that wines are designated by their Lagen and by the year of origin is sufficient indication that in all stages of their development in cask and in bottle—they are dependent on Nature. Anyone therefore who expects the wine-grower to deliver him identical products year after year, as if they were machine-made, is depriving himself of the exquisite enjoyment that can only be provided through the great variety of the offerings from different sites under the changing conditions of different seasons. No year is the same as the next—the degree of sunshine varies and with it the characteristics of that season's wines. The real wine connoisseur makes it his aim and his pride to pick out the finest product among the manifold kinds set before him, and—renewing this delightful occupation every season—to enjoy these 'peak' wines to the full. His cultivated wine-palate may be compared to the finely attuned sound sense of the musician or the colour-conscious eye of an artist, and affords him similar possibilities of artistic appreciation.

The general quality of German wines in recent years—to which we now turn our attention—has been very good. Nature has been very kind to German viticulture. The 1945 and 1946 vintages were fully satisfactory in quality, particularly in view of the fact that the war took heavy toll of German vineyards. During the war, there was very little labour to be had, there was a great shortage of everything needed for protecting the plants etc., and this makes the reasonably good quality of the wines little short of astonishing. In 1945 there were late frosts during the first days of May and the late summer was fine and sunny; but it was July that brought the storms and sudden showers to which we owe the exceptional qualities of that year's vintage. The velvety taste, fruity richness and bouquet of these wines will distinguish them above all others for many years to come. The weather in 1946 was very similar in many respects; that year's wines owe their characteristic traits to the very sunny autumn. Full of body but fruity, they contain more acidity than usual, but are well-balanced and elegant and, in general, fully representative of the typical Rhine wine flavour. Next came the great year 1947, noted for what was almost excessive sunshine. All wine-growers had fine harvests and produced heavy wines of a very pronounced character whose delicious bouquet will be the delight of every wine connoisseur now and in the future, even though many wines of this vintage show a lack of acidity. It was an outstanding year, in which the specific gravity of the must was particularly high. It should however be noted in passing that this quality alone is not sufficient indication of the greatness of a wine. In the harmonious blending of sweetness with sufficient acidity the 1947 is a worthy successor to the famous 1921, and altogether a wine that will long be remembered by producers and consumers.

The 1948 produced a wine which in some places outshone the 1947 in its harmony and raciness. Its quality may be described as great, and quantitatively the crops were outstanding. Both quality and quantity were due to the beautiful weather which prevailed while the vines were in flower. The summer was followed by a mild and sunny autumn. The delightful flavour of the 1948 wines coupled with their general harmony and delicate bouquet have been greatly appreciated by connoisseurs. When allowed a suitable period for ripening, their quality will improve still more.

It is well-known even in lay circles that a rich—and still more an excessively rich—crop is in general obtained at the expense of quality. Despite this undoubted fact, the 1948 can compete on equal terms with its predecessors, even in some cases being preferred to them. Thus, 1945 to 1948 constituted four successive good years, and the 1949 products bid fair to equal with them. Wherever the grapes were able to ripen undisturbed by natural phenomena and wherever their subterranean store or supply of moisture was sufficient to offset the lack of rain in that year, the wine produced had an elegant fullness and harmony that may make it the wine of the century. On the other hand, dry sites produced wines of only medium quality which can at best be compared with the 1928 vintages. A notable feature of the year 1949 was the frequent appearance of the *Edelfaeule*—botrytis cinerea—on the berries, some of which had shrivelled to raisin-like consistency. Wherever this happened and the berries that had been so attacked were gathered or pressed separately and the wine was appropriately treated, a really superb product was achieved.

The 1950 products have been high in quantity, but qualitatively they fall far below those of previous years. When sunshine was needed there were rainfalls, and many berries began to rot before they had reached the required maturity. In consequence they could only be made durable and drinkable by the addition of sugar. If it is true that vintages are repeated every hundred years, we can expect the next 'good' vintage in 1957 and an 'excellent' one again in 1958. Let us enjoy those we have before it is too late !

Shortly before completing this book I came across a little booklet called : *Wine Chronicle. A thousand years of wine on the Moselle, the Rhine and the Main,* by Deichmann and Wolf, published by Rauschenbusch, Stollhamm, Berlin. This book surveys the whole range of the centuries from 300 A.D. to 1949, and leaves the reader breathless with astonishment at the wealth of knowledge of times so long past, shown by the authors. Arranged in chronological order, the seasons are presented with a description of the weather in each case and a short characterization of the quantity and quality of the vintages produced. Examples : 1529. A poor wine. In 1530 it caused the Christian Chancellor an attack of the colic. In 1628 the wine was so bad that even the vinegar was ruined by it. 1125 : Vineyards, people and cattle frozen to death. 1125 : Dead birds fall to the ground out of the air. Quantity and quality of wine poor. 1166 : Favourable wine year, but famine in the land. In Franconia wine was used in place of water for mixing the mortar used in building. 1296 : Favourable weather, good and plentiful wine, so that much of the old wine was poured away'.

If there were any need to prove that wine-growing is a risky business, this book would furnish sufficient evidence. The pleasing booklet has a historical introduction and shows that even a list of vintages can afford material for an amusing study.

Sekt (Sparkling Hock and Moselle)

The inventor of Champagne is said to have been a monk by the name of Perignon who was cellarmaster in the Benedictine Abbey of Hautvilliers, Champagne (France) from 1670 to 1715. It may be remembered however that long before this—in Roman times— many poems and songs were written in praise of 'sparkling' wines.

Dom Perignon bottled young wine and mastered the secret of clearing the sediment formed in the bottle without allowing the carbon dioxide to escape. And that is the vital basis of all sparkling wine production.

Because this effervescent wine was first produced in the Champagne country, it became known as 'champagne' and has retained the name to the present day. In Germany however the word 'Sekt' began some time ago to replace the more general appellation. The change-over from 'champagne' to 'Sekt' in Germany has a somewhat peculiar history. It came about thus :

When in 1815 the actor Ludwig Devrient came to the Berlin Court Theatre, he would often play *Falstaff* in *Henry IV*. In the scene at the 'Wild Boar's Head' when he ordered the servitor to bring a 'cup of sack', he used the German word *Sekt* to denote 'sack'. Obviously this was not meant for champagne, a beverage unknown in the days of Henry IV, but for sherry. The Shakespeare translators had however rendered 'sack' with 'Sekt'. From the stage Devrient carried this nomenclature into his Berlin 'pub', or rather into the wine-restaurant of Lutter & Wegner, where he used to sit imbibing champagne with his friend and crony, the world-famous E. T. A. Hoffmann. The waiter became accustomed to bring Devrient his champagne, whenever he called out, 'Hey, villain, bring me a glass of "Sekt".'. Since then the word has established itself in Germany as the correct designation for sparkling wine.

Theoretically Germany should be able to produce the finest of sparkling wines. No law hampers the activities of their manufacturers who are at liberty to use any wine in the world for their blends in attempts to find the right *cuvee*. They may even use pure still champagnes, and certainly in former times many a brand contained a percentage of real champagne. Nowadays the sparkling wines of the Saar, the Lower Moselle, and the Middle Rhine are used for these brands, blended with the cheaper wines of the producer's home region. Manufacturers of sparkling wines are to be found in all parts of Germany. Some of their products are world-famous and named on the wine lists of good hotels in all countries under the heading 'Sparkling Hock' or 'Sparkling Moselle'. In addition to these, there are the 'Special Cuvees', such as Sparkling Berncastler, Sparkling Johannisberger, etc. These brands of sparkling wines are produced from blends which—were they to be marketed as still wines—would have a right to these names.

It may happen that a *cuvee* is prepared exclusively from wines originating on different sites; if then two-thirds of the blend comes from one site only, the sparkling wine may be (and is) marketed under the name of that site—for example, Sparkling Steinberger.

But unique among the sparkling hocks is Fuerst v. Metternich's sparkling *Schloss Johannisberger*, as it is made solely from wines of this world-famous site and therefore on an equal footing with the German 'Estate Bottled' wines. It shows fully the fine Rheingau characteristics in bouquet and flavour.

Under the name of *Perlwein* (bubbly) a wine containing carbon dioxide is at present being marketed in Germany. Instructions for its manufacture were given by Kielhoefer 25 years ago in his 'Cellarage Reports'. They are as follows:

> Must or sugared still wine is allowed to ferment in tanks until the sugar content has been reduced to 15 to 20 grammes per litre. The liquid is then cooled down to 3-5°C., so that the 'shocked' yeast works with reduced energy. At the same time the pressure is set at 1.5 atm. Most of the yeast is deposited, and the wine, saturated with carbon dioxide, is drained off under counter-pressure into an empty tank. At the same time the necessary finings are carried out. Clearing by filtering is conducted isobarically in order that none of the carbon dioxide may escape, and the final bottling (long-necked bottles) is similarly accomplished with the help of the sterilizing filter. The bottled wine is under approximately 1 atm.

carbon dioxide pressure and is served like sparkling wine at a temperature of 41°F. The bottle needs no wire netting to keep the cork in place.

Perlwein is quite a formidable rival to the lesser brands of sparkling wine because it has hitherto remained tax-free in Germany. A bottle of *perlender Saarriesling* (bubbly Saar Riesling) as supplied by the producer costs about one third to one half the price charged for the cheapest brand of 'Sekt'. 'Perl' wines are greatly in demand in Germany today, and they are certainly very pleasant to drink on a warm summer's day.

Wine Festivals

In the Rhineland, wine is the centre of existence, and wine festivals or wine-markets are the order of the day practically all the year round in one or other of its wine-dedicated localities. I have already mentioned the Berncastel wine festival. About the same time of year an exactly similar festival is conducted at Ruedesheim on the Rhine. The climax of the festivals is always the period immediately following the grape-harvest.

The inns serve the new wine which in its first stage is called *Federweisser* (feather-white). The taste of this beverage—which has approximately the colour of milk—is sweetish on the tongue; it prickles the palate and is somewhat reminiscent of bitter almonds. This 'New' (wine) appears to be very harmless, but can play unpleasant tricks. It is like a mischievous small boy whose possibilities for naughtiness are not always at first apparent. Many a wine novice, led astray by the innocent appearance and charm of the new wine, has had to suffer. *Federweisser* is usually sold only by petty innkeepers who make use of a limited licence allowing them to serve wine for a short period, provided it is from their own crop. The privilege is only exercised when markets are very bad, for 'it is not necessary to hand up an ivy bush where wine is selling well', or, in the words of the French and English proverbs : 'Un bon vin ne faut point de bouchon'; 'good wine needs no bush'.

In these autumn weeks all the vine-lands give themselves up to a series of wine festivals.

There is for instance the Duerkheim Wurstmarkt ('Sausage Market'), the fame of which is spread far beyond the boundaries of the Palatinate; often on these occasions the town—known both for its wines and as a spa—harbours over 300,000 visitors from all districts of Germany. This is the greatest of all German wine festivals—very ancient and in the eyes of the people of the Palatinate what the 'October Festival' is to the inhabitants of Munich. It takes place in the second half of September. The 'sausage market meadows' on the outskirts of the town are invisible under the wine-tents set up by the small wine-growers who here dispense the wines they have produced on their own lands. Side-shows abound, roundabouts of all shapes and sizes tinkle incessantly, musicians blow lively tunes on all kinds of instruments. Innumerable market stalls show their wares.

The wine—the people. These give the festival its individual character.

It was in Duerkheim too that I discovered the following verse:

Palatinate dwellers are queer, I'm thinking,
I'll wager that other folks find us so.
For when we're merry, we go a-drinking,
And when we are sad, a-drinking we go!

Next comes Neustadt on the Wine Highway with its Grape Harvest Festival.

In Neustadt, as the wine metropolis of the Palatinate, it has always been the custom for the large wine-growers to have grape-harvest festivities as autumn draws to its close. These fetes in honour of the new vintage were attended by large numbers of the local population, notably the grape-gatherers of both sexes, who would meet to make merry and dance village dances. In course of time this spontaneous popular custom was organized into large-scale grape-harvest fetes at which popular music is played and numerous old Palatinate customs are revived annually—there are, for instance, the traditional baptism of the wine and the selection of a wine-queen, there are costume and 'cooper' dances, processions of wine-growers, etc. In the last two decades the Neustadt Festival has attained immense dimensions and is attended by ever greater numbers of people from near and far. From a 'Wine-Day' is has grown to be a 'Wine-Week' and is now—under the title of 'German Grape-Harvest Festival'—one of the greatest popular fetes in the Palatinate, reaching its climax with the coronation of a 'German Wine-Queen'. A feature of the 1950 festival was—as I see by the official Report—a 'wine roundabout', built up in such a way that it was possible to 'make the rounds' of the characteristic wines of all German districts, tasting them so to speak 'en route'. The writer

of the Report concluded his observations (Rheinpfalz, 30.9.50) as
follows :

> Anxious to learn all he can about wines, the visitor steps
> up to the 'wine' roundabout. Here he is greeted by a bevy of
> young Hebes with sparkling eyes, each dressed in the tradi-
> tional costume of her own particular bit of wine homeland, and
> pressingly invited to taste their wares. The choice is his—but
> what torment to choose among so many delights! 'May I give
> you Randersacker Teufelskeller—or would you prefer Veits-
> hoechheimer Sonnenschein ?'—'What about an Assmanns-
> hauser Hoellenberg, or a Ruedesheimer Goldschmidt ?' 'Oh,
> do try our Schloss Boeckelheimer from the Nahe . . . our
> Bernkasteler Doktor . . . our Erdener Himmelreich'. Or he
> may be offered an Ahrburgunder, an Achkarrener Schlossberg,
> or any of numerous wines from the Main and from Wuerttem-
> berg. Many a visitor will wish that he had a thousand tongues.
> Small wonder if one journey on the roundabout makes him
> feel a little giddy !'

Another Festival that must not be over-looked is the 'Unterhaardt
Wine Competition'.

This is held annually for four consecutive nights and days on the
first Saturday, Sunday, Monday, and Tuesday in October, and takes
place at Gruenstadt, the centre of the Unterhaardt viticultural
district. The wines for the competition are supplied every year by
fifteen wine-producing communities around Gruenstadt—the best
products of the Unterhaardt. Here is the list of the wines at the
1950 competition :

1949 *Vintage* from cask

Bockenheimer Halde
Bockenheimer Sonnenberg
Albsheimer Bennweg
Kirchheimer Rosskopf
Muehlheimer Angewann
Bisserheimer Steinbuehl
Asselheimer Goldberg
Gruenstadter Roeth

1947 *Vintage* (in bottle)
Kleinkarlbacher Ohligpfad
Asselheimer Goldberg

1949 *Vintage* (in bottle)
Gruenstadter Hoellenpfad
Dirmsteiner Mandelpfad
Bockenheimer Halde
Sausenheimer Huett
Dirmsteiner Muttergarten

A so-called 'Wine-Tribunal'—composed exclusively of hard-drinking citizens—'arbitrates' on the wines submitted, and their award always takes the same form, viz. :

'Judgment postponed till next year's wine competition'. The main purpose is to find a good reason for drinking, for emptying the wine-growers' casks and filling their pockets—and Gruenstadt certainly succeeds in doing this.

Anyone wishing to become acquainted with Rhineland wines would do well to stay away from the wine festivals. Hampstead Heath on an August Bank Holiday is no more unsuitable for the study of good wines than are the Rhineland and Moselle villages during the festivals.

A large number of world-famous spas are situated in the various wine districts. In the first place there is Wiesbaden—a very good centre from which to visit the Rheingau and Rhinehessia; then there are Baden-Baden and many other places in the Black-Forest; Bad Duerkheim in the Palatinate; Bad Kreuznach and Muenster am Stein on the Nahe; Bad Schlangenbad in the Rheingau; Bad Kissingen in Franconia; Bad Wildstein and Bad Bertrich on the Moselle; Bad Ahrweiler on the Ahr. All these places have a Kurhaus in which a number of selected wines can be tasted and enjoyed at leisure.

Then of course there are the wine-trading centres: Neustadt (Palatinate); Mainz and Bingen (Rhinehessia); Ruedesheim (Rheingau); Berncastel and Traben-Trarbach, Trier (Moselle); Stuttgart (Wuerttemberg); Offenburg (Baden); Wuerzberg (Franconia). These afford manifold opportunities for studying the wines of the respective regions.

Still more interesting is the study of wines in wine restaurants (Weinstuben) where they can be drunk to the accompaniment of the local dishes. In this connection the Rheingau is pre-eminent and has been called Germany's 'parlour', Germany's 'wine bar' (lit. 'drinking-hall'), or Germany's 'banqueting hall'. Although the present book is not intended to be a kind of guide-book, I feel obliged to mention a few of these places for the benefit of travellers interested in wines. Here, therefore, are some names of hotels and restaurants where such tourists—if they can spare the time—would have good opportunities of studying wines and tasting some of the older vintages.

First of all there is the Hotel zur Krone in Assmannshausen (Rheingau), to which I would award five stars for food, wine and service. It has a lovely terrace from which to enjoy a view of the beauties of the river. The proprietor of this hotel is also the owner of Jagdschloss Niederwald which, situated right in the midst of woodlands, is in every way equal to the parent establishment.

Assmannshausen and Ruedesheim are full of little wine-inns, well adapted for drinking purposes, less so for a serious study of wines. There are, for example, the Bauernschaenke and the Froehlicher Weinberg in Assmannshausen; the Lindenwirt in der Drosselgass in Ruedesheim, all highly esteemed by thirsty travellers. Establishments to be recommended for the study of wines in the Rheingau are: Hotel Schwan in Ostrich: Hotel Ress in Hattenheim with its branch establishment the Klosterpforten-restaurant in Kloster Eberbach; 'Mutter Mueller' and 'Weinpump' in Eltville.

Similar facilities are to be found in the other German wine regions. As, for instance :—

Rheinhotel in Nierstein. Hotel Starkenburgerhof in Bingen. (Wine inns: Zum Stolpereck; Binger Bleistift; Goldener Kochloeffel).

Hotel Koehler in Neustadt.

Naturweinhaus Henninger in Kallstadt.

Weinstube Kaesbuero, Seebach, 1 mile from Bad Durkheim. Built in the 11th century as Monastery, 14th century as inn for the visitor of the cloister. End of 15th century altered by the Kurfurst Kasmir into a Zehntenhaus for delivery of cheese. Since 17th century family Mayer proprietor and since known as Weinstube 'Kaesbuero'.

Hotel Claus-Feist in Traben-Trarbach, which is on the same level as the Krone in Assmannshausen.

Ratskeller, Doktorstube, Weinhaus zur Post, Hotel Landshut, in Berncastel.

Kreiswasserwerk Trollmuehle (wine-tasting hall of the District of Kreuznach. Here, there is a carefully selected wine-list which enables the tourist to try out the best of the Nahe products.)

Beim Burgwirt in Ebernburg.

In the following hotels, which are of good repute and well worth a visit, the traveller will find a large selection of first-class Wuerttemberg wines :

Zum Alten Rentamt in Schwaigern, near Heilbron. This establishment belongs to Graf Neipperg. It is furnished in good style with many beautiful antiques. Cellar and cuisine are worthy of this setting.

Grafs Weinstuben in Heilbronn (Lenaustrasse). Schwarze Katz. This house is furnished in modern style and has delightful gardens. The best Wuerttemberg wines are served here

Rhineland — Wineland

A GEOGRAPHICAL SURVEY OF CULINARY DELIGHTS.

The Marquise du Deffand, famed in the 18th century for her epistolary wit, and a friend of Horace Walpole's, was still, at the age of eighty, surrounded by admirers. To one of these she is reported to have said: 'Only three things in this world are really worth while. The first is good food'. 'And what are the other two ?' asked her visitor. 'Oh those . . . ." smiled the old lady, 'I'm afraid I don't remember'.

When travelling through Germany's Rhineland, one is irresistibly reminded of the Marquise's delight in food, without necessarily being either quite so aged or quite so oblivious of other pleasant things in life.

Fertility is the keynote of the Rhineland, both for the casual beholder and for the inhabitants of the region. It provides them with delights of the flesh to which they have clung even in the most troublous times. The preparing of food has never forsaken them entirely, and to this day some of the old-time dishes served in Rhenish inns have preserved their traditional characteristics. Many of these—as is to be expected in a wine region—owe their attractions to a happy combination with wine in their preparation. Others show seasonal specialities.

In May and June, for instance, all Rhine and Main restaurants have asparagus (Spargel) on the menu. It the white variety and the best specimens come from the asparagus-beds at Schwetzingen (between Neckar and the Rhine), and from Ingelheim (between Mainz and Bingen). Asparagus, the recognized king of all vegetables, was cultivated thousands of years ago by the Egyptians and has lost nothing of its flavour in the course of time. On the Rhine it is often served with omelettes, or smoked ham and smoked tongue. Connoisseurs, however, insist on eating asparagus served with no other accompaniment than a Holland sauce, made preferably without flour. Its orthodox components are yolk of egg, butter, lemon juice, and a very little of the asparagus water, the mixture being whipped over a low fire until it is sufficiently thick. The asparagus season is short. The vegetable disappears with the song of the nightingale round about the 24th of June. The asparagus season is co-temporaneous with the rich strawberry ('Erdbeeren') harvest. These large luscious berries are cultivated mainly in the Taunus region, and the little town of Kronberg near Frankfurt is famous for producing the best quality.

Strawberries are closely followed by the cherry ('Kirschen') season. On the Bergstrasse and in the Neckar region very popular steamed puddings—known as *Kirschenplotzer* and *Kirschenmichel* are made from eggs, almonds, and cherries, with bread soaked in milk.

The main culinary season starts in the spring and is enriched, among other delicacies, by the crayfish ('Krebs'). These are served hot, boiled to a ripe red hue, and are guaranteed to chase away all winter memories of spotty old potatoes and other hardships of the cold season. In the 17th century crayfish were eaten raw with salt, pepper, vinegar, and oil, but the more refined modern culinary art serves them in boiling caraway- or dill-water, in wine, or even in champagne. The best crayfish are found on soft soil under clear waters, where they can hide in shore-holes. They should really be eaten to the accompaniment of a cool white wine. And if in addition this feast is enjoyed in one of the restaurant gardens of the Taunus or the Odenwald in moonlight, every traveller will be inclined to agree with the little popular verse:

> The R-less months are best for eating cray,
> For travelling, and for your wedding-day.
> (*Die Monde ohne R sind gut zum Reisen,*
> *Zum Hochzeitsmachen und zum Krebse Speisen.*)

But even apart from such things as wedding-days and crayfish, the R-less months present the traveller through south-west Germany with many delights. At such times, for example, he will find on almost all menus a meat-course called *Suppenfleisch mit gruener Sosse.* This is boiled beef served hot with a sauce made from a number of finely-chopped fresh herbs and hard-boiled eggs, well mixed with cream, vinegar, oil, mustard, salt, and pepper. The same sauce, if it has taken your fancy, may be served with cold meat ('Kalte Platte') or with certain kinds of freshwater fish, such as (hot) perch ('Barsch'), or better still, (cold) shed ('Maifisch').

Fish really deserves a paragraph to itself, if only because of Brillant Savarin's remark: 'Fish is a compromise which suits itself to all temperaments'. Can anyone deny that a slice of salmon ('Rheinsalm'), eaten slowly to the accompaniment of a bottle of Rhinewine, is in its own way as romantic as the ruins of the ancient Rhenish castles. Other fish often eaten in the Rheingau and on the Middle Rhine are the pike ('Hecht') and the eel ('Aal'). While the salmon undertakes its honeymoon from the sea inwards to the river, the eel—if it is not caught first—takes the opposite direction, viz., from the rivers back into the sea. Smoked eel ('Raeucheraal') served with bread and butter is a favourite hors d'oeuvre, while Rhine eel ('Rheinaal'), boiled and served with melted butter, is usually a main dish. In Rhinehessia the inhabitants are very partial to fried fish ('Backfische'), such as the rudd ('Orf'). The extensive fish cultures near Baden-Baden in the Black Forest, and the swift-running brooks of the Taunus and the Lahn Valley, on the other hand, provide their neighbourhoods with delicious river trout ('Bachforellen'). The trout ('Forelle') is the chameleon among fish; it changes the colour of its skin, and even that of its flesh, according to the surroundings in which it is placed. Since the year 1101 trout has been reckoned as one of the ten most wholesome kinds of fish. Monastery cooks were wont to pay great attention to its preparation, having regard to the ancient monastic saying that the culinary art is a permissible fleshy indulgence. Actually, however, the elegant sinuous trout tastes best of all when merely steamed and served with fresh butter. Beethoven, born in Bonn on the Rhine, is known to have been extremely fond of trout cooked in this simple manner.

But it would be unjust to confine our observations to the inhabitants of rivers and brooks. What, for instance, has the Lake of Constance to offer the fish gourmet? Tropically beautiful, surrounded by slopes which since Roman times have been planted with vines, Lake Constance forms an intriguing contrast to the cool pine-woods of the neighbouring Black Forest. It is as large as the Lake of Geneva, and holds vast numbers of the delicious fish—a member of the salmon family—known as Blaufelchen'. These fish are usually prepared *a la meuniere* (auf Muellerinnen Art), or else fried quickly in the pan, and served with white potatoes sprinkled with chopped parsley.

Other fish which make good table delicacies are to be found in the lakes of the Westerwald (which forms part of the Rhenish range of slate hills) and the Eifel, on the north side of which the vineyard-lined Ahr has its source. These lakes yield for instance the plump tench ('Schleie') and the still plumper carp ('Karpfen'). Rhine carp ('Rheinkarpfen') is eaten cold with a sauce made of gingerbread and raisins, while the Moselle carp ('Moselkarpfen') is merely steamed (served 'blue', German *blau*). It is advisable not to eat carp except in months whose name contains an R, at other times it is apt to have a slightly swampy taste. And—an important warning—fish dishes should always be accompanied by a dry, medium-dry, or a mild white wine. The wine brings out the flavour of the fish.

Once the months containing an R have begun, fruit harvesting starts in the Rhineland and its surroundings: Grapes are gathered in the vineyards, apples and egg-plums are harvested in the orchards, and chestnuts break out of their prickly coverings. At the same time shooting begins in the game-filled Rhineland woods; the young must made from the new grape-harvest is still richly sweet when the first partridges ('Feldhuehner') appear on the table, each tied up with a piece of bacon fat, rolled in vine-leaves, and softly bedded on a mound of sauerkraut. The sauerkraut is cooked in wine, on special occasions in sekt which is certainly a luxurious way of preparing this vegetable. Incidentally, Lord Nelson thought highly of sauerkraut, to judge by the following anecdote told of him. In order to keep his men in a good humour, he is said to have loaded his men-o-war with lemons and sauerkraut and when he was once asked after a battle what means he had employed to gain the victory, to have answered: 'Lemons and sauerkraut'.

Rather later in the season than partridges come pheasants, wild duck, deer, wild boar, and hares. Anyone boasting a good digestion will certainly enjoy galatine of wild boar ('Wildschweinsuelze') and will also be inclined to sing the praises of the jugged hare *en casserole* ('Dippehas'), the special dish of ancient origin typical of peasant food on the plains. This is prepared as follows: The hare is cut up and put to soak over night in milk and pickles. The next day it is removed to an earthenware vessel with a firmly fitting lid. To it are added: a piece of pig's belly, a crust of black bread, a laurel leaf, cloves and onion, and over this mixture the cook pours a great deal of red wine and a small quantity of oxblood. In order to bring out the strong aromatic flavour and to make the flesh of the hare really tender it is necessary to cook this dish for a full three hours in a good hot oven. After partaking of this succulent dish the real gourmet can finish off his meal with 'Karthaeuser Kloesse' served with a wine sauce, or with 'Arme Ritter', both of which are hot sweets made of baked white bread, previously soaked in egg and milk. Another hot sweet, made with yeast dough put to rise in hot milk in the oven, is known as 'Dampfnudeln', and yet another, made from yeast dough with egg-plums, is called 'Zwetschenkloss'. Dampfnudeln are served with hot vanilla sauce. In the more luxurious hotel restaurants on the Rhine they make a very good wine-cream ('Wein Creme') decorated with sweet whipped cream.

To assist the traveller who may be somewhat bewildered by the enormous selection with which he is faced on the menus presented to him anywhere between the Kaiserstuhl, the hills flanking the plains of the Upper Rhineland, and the Lake of Constance, the following list of dishes has been drawn up. The foods mentioned are not in all cases 'specialities', but they are all prepared in ways typical of the South and West German cuisine. They are arranged under the headings to be found on the German menus.

Vorspeisen

Wildpastete mit Cumberland Sosse...Game Pie with
Cumberland Sauce.
Rindermark auf Toast.....................Fried Beef Marrow on Toast

Zwischengerichte.

Saure Nieren...Pickled Kidneys
Kalbskopf..Calves' Head
Kalbsmilcher .... Sweetbreads
Badische Leberspaetzle........................(Baden) Liver Dumplings

Fleischgerichte.

Rindsroulanden...................................Stuffed Beef Rolls
Sauerbraten.....................................Pickled Beef
Zwischenrippenstuck 'Suppen Fleisch'........................Boiled Beef
Schnitzel Holstein...............................Veal 'Schnitzel'
Paprika Schnitzel.........................Veal 'Schnitzel' with Paprika
Gefuellte Kalbsbrust.............................Stuffed Breast of Veal
Kalbshaxe..................................Knuckle of Veal
Schweinelendchen mit Rahmsosse...Fillet of pork with creamed gravy
Schweinekotelett .... Pork Chop

Beilagen und Gemuese

Steinpilze .... Mushrooms
Edelpilze .... Champignons
Spaetzle...A kind of Dumpling
Schupfnuldeln............Fried Dumplings made of flour and potatoes
Himmel und Erde......Mashed potatoes with mashed apples
and fried onions
Kartoffelkloesse...Potato Dumplings

Suesse Speisen

Kaiserschmarren......A variety of pancake made of
eggs, flour, and sultanas
Omelette mit Kirsch............................Omelette with Kirsch

Kaese............Cheese

The last category comprises a large variety of cheeses. The meal should always be concluded with some kind of cheese, as its alkaline constituents are extremely well adapted to bring out the best qualities of a fine wine.

Apart from these and other dishes, however, served the whole year round at lunch and dinner in the various restaurants, the traveller will find a number of typical snacks for eating between the regular meals. On the Neckar, for instance, or in the neighbourhood of Hanau or Wuerzburg, the tourist may please himself whether he will choose the morning or the afternoon for eating a piece of cake made with onions ('Zwiebelkuchen') solely in order to heighten his pleasure in the drink in which he is indulging; or whether—between the Main and the Rhine—he feels like taking a bite of Mainz cheese ('Mainzer Handkaese') to bring out the taste of his wine. These combinations are partially compulsory. The Handkaese—covered with caraway seeds—is very good with bread and butter, but typically it should be prepared with Musik. This does not mean that it is eaten to music, but with a sauce called Musik made of vinegar, oil, chopped onions, pepper and salt.

A cold salted pork chop with sauerkraut ('Rippchen mit Kraut') is another favourite between-meals titbit. But most popular of all in the Rhine-Main region, as adjunct to the 'sundowner', is the sausage. There are many kinds of sausage, but above all there is the pork sausage ('Fleischwurst') made of fresh pork. It contains no fat and the meat has been passed through a fine sieve. It tastes best when boiled and eaten together with rolls made of flour and water and known as 'Wasserwecken'. Unlike the Fleischwurst, the fried sausages ('Bratwuerste'), always served in large quantities at popular festivals, are smoked, and made of a mixture of beef, veal, and pork.

These are by no means the only varieties of sausage manufactured in this part of Germany. There are, for example, the world-famous 'Frankfurters' ('Frankfurter Wuerstchen') and many kinds of liver and 'blood' sausages. And particular mention should be made of the 'Schwartemagen', if only because Goethe, always loyal to his home town of Frankfurt, was so partial to it. Jean Paul too, was extremely fond of sausages. He is known to have thanked his publisher for a gift of fifty different varieties of smoked and fresh sausages, signing his letter as 'The Author of the book *Heperus* and of other works very different from sausages.

The traveller, however, who may not be quite so addicted to sausages as the two great German authors, or who may not wish to spoil his appetite for the two main meals of the day, will find

other and lighter snacks at hand that may fairly be described as
specialities and which form a pleasant accompaniment to a glass of
wine. Most restaurants, for instance, will provide him with unsweetened rolls or other bakery products made savoury with such
trimmings as salt, caraway or poppy seeds. These are known as
Salzstengel, Kuemmelweck, Laugenbretzel, and *Mohnbroetchen.*

Festivals of all kinds provide not unwelcome opportunities for
baking cakes—in the Rhineland as elsewhere. In some districts of
Western Germany large hares made of sponge-cake and covered with
sugar appear at Easter, while at Christmas effigies of Santa Claus
made of honey-cake (ginger-bread containing honey) take their place.
Christmas is also the time for little spicy gingerbread cakes ('Leb-
kuchen') in the form of hearts and covered with writing in sugary
letters. The Rhine Carnival is celebrated with the help of jam-filled
doughnuts ('Krebbel'). In South Germany a traditional custom
demands the baking of enormous plum tarts made of yeast dough.
Sometimes these tarts are as big as a good-sized table and in peasant
families may form the main dish of a meal. Other cakes in these
gigantic sizes are made instead of with plums, with bilberries, apples,
cream-cheese, or 'Streusel', a concoction of sugar, butter and grated almonds. Among such rather crude and rural products we should include 'Hutzelbrod', a loaf baked from dried fruits and flour, and
many kinds of fancy bread baked from yeast dough in a variety of
shapes. But beside these, the shops always have an assortment of
fine pastries for more fastidious palates.

Somewhere about the year 1800 a man called Grimod de la
Reyniere—whose *Almanach des Gourmands* in the opinion of experts proclaims the joys of the table even more lyrically than Ovid
extols the joys of love—described no less than 534 different ways
of preparing eggs. It was this man's opinion that good pastry-cooks
are almost as rare as good speakers. Few travellers in the Rhineland
will be found to agree with him. They may however be astounded
at the very queer names given to some of the delicacies they find.
The name 'Mannheimer Dreck', for example, (which read literally,
suggests something dirty), is applied to a delicious little mound made
of almonds and white of eggs and covered with chocolate icing;
'Frankfurt Bethmaennchen' (literally, little praying men) is a most
tempting trifle resembling a macaroon. Then there are the well-
known 'Frankfurter Brenten', made of a kind of almond paste to
which oil of roses has been added, while 'Offenbacher Pfeffernuesse'
(literally pepper nuts) are hard-baked and strongly spiced little
cakes resembling the richer kinds of ginger-bread. Another delicacy

which can be recommended to the visitor with a sweet tooth is the 'Wormser Bretzelchen', a tiny very rich short-cake. And—for those who after all are a little tired of sweet things—there are the rusks known as 'Friedrichsdorfer Zwieback'.

'Dost thou think', said Sir Toby Belch, 'because thou art virtuous, there shall be no more cakes and ale ?' The Rhineland certainly lives up to the implied principle. The list of sweet specialities would not be complete without a description of the excellent fruit-tarts to be found all over the region in the appropriate shops, beginning with the pine-apple tart, a Wiesbaden speciality. The base of these tarts is a rich pastry made with butter. This is then covered—according to the season—with strawberries, cherries, red currants, apricots, or grapes. And over the fruit goes another layer—a thick one—made of sugar and white of egg. Whipped cream is served lavishly with each portion.

If we made the permissible substitution of 'wine' for the 'ale' of the Shakespeare quotation, the Rhineland is seen as a still more faithful adherent of the principle that virtue should not be allowed to exclude certain material delights. No one on the Rhine is likely to neglect the joys of the bottle—if only because of its sorely needed cheering qualities—the good food alone demanding it. In fact, the Rhineland is the place *par excellence* to demonstrate the truth of the 200-year old saying that 'Eat-Well is Drink-Well's brother'.

APPENDIX I

German Wine-Growing Centres

Ahr District: Ahrweiler, Bodendorf, Mayschoss, Walporzheim (Ahrbleichert).

Baden: Achern, Achkarren, Affenthal, (red wines), Bischoffingen, Buehl, Durbach, Endingen, Ihringen, Oberkirch, Radolfzell, Rothweil, Weinheim, Zell.

Franconia: Buchbrunn, Dettelbach, Escherndorf, Hammelburg, Iphofen, Klingenberg, Miltenberg, Randersacker, Roedelsee, Sommerach, Sulzfeld, Wuerzburg.

Middle Rhine: Bacharach, Boppard, Caub, Enghoell, Koenigswinter, Linz, Manubach, Niederheimbach, Oberdiebach, Oberheimbach, Ober-Wesel, Perscheid, Steeg, Trechtingshausen, Unkel.

Following is a list of the wine-growing localities in:

1. *RHEINGAU* (all localities are centres).

Assmannshausen (Red Hock), Eibingen, Eltville, Erbach, Geisenheim, Hallgarten, Hattenheim, Hochheim, Johannisberg, Kiedrich, Lorch, Mittelheim, Martinsthal, Oestrich, Rauenthal, Ruedesheim, Schierstein, Walluf and Winkel.

2. *RHEINHESSIA* (the following are the centres only):

Alsheim, Alzey, Bechtheim, Bingen, Bodenheim, Bosenheim, Dienheim, Elsheim, Ensheim, Gau-Algesheim, Gau-Bickeleheim, Gau-Bischofsheim, Gundersheim, Guntersblum, Hahnheim, Laubenheim, Nackenheim, Nieder- and Oberingelheim (red Hock), Nierstein, Ockenheim, Oppenheim, Osthofen, Pfaffenschwabenheim, Selzen, Westhofen, Woellstein, Worms, and Zornheim.

3. *MOSELLE, SAAR and RUWER* (centres are in italics or capitals).

(a) MIDDLE MOSELLE: Andel, Bausendorf, Beckond, *Bernkastel, Brauneberg,* Burg, BURGEN, DETZEM, DHRON, Dreis, Nieder-Emmel, Enkirch, Ensch, Erden, Fastrau, Ober- and Niederfell, Filzen, GRAACH, Hetzerath, Hupperath, Josephshof, Kenn, Keston, Kinheim, Kluesserath, Koewerich, KROEV, Kues, Leiwen, Lieser, Loesenich, Longen, Longuich, Loersch, Machern, Maring, Mehring, Minheim, Monzel, Muestert, Muehlheim, NEUMAGEN, Noviand, Osann, *Piesport,* Platten, Poelich, Rachtig, Reil, Reinsport, Rievenich, Riol Schleich, Schweich, Starkenburg, Thoernich, TRABEN, TRARBACH, TRITTENHEIM, UERZIG, VELDENZ, WEHLEN, Wintrich, Wittlich, Wolf, *Zeltingen.*

(b) Saar and Ruwer. AYL, Beurig, Biebelhause, EITELS-BACH, Filzen, GRUENHAUS, Irsch, KANZEM, KASEL, Koenen, Krutweiler, Mertesdorf, Morscheid, Niederleuken, *Ockfen*, Fiveris, Ruwer-Maximin, Ruwer-Paulin, SAARBURG, Schoden, Serrig, Sommerau, WAWERN, WALDRACH, and *Wiltingen*.

(c) Obermosel and Sauer. Bollendorf, Echternacherbrueck, Fellerich, Grewenich, Helfant, Igel, Koellig, Kreuzweiler, LANG-SUR, Liersberg, MESENICH, Metzdorf, NITTEL, Oberbillig, Onsdorf, Psalzem, Rehlingen, Sehndorf, Soest, Tawern, Temmels, Wasserbillig, Wasserliesch-Reinig, Wehte, Wellen, Wincheringen, Wintersdorf.

(d) District Around Trier. OBEREMMEL, Franzenheim, Heiligkreuz, Irsch, Kernschied, Kommlingen, KONZ, Krettnach, Kuerenz, Nieder- and Ober-Menning, Merzlich, Glewig, Pfalzel, St. Mathias, St. Medard-Feyen, and Tarforst.

(e) Lower Moselle. ALF, Aldegund, Alken, Beilstein, Bremm, BRIEDEL, Briedern, Brodenbach, Bruttig, BURGEN, Bullay, Dieblich, Ediger, Eller, Ellenz, ERNST, Fankel, Niederfel, Oberfell, Gondorf, Guels, Hatzenport, Kaimt, Kattenes, Karden, KLOTTEN, Kobern, Koblenz, KOCHEM, Kong, Lay, Lehmen, Loef, Merl, MESENICH, MOSELKERN, Mueden, NEEF, Nehren, Poltersdorf, Pommern, Puenderich, Sehl, Senheim, Treis, Valwig, WINNINGEN, and Zell.

4. *PALATINATE*

(a) Oberhaardt. ALBERSWEILER, Alsterweiler, Altdorf, Appenhofen, Arzheim, Bellheim, Berghausen, Bergzabern, Billigheim, BIRKWEILER, Boebingen, Boechingen, Bornheim, BUERR-WEILER, Dammheim, DIEDESFELD, Doerrenbach, Dudenhofen, Duttweiller, EDENKOBEN, EDESHEIM, Essingen, Eschbach, Flemlingen, Frankweiler, Freckenfeld, Freimersheim, Freisbach, Geinsheim, GLEISWEILER, Gleishorbach, Gleiszellen, Goecklingen, Godramstein, Graefenhausen, Gross-Fischlingen, Hainfeld, Hanhofen, Heiligenstein, Heuchelheim, Ilbesheim, Impflingen, Ingenheim, Insheim, Kapsweyer, Kirrweiler, Klingen, Klingenmuenster, Knittelsheim, Knoeringen, Lachen, Landau, Leinsweller, Lingenfeld, MAI-KAMMER, Mechtersheim, Minfeld, Mittel-Hambach, Moerzbach, Nieder-Hochstadt, Nieder-Horbach, Nieder-Lustadt, Nussdorf, Ober-Hambach, Oberhausen, Ober-Hochstadt, Ober-Hofen, Ober-Lustadt, Ober-Otterbach, Offenbach, Ottersheim, Pleisweiler, Queichheim, Ranschblach, Rechtenbach, Rhodt, Roschbach, Ridzheim, St. Martin,

Schwegenheim, Schweigen, Schweighofen, SIEBELDINGEN, Steinweiler, Unter-Hambach, Venningen, Vollmersweiler, Wald-Hambach, Walsheim, Weingarten, Westheim, Weyher, Wollmesheim, and Zeiskam.

(b) MIDDLE HAARDT. Alsheim, Assenheim, *Bad-Duerkheim,* Battenberg, Bobenheim a. Berg, Boehl, Dakenheim, Dannstadt, DEIDESHEIM, Ellerstadt, Erpolzheim, FORST, FREINSHEIM, Friedelsheim, Fussgoennheim, GIMMELDINGEN, Goenneheim, Grethen, HAARDT, Hassloch, HERXHEIM, Hochdorf, Iggelheim, KALLSTADT, KOENIGSBACH, Lambsheim, Leistadt, Meckenheim, Mondach, MUSSBACH, Mutterstadt, NEUSTADT, Niederkirchen, Ruchheim, RUPPERTSBERG, Seebach, Schauernheim, UNGSTEIN, WACHENHEIM, Weisenheim a. Berg, Weisenheim a. Sand, and Winzingen.

(c) LOWER HAARDT. Albisheim a.d. Pfrimm, Albsheim a.d. Eis, Asselheim, Bennhausen, Bissersheim, Bischheim, Bolanden, Bubenheim, Colgenstein, DIRMSTEIN, Einselthum, Eisenberg-Stauf, Gauersheim, Gerolsheim, Gross-Niedesheim, GRUENSTADT, Harzheim, Hessheim, Heuchelheim, Immelsheim, Jakobsweiler, Kerzenheim, Kindenheim, Kirchheim a.d. Eck, Kirchheim-Bolander, Kleinbockenheim, Klein-Karlbach, Klein-Niedesheim, Kriegsfeld, Laumersheim, Marnheim, Nauchensheim, Mertesheim, Moersteld, Morschheim, Muehlheim a.d. Eis, Neu-Leiningen, NIEFERNHEIM, Ober-Suelzen, Obrigheim, Orbis, Ottersheim, Quirnheim, Rittersheim, Roxheim, Ruessingen, SAUSENHEIM, Stetten, and ZELL.

NAHE : Altenbamberg, Bretzenheim, Dorsheim, Ebernburg, Gutenberg, Heddesheim, Kreuznach, Langenlonsheim, Laubenheim, Mandel, Meddersheim, Meisenheim, Monzingen, Muenster, Niederhausen, Norheim, Roxheim, Ruemmelsheim, Sobernheim, Waldboeckelheim, Waldhilbersheim, Wallhausen, Windesheim, Winzenheim.

WUERTTEMBERG : Beilstein, Besigheim, Boennigheim, Brackenheim (red wines), Cannstadt, Duerenzimmern (red wines), Edelfingen, Elpersheim, Erlenbach, Fellbach, Geradstetten, Grossbottwar, Grossheppach, Gundelsheim, Heilbronn, Heppach, Hohenhasslach, Horb, Ingelfingen, Laudenbach, Lauffen, Marbach, Markelsheim, Maulbronn, Mundelheim, Neckarsulm, Neipperg (red wines), Obertuerkheim, Reutlingen, Sachsenflur, Schnaith, Schnaitheim, Schwaigern (red wines), Stockheim (red wines), Stuttgart, Uhlbach, Unterbalbach, Unterschluepf, Untertuerkheim, Weinsberg.

APPENDIX II

Vineyard Class Names

BADEN

Names of Villages	Names of Sites (Lagen)
Achkarren and Ihringen	Berg, Griwelgarten
Achkarren and Rothweil	Buechsenberg
Bleckstein and Lauda	Seeb
Bleckstein and Koenigshofen	Kuettwig
Buehlerthal and Altschweier	Altenberg, Engelsbach
Diersburg	Schlossberg, Burggraben
Dietlingen and Elmendingen	Hochstrasse, Klepberg
Dietlingen and Broetzingen	Gauchhelde
Dietlingen and Birkenfeld	Kempf
Elsenz	Tiefenbach
Hagenau a. Bodensee and Stehten	Ilben
Herbolzheim	Ostberg, Tiefengrube
Immenstaad	Hochberg, Herschberg
Kippenheim and Sulz	Galgenberg
Kippenheim and Wintersheim	Fuchsberg
Kippenheim and Schmieheim	Eichert
Unterhelbach and Oberlbach	Rossberg
Werbach and Impfingen	Tauberhellen

FRANCONIA

Boettigheim and Werbach	Buellesleite
Buchbrunn and Kitzingen	Buchbrunner Berg
Bullenheim and Seinsheim	Hoher Buehl
Buergstadt and Miltenberg	Steingrube
Eibelstadt and Randersacker	Alter Berg, neuer Berg
Fahr and Volkach	Berg
Karlstadt and Gambach	Rothenberg
Karlstadt and Stetten	Rossthal
Repperndorf, Koehler and Kitzingen	Berg
Schweinfurth and Mainberg	Mainleithe
Thuengersheim and Vietshoechheim	Ravensburg
Wiesenbronn and Roedelsee	Duerbach, Wachhuegel
Wiesenbronn and Grosslangheim	Kiliansberg

MIDDLE RHINE

Boppard and Oberspai	Hamm
Braubach and Oberlahnstein	Koppelstein and Mainsberg
Hoenningen and Rheinbrohl	Elsberg
Hoenningen and Leutesdorf	Im Olter, An der Ley
Manubach and Oberdiebach	In der Retz, In der Muehle

MOSELLE

Berncastel and Graach	Braunes
Brauneberg and Maring	Brauneberg
Briedel and Kaimt	Bruch, Krammeterrech
Cobern and Winningen	Uhlen
Cochem and Clotten	Wirges
Crettnach and Niedermennig	Euchariusberg
Croev and Wolf	Kahlenberg
Croev and Kienheim	Kant, Halsbach
Dhron and Neumagen	Hofberg
Enkirch and Traben-Trarbach	Hinterberg, Lach, Steffensberg
Ernst and Sehl	Newig
Graach and Wehlen	Muenzlay
Kesten	Niederberg, Braunepichter and Karl
Longuich and Schweich	Probstberg
Mehring and Loersch	Zellerberg
Mertesdorf and Eitelsbach	Wenigbach
Mertesdorf and Casel	Lorenzberg
Minheim and Niederemmel	Grauberg
Muehlheim, Veldenz and Burgen	Bitsch
Nittel and Wellen	Griffel
Puenderich and Reil	Staaden
Oberfell and Alken	Rosenberg
Piesport and Niederemmel	Taubengarten, Michelsberg, Hohlweit
Senheim and Mesenich	Lay, Kolay, Rosenberg, and Kukukslay
Wiltingen and Oberemmel	Scharzberg
Zeltingen and Uerzig	Schoores
Zeltingen and Wehlen	Welbersberg, Bikkert
Zell and Merl	Rossberg

NAHE DISTRICT

Bingerbruck and Weiler	Muethe
Bretzenheim and Winzenheim	Monik, Rosenheck, Metzler, Hof
Burgsponheim and Sponheim	Hinterberg
Dorsheim and Ruemmelsheim	Honigberg
Heddesheim and Waldhilbersheim	Kilb, Ohlig-Muehle
Heddesheim and Langenlonsheim	Liewer, Rote Pfuhl, Im Steinchen
Heddesheim and Winzenheim	Honigberg, Goldloch
Kreuznach and Hackenheim	Galgenberg
Kreuznach and Hargesheim	Kronenberg
Kreuznach and Winzenheim	Erschaft
Muenster bei Bingerbruck and Sarsheim	Pittersberg
Muenster and Traisen	Rotenfels
Niederhausen and Rueffelsheim	Steyger
Ruedesheim and Mandel	Rosengarten
Waldlaubersheim and Schweppenhausen	Auf Haardt

PALATINATE:

Bergzabern and Doerrenbach	Wonneberg, Schlettig
Birkweiler and Albersweiler	Goldgrube
Boechingen, Flemlingen and Burrweiler	Schlittweg
Boechingen and Gleisweiler	Hoelle
Burrweiler and Gleisweiler	Staufert
Burrweiler and Hainfeld	Heide
Dackenheim and Herzheim a. Berg	Doerrling
Dammheim and Nussdorf	Rotenweg
Dammheim and Landau	Grain
Dammheim and Knoerringen	Ueber die Schleid
Deidesheim and Ruppertsberg	Hofstueck
Diedesfeld and Hambach	Hartkopf, Steppeswiese
Diedesfeld and Maikammer	In der Schleife, An der Hitschbach, Heide
Bad Duerkheim and Seebach	Klosterberg
Bad Duerkheim and Wachenheim	Ortwingeert, Fuchsmantel, Schenkenboehl

Bad Duerkheim and Ungstein	Spielberg, Bachel
Edenkoben and Maikammer	Pfeiffer, Stossen
Edenkoben and Venningen	Trappenberg
(see also under St. Martin)	
Edesheim	Hochholz
Frankweiler and Godramstein	Stahlbuehl
Gimmeldingen and Mussbach	Teichwiese
Gleiszellen-Gleishorbach and	Wadenhehl, Kirchbach
Klingenmuenster	
Godramstein and Siebeldingen	Heutal, Im roten Loch, Wegscheid
Godramstein and Landau	Loehl
Hambach and Neustadt a.H.	Hufeisel (or Zwerggewann)
Hilbesheim and Arzheim	Kalmit
(see also under Wollmesheim)	
Ilbesheim and Leinsweiler	Baerenloch, Zehentfrei
Lachen and Duttweiler	Im Grund, Auf der Hoehe,
	Am Kroatenpfad
Lachen and Kirrweiler	In den Haingeschaeften
Leistadt and Harxheim a. Berg	Felsenberg
Moerzheim and Gloecklingen	Haine
Moerzheim and Heuchelheim	Schwarzacker
Nussdorf and Walsheim	Ried
Pleisweiler-Oberhofen and	Im Seigen, Im Spiess
Gleiszellen-Gleishorbach	
Rhodt and Weyher	Kalkgrube
Ruppertsberg and Mussbach	Scheidgraben
Sausenheim and Gruenstadt	Hochgewann
Sausenheim and Kleinkarlbach	Auf der Senn
Sausenheim and Neuleiningen	Gaensbusch
Siebeldingen and Albersweiler	Starkenberg
Schweigen	Hasenberg
St. Martin and Edenkoben	Schrausental, Goldmorgen,
	Kastanienbusch
St. Martin and Maikammer	Ueberfeld, Langgaben, Wolfsloch,
	Speilfeld
Ungstein (See under Bad Duerkheim)	
Ungstein and Karlstadt	Kobnert, Huhneracker
Ungstein and Erpolzheim	Schleut, Hang
Wachenheim and Forst	Neuberg, Altenburg
Wollmesheim and Ilbesheim	Voracker
Weyher and Hainfeld	Letten
(See also under Rhodt)	

RHEINGAU DISTRICT

Eltville and Kiedrich	Sandgrub
Eltville and Rauenthal	Steinmaecher, Wagenkehr, Ehr
Eltville and Erbach	Pellet, Huehnerberg
Erbach and Kiedrich	Steinmorgen
Geisenheim and Winkel	Steinacker
Hallgarten and Oetsrich	Deez
Hallgarten and Hattenheim	Deitelsberg, Mehrhoelzchen
Hochheim and Kostheim	Daubhaus
Johannisberg and Winkel	Schlossberg
Lorch and Lorchhausen	Niederflur, Hoehenberg, Wannen
Lorch and Assmannshausen	Honigberg
Mittelheim and Winkel	Oberberg, Neuberg, Gottesthal
Ruedesheim and Eibingen	Haeuserweg, Kiesel

RHINEHESSIA

Albing and Framersheim	Muellerberg
Albing and Alzey	Vorgemaerk
Alsheim and Mettenheim	Goldberg
Armsheim and Ensheim	Kachel
Aspisheim and Horrweiler	Barkheim
Aspisheim and Gensingen	Waschberg
Bechtheim and Osthofen	Woelm
Bodenheim and Laubenheim	Seckergrund
Bosenheim, Pfaffenschwabenheim and Planig	Am Bosberg
Bosenheim and Hackenheim	Am Galgenberg
Buedesheim and Kempten	Treffelsheim
Dalheim and Friesenheim	Altdoerr
Dienheim and Ludwigshoehe	Modern
Dienheim and Guntersblum	Steinberg
Dienheim and Oppenheim	Kroetenbrunnen, Goldberg, Saar
Ebersheim	Im Sand, Sackenborn, Dechenberg, Lochsteig
Flonheim and Uffhofen	Zwergweg, Muehlenpfad, Kirschgarten
Gau-Algesheim and Appenheim	Duennbach, Abley
Gau-Weinheim and Gau-Bickelheim	An der Platte
Gau-Weinheim and Sprendlingen	Geiersberg

Gross-Winternheim and Ober-Ingelheim	Auf dem Haun
Gundheim and Bermersheim	Hohlweg
Hahnheim and Zornheim	Moosberg
Horrweiler and Gensingen	Warschberg
Koengernheim and Friesenheim	Goldgrube
Loerzweiler and Bodenheim	Hohberg
Loerzweiler and Harxheim	Kuechelberg
Nackenheim and Nierstein	Fritzenhoell
Nierstein and Schwabsburg	Domthal, Schnackenberg
Nieder-Engelheim and Ober-Ingelheim	Auf dem Horn
Ockenheim and Gaulsheim	Langgewann
Siefersheim and Wonsheim	Martinsberg
Siefersheim and Neubamberg	Heerkraetz, Eckelsgrund
Siefersheim and Woellstein	Hoellberg
Schwabenheim and Gross-Winternheim	Landgraben
Sprendlingen and Zotzenheim	Arrach, Horn
Sprendlingen and St. Johann	Geiersberg
Wallterheim and Schimsheim	Finkenberg
Wolfsheim and Vendersheim	Sand
Wolfsheim and St. Johann	Traiss

WUERTTEMBERG

Besigheim and Bietigheim	Brachberg
Boennigheim and Kleebronn	Sonnenberg
Boennigheim and Erligheim	Lichtenberg
Fellbach and Untertuerkheim	Simonrot, Goldberg
Fellbach and Rommelshausen	Haldenbach
Heilbronn, Neckarsulm and Binswangen	Weisshalde
Heilbronn, Erlenbach and Binswangen	Knoller
Reutlingen, Eningen and Pfullingen	Georgenberg
Schwaigern, Nordheim and Neipperg	Heuschelberg
Untertuerkheim and Cannstadt	Blick
Tuebingen and Hagëlloch	Wann, Neuhalde
Tuebingen and Weilheim	Neckarhalde
Tuebingen and Unterjesingen	Kreuzberg
Zuffenhausen and Cannstadt	Vogelberg

APPENDIX III

The Viticultural Regions of the Nahe District and important sites

1. LEFT BANK OF THE RIVER NAHE UP TO BAD KREUZNACH:

Martinstein	Burgwingert
Monzingen	Auf der Lay, Auf der Fels, Rosenbaum, Kronenberg
Waldboeckelheim	Koenigsfels, Muehlberg, Welschberg
Schlossboeckelheim	Kupfergrube, Felsenberg, Muehlberg
Niederhausen	Steinberg, Hermannshoehle, Rossel, Rosenheck, Steyer, Hermannsberg
Hueffelheim	Steyer, Guthoelle, Brauneberg, Hipprich
Norheim	Kafels, Hinterfels, Dellchen,
Bad Muenster am Stein	Kirschheck, Oberberg, Schmalberg Rotenfels, Hoell, Felseneck
Bad Kreuznach,	Kausenberg, Kronenberg, Hinkelstein, Forst, Narrenkappe, Brueckes, Steinweg, Kahlenberg, Galgenberg, Kehrenberg, Monau

2. ELLERBACHTAL:

Weinsheim	Kellerberg, Frohnberg, Schafskopf
Mandel	Kranzwingert, Schlossberg, Dellchen, Rosengarten
Ruedesheim	Rosengarten, Wiesberg

3. GRAEFENBACHTAL:

Dalberg	Schlossberg, Wingertsberg
Hergenfeld	Mayen, Herrschaftsacker, Minchrech
Wallhausen	Johannisberg, Pastorenberg, Hahnenbach, Rebsgrund
Braunweiler	Weingarten, Heide
Sommerloch	Steinrossel, Lett Neuberg, Kaul

St. Katharinen	Berg, Heide, Steinig
Gutenberg	Schlossberg, Stein, Heide, Fels, Vogelsgesang
Roxheim	Birkenberg, Muehlenberg, Huettenberg, Neuenberg, Bangert

4. VALLEY OF THE RIVER NAHE UP TO THE ESTUARY OF THE GULDENBACH

Winzenheim	Rosenheck, Honigberg, Metzler
Bretzenheim	Manik, Kronenberg, Vogelsgesang

5. GULDENBACHTAL:

Schoeneberg	Schaefersley, Eichenreis, Hoelle
Schweppenhausen	Steyerberg, Hoelle, Homberg, Hardt
Windesheim	Hoell, Huettenberg, Sonnenmorgen, Hinkelstein, Rosenberg, Roemerberg
Waldhilbersheim	Roedern, Apostelgraben, Butterberg, Kilb
Heddesheim	Kilb, Hipperich, Geisemann, Bommerich, Honigberg, Goldloch, Hoell, Huttenberg, Scharlachberg, Rosenburg, Roernerberg, Sonnenmorgen
Waldlaubersheim	Domberg, Rosenberg, Wingertsberg
Genheim	Genheimer Berg

6. VALLEY OF THE RIVER NAHE UPWARDS TO THE MOUTH OF THE RHINE:

Langenlonsheim	Rotenberg, Borngraben, Rieth, Grems, Sonnenborn, Loehr.
Laubenheim	Karthaeuser, Hoernchen, Loehr, Remicher, Vogelsgesang
Dorsheim	Burgberg, Goldloch, Pittermaennchen, Honigberg
Ruemmelsheim	Honigberg, Hoell, Hirschhorn, Rotenberg
Sarmsheim	Muehlberg

Muenster bei Bingerbrueck	Pittersberg, Kapellenberg, Moenchberg, Dautenpflaenzer
Weiler	Rechte Mueh, In der Lay, Hungerborn
Bingerbrueck	Elisenhoehe, Muehe, Hoernchen

7. VALLEY OF THE NAHE UPWARDS TO THE MOUTH OF THE GLAN:

Becherbach	Rotenberg
Krebsweiler	Dellberg
Meckenbach	Weidentell
Merxheim	Vor der Burg, Aresberg, Hinterberg
Sand, Nauenberg	Kirschroth
Altenberg, Scherendell, Eisendell	Meddersheim
Hohrech, Grub, Kauzenberg	Staudernheim

8. VALLEY OF THE GLAN:

Offenbach	Hinterberg, Hellenbach, Freifrauenloch
Medard	Rattenfels, Goetzennell
Meisenheim	Altenberg, Heimbach
Raumbach	Raumberg, Allenberg
Lauterecken	Schaefersberg, Oberberg
Odenbach	Bornberg, Lettberg
Callbach	Fastenberg, Im Mai, Delbchen
Rehborn	Raumberg, Eschbach, Hahn
Odernheim	Klosterberg, Sonnenberg

9.—THE VALLEY OF THE NAHE UP TO THE MOUTH OF THE ALSENZ:

Durchroth-Oberhausen	Vogelschlag, Kaisersgrund
Ebernburg	Schlossberg, Weidenberg, Erzgrube, Zennerrech

10. THE VALLEY OF THE ALSENZ:

Hochstaetten	Haeuserweg, Glueckerberg
Feil-Bingert	Kahlenberg, Hochstaetterberg
Altenbamberg	Rotenberg, Schlossberg, Treuenfels

11. VALLEY OF THE NAHE RIGHT BANK, UP TO WHERE THE NAHE MEETS THE RHINE:

Hackenheim	Galgenberg, Heide
Bosenheim	Bosenberg, Honigberg
Planig	Frenzenberg, Ried
Ippesheim	Steiler, Baumann
Gensingen	Muelenberg, Kirschberg
Grolsheim	Nauenberg
Dietersheim	Pfingstweide
Buedesheim	Scharlachberg, Steinkautweg, Rosengarten, Rochusberg, Kieselberg
Bingen	Eisel

APPENDIX IV

BADEN, ITS IMPORTANT WINE-GROWING COMMUNITIES AND SITES.

Villages	Sites
KAISERSTUHL	
Achkarren	Schlossberg, Buechsenberg
Bockensol	Halden, Kaefer, Steinhalden
Bischoffingen	Enselberg, Wittlig
Ihringen	Winklerberg, Fohrenberg, Bankenhornsberg, Haeglinsberg, Lilienhof
Oberrottweil	Eichberg, Kirchberg, Henkenberg

ORTENAU, REGION OF BUHL

Ortenberg	Schlossberg
Fessenbach	Sonnenschein, Altenberg
Durbach	Staufenberg, Steinberg
Oberkirch	Wolfhag, Hungerberg
Tiergarten	Schlossberg
Kappelrode	Kappelberg, Hundsberg
Waldulm	Pfarrberg, Russhalde
Sasbachwalden	Burgunder
Neuweier	Mauerberg
Varnhalt-Umweg	Klosterberg
Sinzheim	
Steinbach	

MARKGRAEFLER LAND

Auggen	Letten, Schaef
Britzingen	Lerchenbuehl
Ebringen	Sommerberg
Ehrenstetten	Oelberg
Haegelheim	Sonnenhohle, Jaegerhohle, Gottesacker
Laufen	Altenberg, Weingarten
Muellheim	Reggenhag, Zielberg
Schallstadt	Batzenberg
Staufen	Schlossberg
Sulzberg	Kastelberg
Wolfenweiler	Batzenberg

BREISGAU

Freiburg	Schlossberg, Lorettoberg
Glottertal	Eichberg
Hecklingen	Schlossberg

APPENDIX V POINTS VALUATION FOR THE TESTING OF WINES BY SIGHT, TASTE AND SMELL

Number of	1	2	3	4	5	6	7	8	9
Colour White Wine	Greenish-yellow	golden-yellow	amber yellow						
Red Wine	Garnet-red	golden-ruby	deep red						
Clarity	clear	bright	starbright						
Aroma	volatile	fresh	pure timbre	delicate perfume	strong perfume	fine bouquet	fruity	spicy	exquisite
Quality	agreeable	distinctive	dainty	robust	harmonious	mellow	fine	noble	superb
Sugar	fermented	delicately faintly sweet	nobly sweet						
Acidity	steely	pungent	vinous						
Carbon dioxide (Effervescence)	sparkling	refreshing	well-balanced						
Extract	thin	delicate	smooth	elegant	broad	juicy	oily	powerful	supremely great
Alkohol	weak	strong	heavy						
Age	young	mature	at its peak						

Grading. White Wines :

10-22	normal consumption wines
23-29	good to superior wines
30-42	fine to noble wines
32-48	superb (great) wines

Wines with less than 10 points are not graded

Glossary

(A) TERMS USED WITH SOUND WINES

Abgebaut-Diminished Acidity	The acidity is diminished, and the wines rendered more harmonious.
Aroma—Aroma	Strongly-marked bouquet of grapes.
Art—Character	Fine, fruity, delicate character when there is an absence of obstrusive elements of bouquet and taste.
Artig—Smooth	AMIABLE wine, smooth to the palate (It. amabile), round.
Ausgebaut—Ready for bottling	Seasoned wine, ready for bottling.
Alt oder Firn—Old	The wine has lost its freshness, it no longer contains carbonic acid, harmonious, spirity.
Ausdrucklos	For ordinary table wines of no distinctive character. OR : for undistinctive table wines.
Blassfarbig—Pale	Pink, light coloured red wines; so-called 'Schiller' wines.
Blume—Bouquet	Aroma according to the individual type of grape, e.g. Riesling, Muscatel, Gewuerztraminer, Gutedel, etc.
Blumig—Good Bouquet	
Bukettreich—Rich Bouquet	Generally called 'Bouquet Wines'; Bouquet depends upon strongly-marked characteristics of the kind of grape and develops favourably after bottling.
Brandig—Brandy Taste Spirity	The alcoholic strength of the wine is very conspicuous in contrast with the acid and other flavouring substances, especially in the case of STRONGLY-SUGARED, ordinary wines. Also found with fine wines (1921 vintage).
Brandeln—Brandy Flavour	Taste of brandy or of caramel (colour or sugar) with wines of little body.
Breit—Broad	Neutral wine, without any special character and finesse.

Bodengeschmack—Taste of soil. Soily, Earthy	Strongly-pronounced earthy, peculiar taste which is often unpleasant; Nahe and Moselle wines sometimes show strong earthy flavour.
Duftig—Fragrant	Exquisite, fine bouquet.
Duenn—Thin	Ordinary, little wine, poor in alcohol and extracts.
Edel—Noble, Extra-fine	Fully ripe (over-ripe) exquisite character.
Edelsuesse—Noble Sweetness Extra-fine sweet	Great natural sweetness in fine and noble wines.
Elegant—Elegant	Very pleasing wine.
Erdig—Earthy, soily	
Fad—Insipid	Wine lacking in extract, body and freshness.
Fett—(lit.) Fat	Full wine with considerable extract and glycerine content.
Feurig—Fiery	Red wine, not a description of the colour but indicating a high content of alcohol ana a fine, mellow character. (Bordeaux and Burgundy wines.)
Finesse—Finesse	Amiable, harmonious, fine type of wine.
Flach—Flat	With no outstanding characteristic.
Fluechtig—Short	
Fuelle—Richness	Ripeness showing harmoniously in the case of noble wines.
Frish—Refreshing	Sound wines with plenty of acidity; carbonic acid may also be present.
Fruchtig—Fruity	Fine-fruity flavour, e.g. peach, strawberry, raspberry.
Gefaellig—Pleasing	All qualities of bouquet and taste are perfectly balanced in this harmonious wine.
Gross—Great	Wine showing a beautiful and harmonious combination of all the fine qualities.
Gezuckert—Sugared (Verbessert) Improved	Wine with sweet bouquet and flavour, mixed with *sugar,* either dry or in a watery solution; as opposed to unsugared or NATURAL wines.
Glatt—Smooth	Equivalent to palatable; pleasant wine without fault.
Gruen—Green	Too young.

Gut—Good	Clean wine, satisfactory in colour, bouquet and taste.
Harmonisch—Harmonious	A completely harmonious combination of all the elements of flavour and aroma.
Hart or Fest—Hard or firm	Acids or tannic elements stand out in high relief (particularly noticeable with ordinary natural wines).
Herb—Bitter	*Tannin* stands out too strongly in high relief above all the rest.
Honigartig—Honey Type Flavour	Aroma and flavour of honey as experienced with best wines prepared from selected grapes.
Huebsch—Nice	Delicate, fine type of wine.
Jung—Young wine, New	An UNMATURED wine which contains a good deal of carbonic acid.
Kernig—Robust	The acids are strongly pronounced, but balanced with alcohol and without unpleasant qualities.
Koerper—Body	Wines with high extract content and of pleasant richness and type.
Koerperarm—Poor in body	The above qualities are not very noticeable.
Kraeftig	Rich in body and alcohol.
Kurz—Short	Aroma and flavour not very noticeable.
Lebendig—Racy	Wine with fresh, pleasant aroma and taste.
Leer—Thin	Water content is high in comparison with flavouring elements; wine is thin, has little taste and is relatively unattractive.
Lieblich—Pleasantly mild	Wine of somewhat light but fine pleasant character.
Mager—Thin : Bodiless	Wine poor in extract, thin; deriving from badly-manured vineyards, or poor soil.
Mandel Bitter—Bitter Almonds Flavour	Reminiscent in flavour and aroma of BITTER ALMONDS. With extra-fine wines often stands out in high relief and is much esteemed. (Ruppertsberger Mandelacker).

Matt—Flat : Insipid	Wine possesses no freshness.
Moussierend—Sparkling	Carbonic acid content is very high. (Not popular with wines, but with Champagne, imperative).
Mundend—Tasty	Nice on the palate.
Naturwein	Natural, not sweetened.
Nervig—Full-bodied	Vigorous, racy, full-bodied wines with a steel tang.
Oelig—Oily	Wine with high alcohol and glycerine content, like oil flowing into a glass.
Rassig—Racy	Elements of aroma and taste are strongly noticeable, but are not obtrusive.
Reif—Ripe	Wine from good, sound, FULLY-RIPE grapes, hence possessing a delicious sweetness.
Reintoenig—Well-balanced	Thoroughly satisfactory wine manifesting complete equilibrium among elements of aroma and taste.
Rein—Clean	Free from all unpleasant ingredients, with clear aroma and taste; can be used for both, unsugared or natural wines.
Rund—Round	Harmonious, beautiful, rounded off wine.
Saftig—Juicy	Wine rich in alcohol and extract content with lovely, pleasant acid and individual character of grape type.
Sauber—Clean	Pure wine without any unpleasant taste.
Schal—Musty	Wine which has lost its freshness, and contains no carbonic acid.
Schoen–Harmonious Balance Harmonious Combination	When aroma and taste elements form a harmonious combination in the wine.
Schwer—Heavy	Wine which lies equally heavy on tongue and palate.
Spiel—Play	Fineness of the substances producing aroma and taste.
Spitz—Thin	Wine which the palate feels to be thin and deteriorating.
Spritzig—Effervescent	Wines with fairly high carbonic acid content which, however, should not be

felt as unpleasant. Carbonic acid content is desirable with Moselle-, Saar- and Ruwer-Wines.

Suffig—Tasty   Fresh, palatable wine.

Suesse—Sweetness

Stark—Strong   Vigorous wines rich in alcohol.

Stahlig—Steely   Strong, typically tasting of metal, but pleasant in their own way.

Stumpf—Lifeless

Trocken—Dry   High *total-acid* content, dry and exhausted taste; in testing it the teeth become 'numbed'.

Unharmonisch—Unharmonious   There is no general harmony among the various qualities, e.g. acid, tannin, or alcohol stands out in high relief.

Vanillen-Geschmack—Vanilla Taste   Aroma and taste of vanilla found with many fine wines.

Verbessert—Improved   Sweetened wines.

Verschlagen   Shortly after racking, the wine tastes 'naked'; also after filtration and bottling. After storage from 4-6 weeks, the wine recovers.

Voll—Full   Opposite to thin and watery; wine shows a somewhat high percentage of alcohol, also wines which possess an *extract above the average*.

Vornehm—Exquisite   Strongly-marked aroma and taste besides mellow maturity.

Weich—Soft   Poor in acid and alcohol content.

Weinig—Vinous   All good qualities of a wine must harmonize.

Wuerzig—Spicy   Wines whose grape is strongly pronounced. Typical taste of Riesling, M u s c a t e l, Gewuertztraminer, etc., grapes.

(B) *TERMS USED WITH UNSOUND WINES*

Bissig—Biting   Too strongly pronounced sharp *acid* and tannin content.

Bitter—Bitter	Reminiscent of taste of *bitter almonds*, especially during warm years; also strong tannin content produces an intense bitterness; found with red wines which have been infected by the Bitter Fungus (Bitterpilz).
Boeckser—Taste of Rotten Eggs	Wines with high sulphuretted water-content. Distinctions are made between sulphur-, yeast-, dung- and soil-taste of rotten eggs. With too strong a sulphur admixture, a taste of rotten eggs ensues upon sulphurizing grapes by means of sulphur powder against grape mould (oidium).
Bruch—Turbidity	A distinction is made between white and black turbidity; diseased transformation by the excretion of iron resulting in milky up to blackish turbidity.
Essigstich—Vinegar Flavour	Acetic acid in wine makes its presence strongly felt.
Faul, Faeulzig—Rotten	Wines from grapes attacked by the 'Rohfaeule' (raw-rot), partly evil-smelling, partly tasting of drugs; difficult to remedy. (1922 vintage and some 1950).
Filtrier-Geschmack—Filter Taste	Wines which have been freshly filtered show a definite 'Asbestos taste' generally diminishing after being stored for some time.
Flaschenkrank—Bottle Sickness	After bottling, some wines taste 'naked' or thin, and cannot be tasted. After keeping for some time (4-6 weeks) the essential nature and bouquet reappear, the thin taste disappearing.
Firn—Madeirish	Special taste and colour after maturation if too much advanced; wines which taste very old and exhausted.
Frostgeschmack—Frosty Flavour	Unpleasant taste caused by *frost* which deeply affects grapes in the autumn; wine from unripe grapes also shows similar flavour.

Hart, Fest—Hard, Firm	Wine with high unpleasant content of acid, also wine with slight vinegar flavour.
Holzgeschmack—Taste of Woody	Wines which have been stored for a considerable time in new casks not thoroughly seasoned, or old casks not thoroughly cleaned.
Hefegeschmack—Taste of Yeast	The wine smells and tastes of yeast and the decomposition agents of yeast through lying too long on the yeast without racking in time.
Kahmig—Ropy	Wines with mould fungus resulting in cloudiness; disease caused through negligent treatment, more especially through storage in casks which are not full.
Karbol-Geschmack—Taste of Carbolic-Acid	Wines deriving from vineyards freshly impregnated with carbolic acid.
Kerngeschmack—Grape-stone Flavour	White wine with flavour of *grape-stones* through having been left too long on the mash.
Kochgeschmack—Flavour of Cooking	Obtrusive taste caused by the over-heating of wine (Pasteurisation) i.e., above 140°F. when feeding with air.
Kreosol-Geschmack—Creosol Flavour	Caused by freshly creosoled vineyard-props whose taste has penetrated into the grapes. Props have not been aired long enough.
Kratzig—Prickly, Bubbly	Wines with high acetic acid and strong sulphur dioxide content.
Lackgeschmack—Taste of Varnish	Wines whose 'must' has come into contact with wine-press glazing varnish which was insufficiently acid-proof; caused also by inadequate equipment of wine-press and insufficient cleaning tools.
Luftgeschmack—Air Flavour	Wines which have been in contact with the air for some considerable time; unpleasant taste which is also observable in unmatured wines that are rich in extract and have been prepared partly from rotten grapes.

Mauseln—Smell of Mouse Urine	Recognizable smell and taste (remains suspended on the palate) when the addition of chemicals is suspected.
Metall-Geschmack—Metallic Taste	This taste which is unpleasant and disharmonious, is reminiscent of iron or zinc. It is caused by the use of badly zinced cleaning tools and carelessly treated cask doors. (Manhole doors).
Pechgeschmack—Taste of Tar	Bitter taste of pitch or tar. Wines possess this unpleasant flavour when they have lain for some time in improperly-treated re-built casks previously used for the storage of beer.
	Wines from vineyards lying near freshly tarred roads are imbued with a taste of tar.
	Wines from vineyards near basalt works where stone chips and tar are mixed at the dumping place, resulting in an abominable taste of pitch and tar in the wines from such vineyards.
Petroleum-Gaschmack— Taste of Petroleum	Wines tasting and smelling of mineral oil or petroleum as a result of incautious and careless handling of petroleum.
Rahn oder Rohnig— White Wine, turning tawny or Red	Full, oily wines with the admission of air, which are not yet ready for bottling turn high-coloured to brown-red with an unpleasant, sickly taste. The fault is remedied by suitable treatment. There is a saying on the Moselle : 'The wine is getting "red hair".'
Rapsig—Stalky Taste	Wines whose unfermented juice has stood too long in grape-vats, become bitter and taste of grape-stones, grape-skins and grapestalks (too much tannin).
Rappen oder Huelsen-Geschmack— Pod Taste	Occurs when grape-skins have come into close contact with the air; the wines show an unripe, grassy unpleasant taste reminiscent of green grape stalks.

Rauh—Raw, Rough	Rough, unpleasant after-taste.
Sackgeschmack—Taste of Sacks	Unpleasant *taste of cloth* resulting from the use of insufficiently treated and cleaned filter bags. Cloudiness and yeast arise in the process of filtration.
Scharf—Fermentative	Fairly ordinary wines with too much carbonic acid become fermentative. Also wines with unfermented sugar-content go through a *secondary fermentation* process.
Schimmelig—Mouldy, Musty	The wine smells *mouldy*. Besides this, the unpleasant taste of unseasoned wine, caused by the decomposition of mould fungi in the cask used.
Spritzig—Effervescent	
Korken-Geschmack—Corky	Musty, mouldy, unpleasant odour and taste of old tannin-bark caused by the employment of poor quality corks. This peculiar taste occurs also with individual *corks* in spite of taking the best materials.
Stichig—Turning Sour	Acetic acid in wine makes itself very noticeable. Wines with volatile-acid content can be used only for the preparation of vinegar; Low volatile-acid content can be checked by filtering through a sterilizing filter or by pasteurization. But even with 0.8-0.10 grammes per litre the sour quality (stich) is so pronounced with ordinary and medium wines that they may be said to be *spoilt*. With fine wines, which often show a much higher percentage of volatile acid, this is a disadvantage only when it affects the taste. This seldom occurs since the high sugar percentage conceals the acid.
Ueberschwefelt—Too much Sulphur	
Unrein—Unclean	

Unsauber—Dirty, with Unpleasant secondary Flavour	Defective, sickly odour and taste unsuitable treatment; wines which have lain in cellars in which meat, cheese, potatoes, etc., are kept, assume this unpleasant taste because odourous subtance make the wine unpalatable by penetrating the cask pores.
Weisser Bruch—White Turbidity	Clouding, partly milky, partly bluish in appearance. The heavy ingress of *air* results in the secretion of Phosphate or iron, which in its turn causes clouding.
Zaeh—Ropy	The wine flows like oil on being poured out and turns at once slimy or thick. Aroma and taste of the wine are covered up.

APPENDIX VII

Appraisement of Vintages in regard to quality for the last hundred years

Year	Inferior	Medium	Good	Excellent
1850	inferior	—	—	—
1851	inferior	—	—	—
1852	—	medium	—	—
1853	inferior	—	—	—
1854	—	medium	—	—
1855	—	medium	—	—
1856	inferior	—	—	—
1857	—	—	good	—
1858	—	—	good to excellent	
1859	—	—	—	excellent
1860	inferior	—	—	—
1861	—	—	—	excellent
1862	—	—	good to excellent	
1863	inferior	—	—	—
1865	—	—	—	excellent
1864	inferior	—	—	—
1866	inferior	—	—	—
1867	inferior	—	—	—
1868	—	—	good to excellent	
1869	—	—	—	excellent
1870	—	—	good	—
1871	inferior	—	—	—
1872	—	medium	—	—
1873	inferior	—	—	—
1874	—	—	—	excellent
1875	—	—	—	excellent
1876	—	—	good	—
1877	inferior	—	—	—
1878	inferior	—	—	—
1879	inferior	—	—	—
1880	—	medium	—	—
1881	—	—	—	excellent
1882	inferior	—	—	—
1883	—	—	good	—
1884	—	medium	—	—
1885	—	medium	—	—
1886	—	—	—	excellent

Year				
1887	—	—	—	—
1888	inferior	—	—	—
1889	—	—	good	—
1890	—	medium	—	—
1891	inferior	—	—	—
1892	—	—	good to excellent	—
1893	—	—	—	excellent
1894	inferior	—	—	—
1895	—	medium	—	—
1896	inferior	—	—	—
1897	—	—	good	—
1898	inferior	—	—	—
1899	—	medium	—	—
1900	—	—	good	—
1901	inferior	—	—	—
1902	inferior	—	—	—
1903	inferior	—	—	—
1904	—	—	good	—
1905	—	—	good	—
1906	inferior	—	—	—
1907	inferior	—	—	—
1907	—	medium	—	—
1908	—	medium	—	—
1909	inferior	—	—	—
1910	inferior	—	—	—
1911	—	—	—	excellent
1912	inferior	—	—	—
1913	inferior	—	—	—
1914	—	medium	—	—
1915	—	—	good	—
1916	inferior	—	—	—
1917	—	—	good	—
1918	inferior	—	—	—
1919	—	medium	—	—
1920	—	—	good	—
1921	—	—	—	excellent
1922	inferior	—	—	—
1923	inferior	—	—	—
1924	—	medium	—	—
1925	—	medium	—	—
1926	inferior	—	—	—
1927	—	medium	—	—
1928	—	medium	—	—

1929	—	—	good	—
1930	inferior	—	—	—
1931	inferior	—	—	—
1932	inferior	—	—	—
1933	—	—	good	—
1934	—	—	—	excellent
1935	—	—	good	—
1936	inferior	—	—	—
1937	—	—	—	excellent
1938	—	medium	—	—
1939	inferior	—	—	—
1940	—	medium	—	—
1941	inferior	—	—	—
1942	—	—	good	—
1943	—	—	good	—
1944	—	medium	—	—
1945	—	—	good to excellent	
1946	—	medium to good		
1947	—	—	good to excellent	
1948	—	—	good	
1949	—	—	good to excellent	
1950	inferior to medium			
1951	inferior			

APPENDIX VIII. *RHINEHESSIAN COMMUNITIES AND THEIR BEST-KNOWN SITES.*

Alsheim	Hahl, Karstweg, Brechtel, Sandhohle, Steinland, Goldberg, Zehnmorgen, Hammel, Rust, Wahlheimerweg, Pappen, Brandehof.
Bechtheim	Geiersberg, Gotteshilfe, Stein, Sarken, Berg, Bende, Bruhlhecke, Kehlmitte, Schild, Karweg, Wolm, Dankental, Haferberg (White Wine). Wolfau, Lowenberg (Red Wine).
Bingen-Stadt :	Schlossberg, Eisel, Schwaetzerchen, and Morsfeld, Rochusberg and Rochusweg, Hungerborn & Rosengarten, Mainzerweg with Rheinberg, Ohligberg, Mittelpfad and Kalbskopf.
Bingen-Kempten :	Kempter Berg, with Gaensberg, Schnack, Wolfskraut, Pfarrgarten, Kapellenberg; Grosse Lies, with Hofwingert, Mauer, Treffelsheim and Moerdershoelle. Hagelkreuz (Red Wine).
Bodenheim :	Westrum, Hoch, Kahlenberg, Ebersberg, Leistenberg, Silberberg, Bock, Braunloch, Burgweg, Hasenmaul, Neuberg.
Dienheim :	Goldberg, Krotenbrunnen, Langweg, Neuweg, Ebenbreit, Bank, Guldenmorgen, Falkenberg, Steig, Gumben, Rosswiese, Kandelweg, Tafelstein, Geierscheid, Mittelweg, Sohlbrunnen, Silzbrunnen, Hahlen, Grasweg, Brunnen, Ganzgrub, Saar.
Gau Bickelheim :	Neuberg, Goldberg, Steinweg, Kapelle, Frohngewann, Fels, Innerst.

Guntersblum :

(White Wines) :
Rost, Kehl, Autental, Wohnweg,
Himmeltal, Kachelberg, M u h l,
Bornpfad, Erbsenbrunnen, Steig,
Gansweide, Oppenheimer Weg,
Eiserne Hand, Vogelsgarten, Stein-
berg, Enggass, Hasenweg, Schoger-
hohl, Sand, Herrengarten;
(Red Wines) :
Hellebaum, Spiegel, Driessigmor-
gen, Reiseberg, Wahlheimergewann.

Laubenheim :

Hitz, Dammsberg, Steig Burg, Edelmann, Seckergrund, Ay, Kalkofen,
Neuberg, Steinerne Brucke, Johannisberg, K l i n k e, Laubenheimer
Hauschen, Heyl.

Mainz :

Michelsberg.

Nierstein :

Glock, Auflangen, Pettental, Hip-
ping, Fuchsloch, Rehbach, Domtal,
Orbel, Heiligenbaum, Findling,
Weissenberg, Rohr, Schlangenberg,
Pfuhlweg, Olberg, Streng, Kranz-
berg, Vockenberg, Flaeschenhahl,
Kehr, Rehbacher Steig, Brudersberg,
Floss, Schmitt, Spielberg, Rehbach,
Spielberg, Unter-Rehbach, Am Hin-
kelstein, Fritzenholl, Mundelpfad.

Oppenheim :

Kreuz, Herrnberg, Steig, Sacktrae-
ger, Goldberg, Kugel, Kroetenbrunnen, Reisekahr, Zuckerberg, Schlossberg, Daubhaus, Kehr, Kette.

Worms :

Liebfrauenstift, Katterloch, Lugins-
land.

178

APPENDIX IX.

*SITE NAMES, THEIR MEANING AND THEIR LOCATION**

Abtei	Abbey	Wehlen (M)
		Graach (M)
Abtsberg	Abbot's hill	Graach (M)
Achtmorgen	Eight-acre	Ruppertsberg (P)
Altar	Altar	Uerzig (M)
Altbaum	Old tree	Geisenheim (R)
Altenberg	Old Hill	Canzem (Saar)
Amorpfad	Lover's Lane	Berncastel (M)?
Altenberg	Old Castle	Wachenheim (P)
Annaberg	Anna-hill	Schweich (M)
		Duerckheim (P)
Auflangen	?	Nierstein (R-H)
Baethel	Little Brook	Wachenheim (P)
Badstube	Bath-room (roman bath)	Berncastel (M)
Baiken	?	Rauenthal (R)
Baumberg	Tree-hill	Aldegund (M)
Berg	Hill	Rudesheim (R)
Biengarten	Bee-garden	Senheim (M)
		Mesenich (M)
Bischofsberg	Bishop's hill	Ruedesheim (R)
Bistum	Diocese	Graach (M)
Bockstein	Buck's Rock	Ockfen (Saar)
Bohlig	Hill	Wachenheim (P)
Bratenhoefchen	?	Berncastel (M)
Braunhals	Brown neck	Wiltingen (Saar)
Bruderschaft	Fraternity	Cluesserath (M)
Brunnen	Fountain, well	Ruedesheim (R)
Burgweg	Castle road	Bodenheim (RH)
		Ruedesheim (R)
Calmont	Hot hill	Eller (M)
		Bremm (M)
Camp	Field	Waldrach
Chor	Choir	Uerzig (M)
Claus	Hermitage	Johannisberg (R)
Clemensberg	Clemens-hill	Trittenheim (M)
Dachsberg	Badger-hill	Winkel (R)
Daubhaus	House where staves were kept	Hochheim (R)
Decker	?	Ruedesheim (R)
Deez	dialect for head, top	Oestrich (R)

* R—Rheingau, RH—Rhinehessia, M—Moselle, P—Palatinate.

Dickerstein	Large rock	Ruedesheim (R)
Doktor	Doctor	Berncastel (M)
		Dexheim (RH)
Dhron Hofberger	Dhron Manor hill	Dhron (M)
Doktorberg	Doctor hill	Hauerstein (MR)
Domdechanei	Deanery of a Cathedral	Hochheim (R)
Domprobst	Provost of the Cathedral	Graach (M)
Domtal	Valley of the cathedral	Nierstein (RH)
Engerweg	Narrow path	Ruedesheim (R)
Engelsberg	Angels hill	Zeltingen (M)
Engelsgrube	Angels quarry or hollow	Neumagen (M)
Erntebringer	Harvest-bringer	Johannisberg (R)
Erzgrube	Ore-quarry	Ebernburg (N)
Eulenberg	Owls hill	Kinheim (M)
Falkenberg	Falcon hill	Trittenheim (M)
		Berncastel (M)
Felsenberg	Rocky hill	Schloss Boeckelheim (Nahe)
Feuerberg	Fire hill	Ediger (M)
		Duerckheim (P)
Flecht	Flat area, plain	Ruedesheim- Eibingen (R)
Freundstuck	Friends' section	Forst (P)
Frauenberg	Our Lady's hill	Neef (M)
Fritzenhoelle	Fred's hell	Nierstein (RH)
Frohnhof	Manor, Landlord's place	Duerckheim (P)
Frohewelt	Gay world	Graach (M)
Fruhenberg	Early hill	Hallgarten (R)
Funkelshoelle	Glittering hell	Reil (M)
Gaisboehl	Goat hill	Ruppertsberg (P)
Galgenberg	Gallows hill	Kreuznach (Nahe)
Geiersbuhl	Vulture hill	Nierstein (RH)
Gehrn	?	Rauenthal (R)
Geierskopf	Summit of Vulture hill (Vulture's head)	Wintrich (M)
Geierstein	Vulture-rock	Rauenthal (R)
Gerumpel	Rubbish dump	Wachenheim (P)
Goldberg	Gold hill	Oppenheim (RH)
Goldbaechel	Little gold brook	Wachenheim (P)
Goldgruebchen	Little gold quarry or Little gold trench	Mesenich (M)

Goldtroepfchen	Little golden drops	Piesport (M)
Goldwingert	Gold vineyard	Graach (M)
Gottesfuss	God's foot	Wiltingen (Saar)
Gottestal	God's valley	Oestrich (R)
Graben	Trench	Berncastel (M)
Graefenberg	Count's Hill	Kiedrich (R)
Grain	?	Deidesheim (P)
Grauberg	Grey hill	Uerzig (M)
Grunhauser	Green house	St. Maximin (Ruwer)
Guldenmorgen	Gold acre or Florin acre	Dienheim (RH) Uerzig (M)
Im Hahnen	at (near) the cocks	
Hahnenboehl	Cock's hill	Forst (P)
Haeschen	Little hare	Dhron, Kroev (M)
Haeuserweg	House road	Ruedesheim (R)
Hamm	Hook, Arc	Boppard (MR)
Hasenlaeufer	Hare run	Brauneberg (M)
Hasensprung	Hare jump or Hare fountain	Winkel (R)
Heiligenbaum	Holy tree	Nierstein (RH)
Heisslay	Hot slate rock	Kroev (M)
Heisser Stein	Hot rock	Reil (M)
Herrenberg	The lord's or master's hill	Wawern (Saar) Ayl (Saar) Enkirch (M) Lomguich (M) Oppenheim (RH)
Herrgottsacker	Our Lord's field	Deidesheim (P)
Herzchen	Little heart	Briedel (M)
Himmelreich	Heaven	Graach Zeltingen (M)
Hinkelstein	Hen stone	Nierstein (RH)
Hinterhaus	Rear house	Rüdesheim (R)
Hipping	?	Nierstein (RH)
Hochberg	High hill	Graach (M)
Hochmess	High Mass	Durckheim (P)
Hoheburg	High castle	Ruppertsberg (P)
Hohenmorgen	High acre	Deidesheim (P)
Hoelle	Hell, "Hot as hell"	Kroev (M) Alf (M) Johannisberg (R) Hofheim (P)
Hoellenpfad	Hell path	Roxheim (RH)
Hofstueck	Manor's section	Deidesheim (P)
Hofberg	Manor hill	Dhron (M)
Honigberg	Honey hill	Erbach (R)
Honigsack	Honey bag	Maring (M)

Jesuitengarten	Jesuits' garden	Forst (P)
Johannisberg	St. John's hill	Muelheim, Bruttig (M)
Jungfer	Maiden	Hallgarten (R)
Juffer	Maiden	Brauneberg (M)
Kalbsflicht	Calf-plain?	Eltville (R)
Kalkofen	Lime kiln	Deidesheim (P)
Kapelle	Chapel	Lorch (R)
Kapellenberg	Chapel hill	Clotten, Pommern (M)
Karthauserhofberg	Carthusians' hill	Eitelsbach (Ruwer)
Katharinenbild	St. Catherine's picture	Deidesheim (P)
Kellerberg	Cellar hill	Oestrich (R)
Kieselberg	Pebble hill	Deidesheim (R)
Kirchenpfad	Church path	Zeltingen (M)
Kirchenrain	Church meadow	Senheim (M)
Kirchenrech	Church slope	Senheim (M)
Kirchenstueck	Church section	Forst (P)
Kirchlay	Church slate rock	Graach, Osann (M)
Klosterberg	Convent hill	many
Klostergarten	Convent garden	Leiwen (M)
		Oestrich (R)
Klosterlay	Convent slate hill	Wehlen (M)
Kranklay		Uerzig (M)
Kranzberg	Wreath hill	Nierstein (RH)
Kreuzberg	Crucifix hill	Hallgarten (R)
Kreuzwingert	Crucifix vineyard	Uerzig (M)
Kroetenbrunnen	Toad fountain	Oppenheim (RH)
Krone	Crown	Lorch (R)
Kronenberg	Crown hill	Kreuznach (Nahe)
Kunk	Shell, Valley	Wittlich (M)
Kupfergrube	Copper quarry	Schloss Bockelheim (Nahe)
Kupp	Hilltop, summit	Wiltingen (Saar)
Koenigswingert	King's vineyard	Wachenheim (P)
Langenacker	Long field	Forst (P)
Langenboehl	Long hill	Forst (P)
Langenmorgen	Long acre	Forst and
Langenstueck	Long piece or section	Deidesheim (P)
Laudamusberg	'Let us praise' —hill	Neumagen (M)
Laurentiusberg	St. Lawrence's hill	Rauenthal (R)
Laurentiuslay	St. Laurence slate hill	Trittenheim (M)
Lay	Slate rock	Leiwen (M)
Leinhoehle	Linen cave???	Berncastel (M)
Lenchen	Tenants piece	Deidesheim (P)
	Little Magdalen or	Oestrich (R)

13

Lilienpfad	Lily path	Graach (M)
Lorenzberg	St. Laurence hill	Casel (Ruwer)
Lump	Rascal	Eschendorf (Franconia)
Magdalenengarten	Magdalen's garden	Oestrich (R)
Mandelberg	Almond hill	
Mandelgraben	Almond garden	Brauneberg (M)
Mannberg	Man hill	Hattenheim (R)
Marcobrunn	St. Mark's fountain	Erbach (R)
Matheisbildchen	St. Mathew's picture	Berncastel (M)
Mauerchen	Little wall	Geisenheim (R)
Maushoehle	Mouse hole	Deidesheim (P)
Maxberg,	Maximin's hill	Uerzig (M)
Maximinsberg		
Maximin	Maximin	Ruwer
Maximin Gruenhaeuse.	Maximin green house	Mertesdorf (M)
Mehrhoelzchen	Mare's wood?	Hallgarten (R)
Messwingert	High mass vineyard	Rauenthal (R)
Michelsberg	Michael's hill	Bad Duerckheim (P)
		Cluesserath (M)
		Eller (M)
Michelsripp	?	Uerzig (M)
Monteneubel	Noble hill	Enkirch (M)
Muehlweg	Mill way	Koenigsbach (P)
Munzlay	Mint slate rocks	Graach (M)
Nacktarsch	Nude bottom	Kroev (M)
Neuberg	New hill	Forst (P)
Neufeld	New field	Hallgarten (R)
Neustueck	New section	Wachenheim (P)
Niederberg	Lower hill	Lieser (M)
Nieschen	Little Agnes	Casel (Ruwer)
St. Nikolauslay	St. Nicolas Slate hill	Graach (M)
Nonnenberg	Nuns' hill	Wehlen (M)
		Rauenthal (R)
Nonnenlay	Nuns' slate rock	Brauneberger (M)
Nussberg	Nut hill	Zell (M)
Nussbrunnen	Nut fountain	Hattenheim (R)
Oberberg	Upper hill	Winkel (R)
Ohligsberg	Oil hill	Leiwen (M)
		Wintrich (M)
Ohligswingert	Oil vineyard	Waldrach
Orbel	?	Nierstein (RH)
Palmberg	Palm hill	Walwig, Bruttig (M)
Palmenberg	Palm hill	Aldegund (M)
Paradies	Paradise	Kroev (M)
Petrus	St. Peter	Graach (M)
Pechstein	Pitch stone	Forst (P)

Pettental	?	Nierstein (RH)
Pfaffenberg	Parson's hill	Hattenheim (R)
Pfalzgraben	?	Rauenthal (R)
		Berncastel, Eiger (M)
		Berncastel (M)
Pichter	'Petitura' Common	Longuich (M)
		Forst (P)
Pomerell	Apple-orchard	Zell
Praelat	Prelate	Erden, Pommern (M)
Probstberg	Provost hill	Longuich (M)
Rauchloch	Smoke hole	Hochheim (R)
Rehbacher Steig	Little Bridge across the Reh brook	Nierstein (RH)
Reiterpfad	Riders' path	Ruppertsberg (P)
Rheinhell	Rhine hell or Rhine clear ?	Erbach (R)
Ritterpfad	Knights' path	Wawern (Saar)
Rochusweg	St. Rochus' path	Bingen (RH)
Roemerpfad	Roman's path	Maring (M)
Rosenberg	Rose hill	Berncastel, Wehlen (M)
Rosengarten	Rose garden	Kreuznach (Nahe)
Rosengaertchen	Little rose garden	Neumagen (M)
Rosenkranz	Rose wreath	Uerzig (M)
Rotenberg	Red hill	Geisenheim (R)
		Nackenheim (RH)
Rotert	Red soil	Dhron (M)
Rotkirch	Red church	Erden (M)
Rotlay	Red slate rock	Zeltingen (M)
Rottland	Red or roded land	Ruedesheim (R)
Sandgrub	Sand quarry	Kiedrich (R)
Saengerei	Choir	Dhron (M)
Schafboehl	Sheep hill	Deidesheim (P)
Scharlachberg	Scarlet hill	Bingen-Buedesheim (Nahe)
Scharzberg Scharzhofberg		Wiltingen (Saar)
Schlangenwingert	Snake vineyard	Longuich (M)
Schwanen	Swans	Berncastel (M)
Schwarze Katz	Black cat	Zell (M)
Schwarzlay	Black slate rock	Uerzig, Zeltingen (M)
Schenkenboehl	?	Wachenheim (P)
Schlossberg	Castle hill	Ebernburg (Nahe)
		Nierstein (RH)
		Lieser (M)
Schoenhell	Beautiful 'hell' or beautifully hot	Hallgarten (R)

Sechsmorgen	Sox Acre	Forst (P)
Siebenmorgen	Seven acre	Rauenthal (R)
Siegelsberg	Seal hill	Erbach (R)
Spielberg	Games hill	Bad Duerckheim (P)
Soehnchen	Sonny	Oestrich (R)
Sonnenberg	Sunny hill	Canzem (Saar)
		Eltville (R)
Sonnseite	Sunny side	Wintrich (M)
		Bremm (M)
Sonnteil	Sun section	Trittenheim (M)
Sonnenuhr	Sun dial	Wehlen,
		Zeltingen (M)
Spitzenlehn	?	Geisenheim (R)
Steeg	Path or bridge	Kiedrich (R)
Steffensberg	St. Stephen's hill	Enkirch (M)
		Kroev (M)
Stephansberg	St. Stephen's hill	Zeltingen (M)
Stein	Stone	Hochheim (R)
Steinberg	Stone hill	Hattenheim (R)
Steinmorgen	Stone acre	Erbach (R)
Strasse	Street	Forst (P)
Taubenberg	Pidgeon hill	Casel (M)
Taubengarten	Pidgeon garden	Piesport (M)
Thomasberg	Thomas hill	Uerzig (M)
Treppchen	Little stairs	Erden (M)
Turmberg	Tower hill	Kiedrich (R)
Uhlen	Owls	Winningen (M)
Ungeheuer	Monster	Forst (P)
Unterberg	Lower hill	Canzem (Saar)
Urglueck	Uer-zig bliss	Uerzig (M)
Urlay	Ur-erzig Slate rock	Uerzig (M)
Vogelsang	Bird song	Serrig (Saar)
		Bremm (M)
Weiher	Pond	Hochheim (R)
Weg	Way	Oestrich (R)
		Hallgarten (R)
Weinbach	Wine brook	Deidesheim (P)
Weissenstein	White stone	Kues (M)
Wieshell	?	Rauenthal (R)
Wiesberg	?	Rauenthal (R)
Willborn	Deer fountain	Hattenheim (R)
Wolfsberg	Wolf hill	Kanzem (Saar)
Wolfsdarm	Wolfs' intestine	Wachenheim (P)

Wuelfen	Wolves	Rauenthal (R)
Imwuesten	Wilderness	Uerzig (M)
Wuerzgarten	Herb garden	Uerzig (M)
		Hallgarten (R)
Zederberg	Cedar hill	Trier (M)
Zeppwingert	Summit-vineyard	Enkirch (M)

ACKNOWLEDGEMENT TO PHOTOGRAPHERS

10, 11, 12, 13, 14, 15, 16, 17, 19, 20, 23, 27, 28, 29, 30, 33, 49, 50, 53, 55, 59, 62, 65, 70, 78, 79, 80, 81, 84, 85, 86, Dr. Wolff & Tritschler, Frankfurt am Main ; 8, 18, 24, 25, 35, 36, 37, 56, 58, 61, 64, 90, 91, Photo-Graphik, G.m.b.H., Wiesbaden ; 68, 72, 73, 89, Photo-Zentrale Knippenberg, Bacharach a.Rh. ; 87, 88, Fotohaus Groote, Bad Duerckheim ; 54, 82, 83, Walter Frentz, Esslingen ; 57, 66, 67, 69, 75, 76, Cramers Kunstanstalt K.G., Dortmund ; 2, 3, 4, 6, 9, 21, 26, 31, 32, 34, 43, 44, 45, 46, 48, 51, 52, 71, Foto-Gerspach, Neustadt a.d. Weinstr ; 1, 5, 7, 22, 38, 47, 60, Herrn. Jung, Frankfurt.

WORKS OF REFERENCE

The following is a list of the books from which the writer has quoted, or which he has consulted.

Allen:
The Romance of Wine   London 1931.

Bassermann-Jordan:
Die Geschichte des Weinbaus   Frankfurt 1923.
Das Weinmuseum etc., zu Speyer am Rhein   Speyer 1947.
Der Weinbau der Pfalz im Altertum   Speyer 1947.

Berlet:
Pfalz und Wein   Neustadt 1928.

Bewerunge:
Deutscher Wein an Donau und Rhein

Binding:
Moselfahrt aus Liebeskummer.   Potsdam 1941.

Christoffel:
Trost u. Weisheit des Weines   Heidelberg 1949.
Rebe und Wein in Goethes Weltbild   Heidelberg 1948.

Deichmann:
Weinchronik   Berlin 1950.

Deutsche Weinzeitung:
(Periodical, Mainz)
Von der Traube bis zur Flaschenfullung   Mainz 1950.

Engel:
Die Weinbehandlung   Wein 1950.

Foreign Office:
Vine Culture and Wine Trade of Germany   1907.

Gareis:
Die Staatlichen Domänenweingüter im Rheingau

Goldschmidt:
Weingesetz   Mainz 1933.
Deutschlands Weinbauorte und Weinbergslagen   Mainz 1920.

Harpers:
Wine Gazette (Periodical)

Hennig:
Chemische Untersuchungsmethoden fuer
        Weinbereiter   Stuttgart 1950.

Heuss:
    Weinbau und Weingärtnerstand in Heilbronn Neustadt 1950.

Hofbauer:
    Handbuch der praktischen Kellerwirtschaft

Holscher:
    Das Buch vom Rhein   Köln 1925.

Jung:
    Wenn man beim Weine sitzt   Duisburg 1949.

Kayser:
    Weinbau und Winzer im Rheingau   Wiesbaden 1906.

Klenk:
    Die Weinbeurteilung   Stuttgart 1950.

Klingner:
    Fuehrer durch das Weinbaugebiet der Rheinpfalz

Kloster Eberbach:
    Deutscher Kunstverlag   Berlin 1947.

Matuschka:
    Neuzeitlicher Weinbau   Frankfurt 1927.

Meissner:
    Praktische Behandlung kranker Weine   Stuttgart 1924.

Merck:
    Kellerbehandlung von Wein u. Traubensaft   Darmstadt.

Meyer:
    Rhein-Mosel-Pfalz   Wiesbaden 1926/7.
    Weinbau u. Weinhandel an Mosel,   Koblenz 1926.
        Saar und Ruwer

Müller:
    Rhein-Main   Frankfurt 1940.

Nessler:
    Die Bereitung, Pflege u. Untersuchung des
        Weines (9)   Stuttgart 1930.

Popp:
    Das Moselland und sein Wein   Berncastel 1948.

Puls:
    Die Weinkostprobe   Punderich 1940.

Redding:
    History and Description of Modern Wines   London 1851.

Rheinlands Weine

Köln 1928.

Rheinweine Hessens

Mainz 1927.

Rouel :
    La Vigne et les Vins Allemands   Coblence 1950.

Rudd :
    Hocks and Moselles   London 1935.

Rupp :
    Staatliche Weinbaudomane Mainz   Mainz 1951.

Ruthe :
    Flaschenweinmuseum im Kurhaus Wiesbaden   1948.

Saintsbury :
    Notes on a Cellarbook   London 1921.

Schätzlein :
    Die Gewinnung des Weines (6)   Neustadt 1946.
    Der Ausbau der Weine   Neustadt 1946.
    Tätigkeitsbericht der Landesanstalt fuer Wein-,
        Obst-, und Gartenbau   Neustadt a.d. Haardt 1950.

Scheu :
    Mein Winzerbuch   Neustadt 1950.

Schönberger :
    Geschichte von Zeltingen u. Rachtig
        an der Mosel   Neustadt 1939.

Sneets :
    Die Abtei Eberbach   1943.

Spang :
    Vom Weinbau in Gau-Bickelheim

Sprater :
    Rheinischer Wein u. Weinbau   Heidelberg 1948.

Steinberg :
    Die Lehr-und Forschungsanstalt Geisenheim Wiesbaden 1949

Tovey :
    Wine and Wine Countries   London 1877.

Vogt :
    Weinbau   Freiburg 1952.

Weihrauch:
  Umgang mit Wein   Stuttgart 1950.

Der Weinbau
  (Periodical Mainz)

Welte:
  Der Weinbau Frankens   1933.

Will:
  *Des Weinbau im Gebiete der Mosel, Saar
    und Ruwer*   Dresden 1939.

Winckler:
  Wo der deutsche Wein wachst   Königsberg.

INDEX

Rhineland—Wineland

For site names not contained in the index see Appendix p. 176, for village names Appendix 1, P. 147 ff.

A

B

C

D

196

Yeast 13

X Y

Z

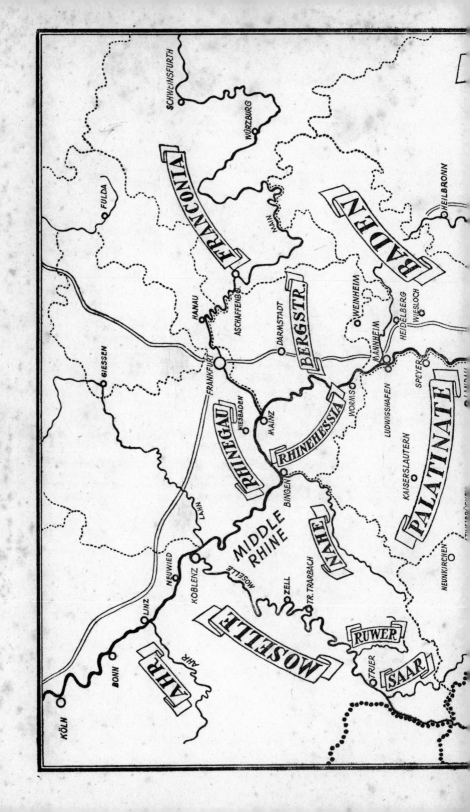